T0389536

Political Trust and Disenchantment with Politics

International Studies in Sociology and Social Anthropology

VOLUME 125

The titles published in this series are listed at *brill.com/issa*

Political Trust and Disenchantment with Politics

International Perspectives

Edited by

Christina Eder
Ingvill C. Mochmann
Markus Quandt

BRILL

LEIDEN | BOSTON

This publication has been typeset in the multilingual "Brill" typeface. With over 5,100 characters covering Latin, IPA, Greek, and Cyrillic, this typeface is especially suitable for use in the humanities. For more information, please see http://www.brill.com/brill-typeface.

ISSN 0074-8684
ISBN 978-90-04-26394-9 (hardback)
ISBN 978-90-04-27606-2 (e-book)

Contents

Acknowledgements VII
List of Figures and Tables VIII
List of Contributors XI

Editors' Introduction
Political Trust and Political Disenchantment in a Comparative Perspective 1
Markus Quandt, Christina Eder and Ingvill C. Mochmann

1 Trust and Political Disenchantment
An Overview 19
Ken Newton

2 Trends in Conventional and Unconventional Political Participation in Europe, 1981–2008 31
Rik Linssen, Hans Schmeets, Peer Scheepers and Manfred te Grotenhuis

3 Rethinking the Meaning and Measurement of Political Trust 59
Suzanne L. Parker, Glenn R. Parker and Terri L. Towner

4 When Citizens Lose Faith
Political Trust and Political Participation 83
Christina Eder and Alexia Katsanidou

5 The Role of Electoral Systems for the Translation of Political Trust into Electoral Participation 109
Christoph Arndt

6 Social Risk, Political Detachment and Welfare State De-Commodification 130
Maria Oskarson

7 Contextual Income Inequality and Political Behavior 156
Michael P. McDonald

8 Thinking Outside the Democratic Box
    *Political Values, Performance and Political Support
    in Authoritarian Regimes: A Comparative Analysis*   184
        Wiebke Breustedt and Toralf Stark

    Index   223

Acknowledgements

The open call for contributions that laid the foundation for this volume was followed by a double-blind review process over several stages. We are indebted to the members of our external review board, who carried most of the evaluation process. Based on the reviews, contributions were selected to be presented at an authors' conference held at the GESIS Leibniz Institute for the Social Sciences in Cologne in January 2012. Review board members were (in alphabetical order): Wolfgang Jagodzinski, University of Cologne; Hans-Dieter Klingemann, Wissenschaftszentrum Berlin;[1] Ken Newton, University of Southampton and Wissenschaftszentrum Berlin; Pippa Norris, Harvard University, Cambridge; Jacques Thomassen, University of Twente, Enschede; and Christian Welzel, Leuphana University, Lüneburg. Most members of the review board attended the conference and inspired the discussions with their comments. With this input, the editors employed a second round of evaluations and reviews after the conference.

---

[1] We are indebted to Hans-Dieter Klingemann also for opening the conference with a keynote speech.

List of Figures and Tables

Figures

Linssen et al. (Chapter 2)

1 Change in item ordering before and after the turn of the millennium: Average item difficulties by year   43
2 Difference in item popularity for voting vs. membership of and working for political parties   44
3 Trends in unconventional political participation, 1981–2008 for equivalent countries   52

Towner (Chapter 3)

1 Trust in the government in Washington, D.C. and trust in state government in Florida: A measurement model   68
2 Trust in government and trust in incumbent political leaders: measurement models   69–71
3 Trust in government, trust in clinton, and clinton job evaluations: A measurement model   73
4 Trust in government, trust in clinton, and clinton job evaluation: A causal model   76–77

Eder & Katsanidou (Chapter 4)

1a Traditional political participation (mean and confidence intervals)   94
1b Non-institutionalized political participation (mean and confidence intervals)   94

Arndt (Chapter 5)

1 Visualizing the coefficients from Model 3 in Table 1   121
2 Predicted probabilities for three typical countries, probabilities derived from Model 3, Table 1   122

Oskarson (Chapter 6)

1 Effect of social risk position on political detachment and reduction of risk of poverty in 2008   145
2 Effect of social risk position on political detachment and social expenditure as a percentage of GDP in 2007   145
3 Effect of social risk position on political detachment and income inequality   146
4 Effect of social risk position on political detachment and GDP per capita   146

McDonald (*Chapter 7*)

1 Three causal models linking income inequality and political participation 157
2 Gini income inequality coefficient for U.S. counties, 2000 162
3 Gini income inequality coefficient for U.S. states, 2000 163
4 Transformed predicted contact propensity for lowest and highest family income categories across meaningful ranges of county-level income inequality 173

Breustedt & Stark (*Chapter 8*)

1 Dimensions of political support in authoritarian regimes 190
2 Constitutional and actual rights of freedom and participation 192

Tables

Linssen et al. (*Chapter 2*)

1 Participating countries and sample size in EVS and ESS surveys, by year 37
2 Question-wording and answer categories for items conventional and unconventional political participation in EVS and ESS 38
3 ANOVA unconventional political participation: Proportions active respondents before and after the turn of the millennium, equivalent and non-equivalent countries 48–49
4 ANOVA membership and working for political parties and voting: Proportions active respondents after the turn of the millennium, equivalent and non-equivalent countries 50–51

Eder & Katsanidou (*Chapter 4*)

1 Voting 96
2 Party engagement 98
3 Petitioning 99
4 Protest 100
5 Variable overview and descriptive statistics 103–104

Arndt (*Chapter 5*)

1 Political trust and turnout across electoral systems 117
2 Effects of political trust and electoral systems on electoral participation, random effects logistic regression 119
A1 Classification of electoral systems according to thresholds and average district magnitudes 126

Oskarson (*Chapter 6*)

1   Political interest, political trust and political detachment
    index. (means 0–10)   138
2   Social risk, government satisfaction and political attachment
    2008, by country. OLS regression, unstandardized b-coefficients   142
3   Correlations between social risk position, political detachment,
    de-commodification, inequality and wealth. (Pearson's r)   148
4   Linear random-intercepts-random coefficients multi-level models
    of the effect of social risk on political detachment   149–150

McDonald (*Chapter 7*)

1   2004 presidential election vote, CPS & ANES logit models   165–166
2   Trust, conflict & mobilization models, ANES pooled logit models   168–169
3   Contextual Income Inequality and Presidential Voter Turnout, 1992–2004   175

Breustedt & Stark (*Chapter 8*)

1   Calibration of three-point scales   196
2   Calibration of four-point scales   196
3   Calibration of five-point scales   197
4   Conditions included in the analysis of sufficiency   199
5   Kazakhstan   201
6   Kyrgyzstan   201
7   Tajikistan   202
8   Uzbekistan   202

List of Contributors

Christoph Arndt
is Assistant Professor in Comparative Politics at the Department of Political Science and Government, Aarhus University. His research interests include electoral behaviour, the political sociology of the welfare state, welfare state reform and party politics.

Wiebke Breustedt
is Research Assistant at the Chair for Comparative Politics at the University of Duisburg-Essen and PhD student at the University of Cologne. Her main research interests are political culture, political psychology, empirical democratic theory and social research methods.

Christina Eder
is Head of the Research Data Center 'Elections' at GESIS. Her research focuses on electoral and non-electoral political participation, in particular direct democracy, gender politics, and the measurement and effects of political institutions.

Manfred te Grotenhuis
is an Assistant Professor of Quantitative Data Analysis at Radboud University Nijmegen and an affiliate of the Interuniversity Center for Social Science Theory and Methodology (ICS). He does research and teaching in inferential statistics, age-period-cohort models, multilevel modeling, event history analysis, and SPSS syntax.

Alexia Katsanidou
leads the International Data Infrastructures Team at GESIS – Leibniz Institute for the Social Sciences. She has published on political behavior, representation, and protest as well as on issues of data management, analysis and replicability.

Rik Linssen
is a PhD-candidate in the department of political science at Maastricht University, the Netherlands. His dissertation focuses on conventional and unconventional modes of political participation in international and longitudinal comparative perspective.

Michael P. McDonald
is Associate Professor in Political Science at University of Florida. His research focuses on political participation and election administration, with emphasis on the United States.

Ingvill C. Mochmann
is Head of the EUROLAB at GESIS and Vice-President for Research and Professor of International Politics at the Cologne Business School. She has published widely in the area of democracy and minority rights.

Ken Newton
is Professor Emeritus at the University of Southampton. His recent work deals with social and political trust, democratic innovations, media politics, and country family patterns of social and political participation in west Europe.

Maria Oskarson
is Associate Professor (PhD, 1958) at the department of Political Science at the University of Gothenburg, Sweden. Her research focuses on Social and Political Cleavages, Voting Behavior and Political engagement.

Suzanne L. Parker
is an Associate Professor of Political Science at Purdue University (West Lafayette, IN). Her research focuses on American politics, public opinion and political attitudes, and in particular the study of trust in government.

Glenn R. Parker
is a Distinguished Professor of Political Science and a Professor of Economics at Purdue University (West Lafayette, IN). His publications span the areas of American Politics and Public Choice, with an emphasis on the economics of political institutions.

Markus Quandt
is Head of the Research Data Center 'International Survey Programmes' at GESIS. He has published on political participation, electoral campaigning, collective goods problems, and measurement problems in comparative surveys.

Peer Scheepers
is Professor of Comparative Methodology, Vice-Dean in the Faculty of Social Sciences at Radboud University Nijmegen the Netherlands. He is member of the Dutch Royal Academy of Arts and Sciences. He has published extensively

in international journals on political voting, social capital and ethnic exclusionism.

Hans Schmeets

is part-time Professor in social statics at Maastricht University and is also employed at Statistics Netherlands. He also works with the OSCE. His research focuses on social cohesion, social capital, national elections, election observation, well-being, survey methodology and public opinion research.

Toralf Stark

is Research Assistant at the Chair for Comparative Politics at the University of Duisburg-Essen. His research focuses on political participation, political culture, political regime and transformation studies and social research methods.

Terri L. Towner

is an Associate Professor in the Department of Political Science at Oakland University in Michigan. She has published on the role of race and ethnicity in politics, the influence of new media on political attitudes, and the pedagogical value of social networks.

Editors' Introduction
Political Trust and Political Disenchantment in a Comparative Perspective

Markus Quandt, Christina Eder and Ingvill C. Mochmann

Approach of This Book

Over the last three decades, disenchantment with politics has increasingly become an issue in public as well as in scientific debates. When asked, many citizens state that politicians do not listen to what 'the people' say, causing some to turn away from politics in frustration. Others voice their opinion in the streets, protesting against political decisions, thus demonstrating that they want to have their say in politics not only on Election Day. At the same time, public opinion surveys from a substantial number of long established democratic polities suggest that political trust is rather low and has been declining over the last decades, meaning that people are less and less confident in their governments and various other political institutions. Following the view that there is a positive feedback loop between high trust and good governance, and that the latter is certainly required to maintain the overall welfare of societies, the apparent slump of trust levels in most Western democracies has even attracted the attention of the United Nations (Blind 2007).

Common sense as well as previous research offer a variety of economic, social, cultural, and political explanations for declining levels of trust. Similar factors are usually mentioned when disenchantment with politics is concerned, and it is only too plausible to relate the two. However, both political trust and disenchantment with politics have often been described as messy concepts that are difficult to handle both in theoretical and empirical terms. That observation is reiterated in most reviews on the topic (see e.g. Newton, this volume, and Levi and Stoker (2000)). We appear to be confronted with a whole syndrome of correlated oscillations in variables related to aspects of political support, where the individual conceptual components are hard to distinguish, and mutual causal relationships are fraught with endogeneity problems. What seems straightforward in common sense terms becomes complicated when systematic empirical research is the goal.

Accordingly, our guiding research question – what is the relationship between political trust and disenchantment with politics? – inevitably breaks up into a maze of sub-questions, each of which could be pursued from different angles. We shall later review what these questions are, and which of them our volume might help answering in the end. Before that, we would like to introduce the particular approach that we choose in producing this collection. The present volume is but one among a number of recent books that focus on trust and related behaviours and attitudes. Seen as a whole, this volume probably reflects the complexity and 'messiness' of the overall topic even more clearly than other works in the field. The individual chapters collect many pieces of empirical evidence that may be put together to reconstruct parts of a larger mosaic, but even this rather wide collection cannot be expected to automatically yield a coherent picture. That kind of picture could only be developed on the foundations of a theory that integrated the various relationships not only *between* the many operational varieties of trust and participation one finds under the umbrella of the two general terms. That wider theory would also have to clarify the nature of many relationships that trust and participation *share* with other factors. Even if we only look at the societal level, some of these shared 'external' factors would be cultural contexts, levels of social capital, economic development and performance, institutional configurations, etc. The contributions collected here tap into several of these external-variable relationships, often producing new insights into that specific section of what ideally would be the unified large picture. But lacking the over-archiving integrative theory, we had to confine ourselves to more modest goals than painting the full picture.

The ambition of this collection therefore is not more, but also not less than adding useful pieces to the more or less continuous stream of new empirical evidence on political trust. The methodological perspective we have chosen as the pivot of our approach, however, is partly special and should favour empirical results of a certain general relevance. The collection was initated with a call for papers on trust and disenchantment that specifically invited researchers to tap into the ever growing wealth of national and in particular of *comparative data sources*. There was intentionally no specification of a particular theoretical approach to follow, a particular scope of countries or political systems to look at, or a particular data collection programme to use as empirical input.

Still, one thing that this book shares with several other works on the topic is the reliance on data from population sample surveys as a main pillar of the empirical analyses. If we aim to look at the attitudes and behaviours of 'the citizens at large', there is still no equivalent way of tapping into the reality of society. But by targeting comparisons either across geographical space, or across points in time, or even across both dimensions at the same time, most of the contributions to this book have a level of generality beyond that of national case studies. Applying the same hypotheses to data from different countries allows investigating whether and how they react to variations in the cultural, political, economic, or institutional contexts that usually prevail across those countries. If we use a longitudinal perspective within one or several countries, we further can try to identify the possible association of political trust and behaviours with external trends – such as changing societal values – or events – such as economic crises or external threats. Thus, comparisons over space and time facilitate the study of such factors at the societal level that single-shot, single-country studies cannot systematically take into focus. At the very minimum, both comparative perspectives should help protect us from the risk of over-interpreting observations made in one-time, single-country studies.

The attention to contextual factors at the national level implies that context factors and the individual attitudes and behaviours that we measure through surveys on population samples are ideally analysed simultaneously. This often requires that advanced statistical methods are applied. Whereas the analysis of conditionality and contingencies focused *either* on identifying interactions among individual-level attributes *or* among macro-level attributes until about a decade ago (Levi and Stoker 2000), researchers now increasingly utilize quantitative macro-level data as contextual information for micro-level models and new analysis procedures to work with these. Although methodology is by no means the subject of this book, the choice of appropriate methods was an important criterion in selecting the contributions that were to be published.

Through this combination of broad topical scope and comparative analyses at the state of the art, the collection contributes new empirical findings to the field of trust and participation research across the board.

Some Remarks on Theory

Stating the absence of an overarching theory that integrates the many possible mechanisms operating between and around trust and disenchantment does not imply that some rough theoretical framing is entirely impossible. We shall therefore provide a few theoretical building blocks, not because we assume their validity or intend to test them, but to use them in organising some of the hypotheses and outcomes of the research presented in this volume.

Trust as a concept of social theory has at least three necessary referents: the first referent is the *person* holding trust into someone or something, the second referent is the *person or entity into which* the holder of that trusting belief is investing her or his expectations, and the third referent is the '*something' about which* the holder of trust is forming her or his expectations – a particular intention that the trusted person is believed to follow, or a reaction that a trusted institution should produce in case certain events occur (Coleman 1990). Each one of these three referents and their properties can independently contribute to the quality and intensity of beliefs of trust, and they can produce complex interactions. Persons may be of a generally trusting or of a distrusting nature; the recipients of trust may previously have demonstrated to deserve trust to a higher or lesser degree; and the action expected of a trusted person or institution may carry in itself more or fewer incentives and opportunities for betrayal of trust.

To add a necessary fourth analytical component, the relationship between trust and behaviour is highly dependent on situational conditions, the description of which often requires a whole array of variables. For example, citizens aspiring to acquire a building lot in an attractive suburban development area might perfectly trust the local authorities to treat them fairly in the allocation procedure – as long as they are ignorant about a close relative of the city's mayor being among the competitors for the scarce lots. After learning about this, they might, however, try to activate personal contacts themselves, if they can avail of such – so there are resource and efficacy considerations coming in, where efficacy is always relative to the restrictions imposed by the situation at hand.

Similarly, trust in government is probably a general attitude about the incumbent government only as long as no differentiation of the object of trust is triggered by the particular decision situation. But as soon as the government's likelihood of following certain courses of action in a given domain is at stake, trust will become more specific, too. A government that is trusted by particular citizens in matters of economic policy may easily be distrusted when it comes to foreign policy. And ultimately, a lack of trustworthiness can either relate to a lack of good intentions on part of the trustee, or to a lack of capability to pursue such good intentions. The formation of trust attitudes, therefore, is inherently relational, multi-facetted, and contextually embedded. Making predictions about the relationships of trust attitudes to behaviours such as political participation should probably involve accounting for as many of these different facets as possible.

One classic work that may help systematising the complex relational possibilities somewhat is that of the economist Albert O. Hirschman (1970) on "Exit, Voice, and Loyalty." Although there is no one-to-one mapping of the triangle drawn by exit, voice, and loyalty to the pair of trust and participation, Hirschman's work by analogy tells us a lot about the motivational and situational mechanisms that may be at work in explaining participation. Indirectly, we can derive how trust conditions these mechanisms. Hirschman's starting point is a loss of satisfaction (with the producer of certain goods, with one's employer, with an organisation of which one is member, with political parties, etc.). Ideal-type reactions to growing dissatisfaction can be 'voice' or 'exit'. Raising one's voice means doing something outside the usual routine to influence how things go. In the relationship to a supplier of products this is raising complaints, in the relationship to an employer it may be participation in employee suggestion schemes or participation in workers' council, in the relationship between citizens and their governments, this is often the option of so-called 'unconventional' participation, which commonly refers to behaviours such as joining boycotts, signing petitions, and participating in demonstrations. Or our citizen finds that her chances of working towards improving the outcomes of the political system are so slim that they would not be worth investing any time, effort, or resources – 'exit' therefore implies that no benefit is expected from contributing to the system's working, neither through conventional nor through unconventional participation.[1]

Hirschman's central claim is that the choice between these reactions to dissatisfaction can be predicted much better if the motivational trait of loyalty is accounted for. The presence or absence of loyalty towards the object of dissatisfaction – which citizens can feel independently of their current negative assessment – is postulated to be a crucial moderator variable. It should be noted that Hirschman early on explicitly enlists further relevant variables that operate in addition to or in interaction with loyalty: That is, firstly, the subjective probability for one's 'voice' to improve on the causes of dissatisfaction; this is what is nowadays called 'efficacy'. That is, secondly, the subjective, time-discounted value of that uncertain improvement, especially in comparison to alternatives (Hirschman 1970, 31, 77). Hence, the behavioural results in response to dissatisfaction can only be understood if researchers look at all components of the motivational and situational matrix. For our purpose, loyalty will however remain the object of interest.

The application of Hirschman's ideas to the area of political trust is not entirely self-evident, because 'trust' does not appear as a concept or variable in Hirschman's work. Accordingly, none of the authors of this volume explicitly refer to Hirschman. But some much-cited articles on political trust do, even if only to gloss over the reciprocal relationship of support for the administration

---

1 Note that our usage of the terms 'conventional' and 'unconventional' participation is itself a matter of convention here. With so-called unconventional forms of participation such as attending demonstrations or personally contacting politicians becoming more common, the aspect of 'unconventionality' probably has long been lost and alternative terms like formal vs. informal or institutional vs. non-institutional have been proposed (Marien, Hooghe, and Quintelier 2010).

or political system and their observed performance (Hetherington 1998, Mishler and Rose 1997). That implicitly assumes that loyalty and trust have the same effect. In the presence of political trust, governments, parties, or generally political actors are given a degree of credit that of course initially derives from past performance, but also allows current and future actions not to be bogged down by a continuous need for public self-justification for any single measure, big or small. The ability to trust elected politicians is at the heart of representative democracy. Trusting citizens will usually not take to the streets for demonstrations to fight tax rises set forth by their elected government. This buffer function of trust is regarded as a condition for future satisfactory performance. The function of loyalty is, according to Hirschman, very similar: loyalty allows a firm or other organisation to sustain their customer base (and thus, their existence) even if the customers or members have momentary reasons for dissatisfaction. Loyal customers often hope that the firm's product will return to its old quality levels, and therefore refrain from 'exit' in the form of switching to a competitor's product, or from avoiding the purchase of the good in question at all. Hence, trust and loyalty have the common function of bridging any gaps until positive expectations can be proven true. Hirschman's further treatment of the concept of loyalty makes it appear so encompassing that it could be understood to include almost any form of attachment to an organization, and even has been described to become ambiguous with regard to its nature as an attitude, as opposed to a behaviour (Leck and Saunders 1992). We need not follow these elaborations here and postulate that trust, in particular political trust, can to some degree be treated as a special case of loyalty. Political trust is much less general than loyalty in that it clearly relates predominantly to the cognitive aspect of attitudes, and of course is per definition confined to political actors and actions. We would also expect that trust – being a cognitive construct – is often less stable, and more prone to short-term reactions to new perceptions than those forms of loyalty that come with deep affective anchoring through socialisation or frequent personal interactions. Nevertheless, it has the same general place in explaining (political) behaviour that loyalty has: it originally grows in a setting of satisfaction with the outcomes, it helps bridging temporary phases of dissatisfaction, and its absence or presence in the minds of people explains different behaviours under otherwise similar conditions of dissatisfaction.

On a slightly more granular level, an interesting aspect of Hirschman's theorizing for the application to political behaviour is that the intensity of loyalty – or trust – plays a role for the effort or other cost that citizens are ready to invest into different paths of action. One implication is this: if we use the dichotomy of exit and voice for categorizing actions taken in response to dissatisfaction, it is often the behaviours classified as voice that are indicative of a higher degree of loyalty towards the political system at large. This is because unconventional participation (=voice) is usually more costly to the citizens than voting as the standard option of conventional participation (vote switching as a moderate form of exit), or as the technically also 'conventional' option of not participating at all (=exit). Any form of protest usually requires a higher investment of time, energy, wit, and other resources than the mere withdrawal of support does. A typical reason for incurring that added individual cost would be higher 'loyalty' to the political system. This may at first look somewhat counterintuitive, as it posits that sometimes emotionally articulated and enacted protest is to be understood as a sign of loyalty in some way, whereas silently tolerating elite decisions may be not.

To avoid confusion over the postulated mechanisms, it is important to note that there also can be blind trust, as there can be blind loyalty, when citizens are ignorant to or deny reasons for dissatisfaction. In these cases, neither 'voice' nor 'exit' are predicted, but continuation of the previous behaviour (Hirschman 1970, 91). Hence, it is important for empirical analyses to directly measure the levels of (dis-) satisfaction, the levels of loyalty or trust, and the behavioural outcome. Only the joint occurrence of conscious dissatisfaction and continuing trust supports the conclusions made above. The almost routinely performed measurement of trust in various comparative survey data bases is therefore a major asset. The ability to assess satisfaction and trust at the individual level gives a glimpse into the subjects' minds that were not possible if we based our analyses on observed behaviours alone.[2]

Further, there are functional equivalents for loyalty in the explanation of exit vs. voice, and we should expect the same for trust. One important class of cases is where real exit is not a feasible option, which holds for many political issues (Hirschman 1970, 100). For most citizens, migrating to a different country as a reaction to particular measures in defence policy or to tax raises is out of the question. When dissatisfaction with the general policies of a country occurs, this will push many citizens either into less effective forms of exit, or into voice, even without feelings of loyalty or trust. Things are different when the dissatisfaction is targeted at specific actors in the political system, such as parties. Here, 'exit' is possible through abstaining at elections or electing other parties. The conventional reasoning for loyalty decreasing the likelihood of exit then typically applies.

---

2 We note in passing that rather direct measures of the more general 'loyalty' to political parties are also available in those surveys that ask for 'party identification'.

One question for empirical analysis then is which constellations of real-world conditions make people chose the exit route if they are unhappy with the performance of political institutions, which conditions make them increase their investment (through unconventional participation), and which conditions allow them to vent their dissatisfaction even within the normal system routine.

It shall not be forgotten that each of the variables discussed above may be subject to influences from outside the Hirschman model. We have so far followed the model in the assumption that dissatisfaction is at the root of changes in political attitudes and behaviours, conditioned by trust. But it has been argued that the choice of political actions is not only a matter of immediate situational restrictions and opportunities, but also one of preferences for political styles, which may, for example, be either more or less individualistic or collectivistic, or order-accepting vs. order-questioning. A long-term change in political values may affect the levels of satisfaction with a given performance level of governments to the negative, but may at the same time bend the preferences for political styles towards more individualistic and expressive, and that tend to be 'unconventional', behaviours (Dalton 2008, Inglehart and Oyserman 2004). Although such a long-term co-variation between dissatisfaction and unconventional behaviours seemingly matches a 'dissatisfaction-leads-to-voice' hypothesis, the co-variation could also be explained by a common third factor 'value change'.

To the degree that trust could strictly be regarded to be a *moderator* variable in the relationship between dissatisfaction and participation choices, we need not be interested in the many-faceted causes and correlates of trust as such. If one were to pursue only this narrower research perspective, the messiness of the trust concept that Newton points to in the next chapter would be less of a problem for our research question. In a straightforward application of the Hirschman model trust is an external variable, for which valid measures are required, but *not* a prediction from within the model, as there are no direct causal connections between trust and the other variables. However, that probably is an over-simplification when we again move to longer time horizons. More time means more opportunities for citizens to react to environmental cues and experience, and to revise their assessments of the trustworthiness of political actors. One should then be mindful of all sorts of feedback between changes in satisfaction, changing trust levels, and political behaviours. Therefore, most authors of this collection follow the mainstream of Political Science and treat trust as a variable in its own right. Still, the above discussion allows us to better understand the exact meanings of trust that are employed across the contributions.

Finally, things are not made easier for researchers by political participation being no less context-dependent than trust. Besides skills and resources,[3] the key drivers for any participatory act are motivation and opportunity (Brady, Verba, and Schlozman 1995, Schlozman, Verba, and Brady 1995). As mentioned above, motivation does not only lay in the presence or absence of dissatisfaction, and opportunity is not fully described by looking at the presence or absence of exit options. Motivation and opportunity to perform a specific political act are naturally reflections of the specific situation a citizen is confronted with.

An Overview of the Contributions and Their Research Questions

The first chapter is by Ken Newton and gives a short general overview of empirical research on the topic of trust. He sketches major issues and developments in the field of political and social trust, disenchantment with politics and its impact on public policy over the past decades. All remaining chapters then present new empirical analyses on various issues. The sequence starts with a look at basic descriptive and methodological topics and then moves on to substantive analyses. For the latter, the opening is made by an analysis with a broad set of hypotheses on trust and participation; then narrower topics are addressed in turn over the remaining chapters. We shall briefly list the main topic of each chapter and then enter into a deeper discussion of the designs and results. We shall finally venture to suggest a few theoretical conclusions.

In Chapter 2, *Rik Linssen, Hans Schmeets, Peer Scheepers,* and *Manfred te Grotenhuis* focus on our dependent variable alone, by presenting European trend data on conventional and unconventional forms of political participation. The validity of the data is evaluated by Mokken analysis, a scaling technique for ordinal indicator variables.

In Chapter 3, *Suzanne L. Parker, Glenn R. Parker* and *Terri L. Towner* turn to the problem of measurement of trust. By structural equation modelling of u.s. data on state and federal level electoral contests, they test whether citizens are indeed capable of consistent and differentiated trust judgments.

In Chapter 4, *Christina Eder* and *Alexia Katsanidou* look at a large set of European countries through the lens of a multi-level regression model. The main topic here is how trust levels, but also different institutional configurations,

---

3   Note the common sets of control variables used in predicting participation in Arndt, Eder and Katsanidou, and McDonald, all in this volume.

influence the choice between 'conventional' and 'unconventional' forms of political participation.

In Chapter 5, *Christoph Arndt* looks at the differential effects that trust can have under varying institutional conditions. Specifically, by comparing European polities he investigates why different electoral system types tend to generate different electoral participation rates.

In Chapter 6, *Maria Oskarson* takes a new angle to explaining how a lack of trust (among other things) can evolve from deeply engrained societal structures. Looking at different European welfare regimes, she follows up on the diagnosis that the cleavage between the 'haves' and the 'have-nots' in the economic realm corresponds to a cleavage between the engaged and the disengaged in the political realm.

In Chapter 7, *Michael P. McDonald* continues on the topic of how income inequality affects participation levels, here in the form of electoral participation and with trust in a particular moderator role. His analyses with u.s. data once more showcase the complexity of the mechanisms at work. Apart from testing three substantive hypotheses on the link between inequality and participation, a methodological aspect of this contribution is how contextual analyses can be sensitive to the granularity of the contextual units.

In Chapter 8, *Wiebke Breustedt* and *Thoralf Stark* direct our attention to the role of trust in authoritarian systems. Studying four Central-Asian countries, they find that levels of trust vary markedly also between different autocratic systems. The book thus concludes with an impression of the importance of trust-based mechanisms even outside the Western world and its democratic tradition.

Although the contributions to this book were not designed to follow a unified theoretical model, the discussion in the previous section still helps to classify a number of the research questions and hypotheses recurring across various chapters. In the remainder of this chapter, we shall specifically hint at the role and position in the causal chain that trust has in each chapter, compared to the Hirschman model as a reference. But the first two chapters are reserved to establishing that the measures of participation and trust typically used in the following analyses provide a sound empirical foundation.

With data from two large European survey programmes (European Values Study and European Social Survey), Linssen et al. look at the trends in unconventional participation behaviours in 22 European countries in a time span of almost 30 years up to 2008, and in conventional participation between 2002 and 2008. They start with analysing the viability of valid measurement; not only per each sample, but also for the comparisons over time and countries. The scaling method they use (Mokken) assesses whether the associations between different ordinal indicators of political participation are stable enough to claim that they describe a consistent phenomenon. Although this study is not exempt from the common problem of comparative analysis that the data from at least a few countries do not fully meet the criteria of the formal scaling procedure, the general picture is convincing enough. The descriptive results then contradict the conventional wisdom on the trends in political engagement. First, there is no clear trend in participation at the voting booth, but certainly no marked decline for the post-2000 period. Second, for the so-called unconventional participation through acts such as petitioning, demonstrating, and boycotting, there is a clear upwards shift between 1981 and 1999, which certainly confirms the assertion that what used to be unconventional is no longer so. After 2000, there appears to be almost perfect stability in these forms of participation, if Europe is taken as a whole. Third, this stability over time has to be seen on the backdrop of substantial differences in the typical levels of participation between countries: between-country variation dwarfs over-time variation. So the first thing to conclude is that, in spite of previously observed decreasing levels of political trust in many Western countries, there is no overarching decrease in levels of participation that would correspond to the decrease in trust. A second conclusion relates to the notion of a substitution process going on between conventional and unconventional forms of participation. This is not only not visible in the aggregate levels for both forms, it is also rejected by a correlational analysis at the individual level: the association between both forms of participation is (moderately) positive for virtually every usable national sample in this study.[4] If citizens do substitute one form of participation against the other at all, it cannot be described as a simple trend, but might become visible only if citizens' criteria for choosing one participation form over the other are brought into the equation.

Parker et al. in Chapter 3 address the issue of measurement of different objects of political trust. The distinctions that respondents were required to make concerned trust in the holders of office at different constitutional levels of the U.S., and trust in institutions. They cover a typical range of objects in the political system that could attract more or less 'specific' support, in Easton's terminology. A question of eminent importance to justify any further analysis with survey data is whether citizens are at all capable of providing differentiated trust judgments for these objects. Using a full-fledged latent-variable measurement model with multiple indicators, Parker et al. find that this is clearly the case. The respondents of their survey give consistent and

---

4 Only data of the ESS 2002–2008 have been used for this analysis with both forms of participation.

usefully differentiated evaluations on the trustworthiness and policy performance of two senators at the state level, which they again distinguish from performance and trustworthiness of the incumbent president and policies at federal level. According to their results, citizens are capable of providing highly differentiated trust evaluations, with general trust in government being far from being an amorphous catch-all concept. Although these results were only demonstrated for a sample from the state of Florida, not much speaks against assuming that citizens of other democratic polities should be as capable of providing such judgments as Florida residents are.

In the first chapter with substantive analyses, Eder and Katsanidou look at various possible routes that might lead citizens into different forms of participation. In relation to the effect of trust, they hypothesize that a lack of trust into political institutions affects conventional and unconventional forms of participation in different ways, with for example electoral participation becoming less attractive, but protest behaviour becoming more likely when trust levels are low. The cross-national perspective they take (using European Values Study 2008 data) enables them to investigate the effects of deteriorating economic conditions at the national level, with a particular interest in the short- and intermediate-term effects that the financial and economic crisis might have that was shaking Europe at that time. The comparative design also allows for controlling effects of the institutional context. They find that confrontation of societies with economic crisis apparently leads to higher participation over all four of the participatory acts they analyse (two of them party-related and dubbed traditional here, two of them being petitioning and protesting, dubbed non-institutionalised). The dominant reaction to decreasing performance of the societies in this case seems to be 'voice'. Further, this analysis with a maximal number of control variables confirms the result of Linssen et al.'s simpler design which found conventional and unconventional forms of participation positively correlated to each other. Further to that, conventional and unconventional forms are mostly related to the same control variables, with the same signs for the statistical effects. In essence, that means that conventional and unconventional participation are additive at the individual level. According to Hirschman, this concentration on voice, even in presence of distrust, would be particularly plausible when there is no viable exit option. It is probably fair to say that this applies to societies under crisis conditions. So, when times are seriously bad, people do choose protest more often. But for most, that is no reason to abstain from voting (although it might be a reason to change one's voting preference, which could be tested in none of the studies in this book). If 'voice' is chosen, then this happens through all available routes.

The notable exception to that uniformity is the effect of political trust: this is significantly positive for traditional participation, but significantly (albeit weakly) negative for non-institutionalised participation acts. The authors' argument about the trust-based distinction between alternative forms of participation is thus confirmed. Those who do trust the institutions that were installed through electoral processes have a lower tendency to choose alternative participation forms than those who do not trust these institutions. This extends the finding from Parker et al., in that citizens are not only able to make differentiated trust judgments, they also act upon them.

The European level comparative study of Arndt (chapter 5) points us to the role of the electoral system for offering behavioural channels either into the 'voice' or the 'exit' option of the Hirschman framework. Arndt's hypothesis is that the well-known property of proportional voting regimes to elicit higher participation at the polls should be particularly visible among those citizens that show little trust and attachment to political parties. For these, the better availability of other voting options in proportional systems offers a route to 'exit' from their previous electoral choice, without them being forced into abstention, meaning 'exit' from the electoral process altogether. Vote switching is exit from the previous party, but voice to the overall society. Correspondingly, Arndt finds that in majoritarian systems distrusting citizens indeed more often choose abstention than in proportional systems. The latter can be considered to be more successful at including the dissatisfied in the electoral process. Systems with proportional representation and sufficiently large electoral district sizes typically give room for new and more extreme parties to obtain seats in parliament. Presence in parliament is often sufficient to have at least some items from their agenda influence actual policy outcomes. It could well be an outcome of a long-term feedback from this increased chance of effective participation that citizens in the most open electoral system also display higher average trust levels.

In a comparison of European countries based on data from the European Social Survey of 2008, Oskarson (chapter 6) focuses on the effect that different welfare systems might have on how individual socio-economic positions predicate individual levels of attachment to or detachment from politics. Here, political trust is used as one among several indicators of political involvement. This study thus applies the previously described view that trust, disenchantment, and participation form a syndrome for which internal differentiation might not always be necessary, or feasible. Oskarson asks whether more egalitarian types of welfare systems are able to ameliorate the unlucky correspondence of economic and political marginalisation processes and finds a slightly paradoxical result: the more generous the national welfare system, the higher is the subjective political detachment of those who still find themselves in a disadvantaged socio-economic position in these societies. The author suspects relative deprivation mechanisms to be at work here. The experience of economic problems might be all the more frustrating and alienating in an environment where it is the clear exception; it may also expose the people affected to more ostracism.[5]

McDonald (in chapter 7) continues on the issue of economic inequality. The presence of high inequality is – among other things – a symptom of large parts of the population being in disadvantaged socio-economic positions. As already described, this alone might be reason enough for low participation levels. But inequality also influences which kinds of conflicts are possibly brought into the political arena, and which coalitions can be formed to support the political goals of the relatively disadvantaged. McDonald's study of the contextual effects of inequality on voting abstention in the u.s. therefore postulates three possible causal pathways from inequality experiences to electoral participation. Among these, a 'trust model' posits that long-standing inequality experiences decrease trust in the performance of the political system and thus increase abstention. Hence, trust is understood (and indeed, explicitly modelled) as an intervening variable between inequality and abstention here.[6] The analysis provides some empirical support for this reasoning. However, the strongest effects of both contextual inequality and trust on abstention remain with the direct paths.

Another aspect of the study also deserves mentioning. That aspect is becoming more visible when the other two causal pathways, a 'conflict' model and a 'contact' model, are investigated. Depending on which of two context levels inequality is measured at, it can have very different effects on individual participation. The magnitude and even the direction of the effects can depend on the level (or size) of the contextual unit to which the inequality measure relates. For the present case, the contextual data are available both at the level of states as the larger units and at the level of counties as much smaller units. Interestingly, it is by no means the case that contextual effects are stronger if

---

5   An alternative explanation still to be checked might be that the more generous welfare systems are usually more successful in protecting people from exposure to economic disadvantages, leaving only the most difficult cases to fall through the security nets – with these cases representing a 'negative selection' in many respects, including that of disinterest and distrust in politics.

6   Notably, McDonald's study is the only one in this book that is using general social trust instead of trust in political institutions or politicians, the latter two not being consistently available in his data. One might expect that the trust effect would appear even more clearly if the more relevant measure of political trust could have been applied.

they are measured at the smallest unit level, although one might expect that the smaller size would mean that the context data describe the individuals' immediate environment much better. Rather, it is the case that different context levels can have different substantive implications. For one dependent variable in the present analysis, namely the frequency by which party canvassers contacted respondents' households, inequality at the state level even has regression effects with signs opposed to those of the effects for inequality at county level. And across the board, state level context effects are stronger than county level context effects. Apparently, the relevance of state level politics is simply higher for the variables treated here.

Another view on the relevance of trust is granted by the study of Breustedt and Stark (chapter 8), who investigate factors influencing trust in government in four autocratic countries in central Asia, surveyed by the Asia Barometer series. They use "fuzzy set Qualitative Comparative Analysis" as a procedure to identify the logically sufficient and necessary conditions for explaining trust in these countries. Unusually, the method is applied directly to the individual level data.

Once more, trust is here being treated as a component of general political support. This support is hypothesized to be higher if respondents have autocratic values themselves, are contend with the economic performance of the nation, and have trust in local official institutions. In two of the countries, Kazakhstan and Tajikistan, a model with the variables above achieves acceptable fit by QCA standards. It is particularly institutional trust, mostly indicating the perceived absence of corruption, which makes for the association between performance and government trust. In Kyrgyzstan and Uzbekistan, the models fit less well and the authors caution that further factors should be sought. Still, the varying ability of autocratic governments to provide their citizens with food and with order seems to have a clear effect on trust.

Summary and Conclusion

To begin to the left on the causal path, our authors usually relate to some form of experience to explain individual levels of trust into political actors or institutions.[7] Reassuringly, whenever our authors test for it, they find that the conditions both at the individual level such as one's own economic position,

---

7   In this book, the sole exception is the study of Parker et al., who postulate the evaluation of presidential performance to *depend* on trust in the incumbent president. They do not discuss this choice in detail.

and at the societal level such as overall economic inequality, or the trend in unemployment rates, seem to tell many citizens how well political actors deliver on their promises, or rather on the expectations into politics that citizens nurture. Trust in government and in politicians usually goes down in response to poor individual conditions and to lacking societal performance. This is reassuring from a research perspective because it fits in with previous research, and it is reassuring from a normative perspective because it basically tells us that a relevant number of citizens apply a very plausible logic in forming their trust attitudes. Remarkably, with the necessary deductions the pattern even appears to hold under autocratic regimes (Breustedt and Stark) and can thus be seen as one of the universals in the study of political trust.

As an important qualification to the general role of societal performance in informing trust and then participation, it often appears to be the *relative* position of citizens in comparison to others that makes them trust political institutions and actors more or less, and act on that correspondingly. When looking at socio-economic inequality, Oskarson and McDonald relate to arguments of relative deprivation and of differential political efficacy. Both start from the observation that individual socio-economic disadvantages very often go along with political marginalisation, because it is typically the less educated and less wealthy who are also less prone to political participation.

As another over-arching observation, we can identify a tacit consensus among our authors in one important question. Although a few references are made to possible reciprocal or feedback relationships between trust and participatory behaviour in the long term, all studies seem to assume an asymmetrical relationship between trust in its different incarnations on the one hand and political participation on the other hand in the short term. With the partial exception of Oskarson's study, trust, in a variety of specifications of statistical models, is treated as a *predictor for,* or as *moderator* of the effect of preceding variables on participatory behaviour.[8] The study of McDonald even specifically tests for endogeneity and comes out negative.

This analytical position of trust is what our adaption of the Hirschman framework suggested, where trust inherited its status as an exogenous moderator variable from loyalty. Looking back at the explanatory models for participation that the authors of this collection used, we find this specific placement of

---

8   Oskarson treats trust as one among other indicators of engagement. This is not in breach of the stated causal ordering because her analysis concentrates on the 'left' half of the causal path, leading from deprivation conditions to trust. Her packaging of trust and participatory behaviours – which constitute the 'right' half of the causal path – into one index therefore owes to the main interest lying with the effects of economic and institutional structure.

trust in the causal chain *between* dissatisfaction and participation only in the work of McDonald (with trust technically treated as an intervening variable, not as a moderator), and indirectly of Arndt (who puts trust in interaction with features of the electoral system that determine the efficacy of voting). The remaining authors, with no less plausibility, treat trust as part of the rank-and-file of further predictors.

Although the books are still open on whether there is a single 'correct' analytical treatment of political trust, it is striking how little consequence the differences of treatment found among the studies collected in this volume have on the substantive interpretations. The analyses clearly converge once more in the observation that citizens invest their feelings of trust into institutions and politicians in largely reproducible and sensible ways, thereby creating a useful heuristic to guide their own political actions. Whether these actions have the thrust of 'loyalty' or 'voice' – more participation of the conventional or of the unconventional kind – or of 'exit' – less participation of any kind – could often be re-constructed in terms of reasonable decisions, given enough situational cues.

The very notion of citizens and politicians reacting to situational conditions and to each other's displayed and expected behaviours in sensible patterns makes both trust and participation highly contingent – contingent on each other, but also on any number of outside factors that define a particular situation. It appears that trust is an encompassing heuristic to evaluate such complex situations not only for the actors confronted with the situations. Many analysts trying to understand political attitudes framed in the terminology of trust may initially be tempted to see trust as a self-contained, one-dimensional concept. But even calling trust a 'concept' could already be deceptive, if we understood the concept of trust to mean an attribute that can be captured in a single variable, assigning static values to single objects. Rather, the relational and conditional nature of trust should always be taken into account. It is in its very nature to remain a moving target. Thus, it may be the fate of any empirical analysis in the field of political trust to be a singular snapshot, freezing a particular moment in time that is unlikely to reoccur with the same parameters again at another time.

Still, after once more confirming the general notion that political trust summarises citizens' impression of how well politics works for them, one may of course conclude that this will continue to be true. Levels of trust will also in the future co-vary with how well institutions and politicians perform. In our view, this points to the role that political trust should have in our analytical models: it appears to be a very useful indicator of perceived system performance, and can be targeted at very specific political objects, if needed.

In that respect, researchers should trust their measures of trust. In a normative perspective, and returning to Hirschman's (1970) argument about dissatisfaction being at the heart of decreasing loyalty, we would conclude that "where there is smoke, there is a fire." Low levels of trust most certainly indicate that something is amiss – but it is typically not the level of trust as such that is the problem. Decreasing trust is the smoke, but the fuel for the fire comes from poor socio-economic conditions and unsatisfactory policy outcomes.

References

Blind, Peri K. 2007. "Building trust in government in the twenty-first century: Review of literature and emerging issues." 7th Global Forum on Reinventing Government Building Trust in Government.

Brady, Henry E., Sidney Verba, and Kay Lehman Schlozman. 1995. "Beyond SES: A Resource Model of Political Participation." *American Political Science Review* 89:271–294.

Coleman, James S. 1990. *Foundations of Social Theory*.

Dalton, Russell J. 2008. "Citizenship Norms and the Expansion of Political Participation." *Political Studies* 56:76–98.

Hetherington, Marc J. 1998. "The Political Relevance of Political Trust." *The American Political Science Review* 92 (4):791–808.

Hirschman, Albert O. 1970. *Exit, Voice, and Loyalty. Responses to Decline in Firms, Organizations, and States*. Cambridge, Mass.: Harvard University Press.

Inglehart, Ronald, and Daphna Oyserman. 2004. "Individualism, autonomy, self-expression: The human development syndrome." In *Comparing Cultures. Dimensions of Culture in a Comparative Perspective*, edited by Henk Vinken, Joseph Soeters and Peter Ester, 74–96.

Leck, Joanne D., and David Saunders. 1992. "Hirschman's Loyalty: Attitude or Behavior?" *Employee Responsibilities and Rights Journal* 5 (3):219–230.

Levi, Margaret, and Laura Stoker. 2000. "Political Trust and Trustworthiness." *Annual Review of Political Science* 3:475–507. doi: 1094-2939/00/0623-0475$14.00.

Marien, Sofie, Marc Hooghe, and Ellen Quintelier. 2010. "Inequalities in Non-Institutionalised Forms of Political Participation: A Multi-Level Analysis of 25 Countries." *Political Studies* 58:187–213.

Mishler, William, and Richard Rose. 1997. "Trust, Distrust, and Skepticism: Popular Evaluations of Civil and Political Institutions in Post-Communist Societies." *The Journal of Politics* 59 (2):418–451.

Schlozman, Kay Lehman, Sidney Verba, and Henry E. Brady. 1995. "Participation's Not a Paradox: The View from American Activists." *British Journal of Political Science* 25:1–36.

CHAPTER 1

Trust and Political Disenchantment
An Overview

Ken Newton

Trust is an age-old topic in social and political theory, dating back at least to Confucius, who identified it as an essential ingredient of government, together with food and arms. In the past two decades or so, however, it has attracted vast and diverse research activity in the social sciences and beyond – psychology, sociology, economics, politics, management, education, development studies and medicine. Widespread interest in the topic is not just an academic matter, either. Following the academic work that shows trust is a general benefit to the society, the economy and the polity, Government agencies and policy-making institutions such as the World Bank, the OECD and the EU started their own work on trust and a broad array of practical problems of public policy. They have also investigated the problem of how to increase levels of trust, especially among groups in society where it is low.

The resulting research has uncovered strong associations between trust, in both its social and political forms, and a wide variety of important phenomena in modern society. People who trust others, it seems, are healthier, happier and wealthier and they tend to live longer and feel more satisfied with their own lives (Helliwell and Putnam 2004). They are more tolerant, more likely to help others and co-operate with them, and more likely to support aid for minorities and the poor; as a result, trusting societies are generally more integrated and cohesive and less likely to suffer from illegal behaviour, social strains and deviant behaviour (Uslaner 2002; Marien and Hooghe 2011). Trusting individuals have higher rates of civic participation, volunteering and giving to charities (Uslaner and Brown 2005) and trusting communities have lower crime rates and higher levels of school attainment (Putnam 1993).

Political trust is also associated with many forms of political attitudes and behaviour. Those who distrust their government are more likely to vote for opposition and third parties (Hetherington 1999), and they often display less interest in politics, and are less likely to be active in civic life and they are more likely to engage in illegal activities and to condone improper behaviour such as not buying tickets for public transport or parking illegally (Brehm and Rahn 1997; Uslaner 2002). At the country level there is evidence that higher levels of both social and political trust are associated with democratic development and stability, the rule of law, social and economic equality, economic development and belief in democracy, as well as satisfaction with the way that democracy works in any given country (Knack and Keefer 1997; Inglehart 1997: 188; Keele 2007; Zak and Knack 2001; van der Meer and Dekker 2011). Trusting nations have more equal income distributions (Delhey and Newton 2005) and less corruption (Della Porta, 2000). Their citizens are more likely to pay their taxes, and in return get better and more efficient public services (Sholtz and Lubell 1998).

In short, government and society seems to work more smoothly and effectively if it is built on the twin features of social and political trust. At the other extreme it is rightly said that the person who trusts nobody and trusts nothing should not take the risk of getting out of bed in the morning. Such people are exceedingly rare in modern society (Newton and Zmerli, 2011: 15). In this sense, Confucius is right: trust is one of the core features that make social and political life possible. More recently trust has been described as the glue that holds society together and the lubrication that makes it work more effectively, and for this reason trust is often treated as the core component of social capital and its best empirical indicator. Trust may not be the 'chicken soup of social life', as Uslaner (2000–2001) puts it, but it certainly seems to be mixed up with a great many social 'goods', just as lack of trust seems to be accompanied by many social 'bads'.

However, a difficult problem was presented by survey results in the earlier stages of social capital research. Although theory suggested that there should be a close connection between social trust and political trust, empirical results could not find this at the individual level, although statistically significant correlations were discovered at the national level. Later work, however, confirmed the theory. A strong statistical association appears at the individual level as well when the two are measured more accurately, notably by means of multiple, scalable questionnaire items, in particular the Rosenberg (1957) scale for social trust and batteries of questions for confidence in political institutions. It helps if respondents are given an eleven-point rating scale when answering the trust questions. This work also found a close association between social and political trust on the one hand, and measures of political attitudes, on the other (Glanville and Paxton 2007; Freitag 2003; Zmerli and Newton 2008; Freitag and Bühlmann 2009). In other words, there is a close three-cornered relationship between social trust, political trust and measures of democratic satisfaction and confidence in the institutions of government.

Confirmation that social and political trust are connected and associated with an array of political attitudes and behaviour solves an important problem in research, but news from the trust front is not all good. A persistent refrain in political science, at least from 1968 onwards, has been that democracy is in a crisis that is closely associated with a decline in social and/or political trust and a rise in political disenchantment and disaffection. Thus, we have a series of books and articles with titles like *The Crisis of Democracy* (Crozier et al. 1975), *Why People Don't Trust Government* (Nye, et al., 1997), *Disaffected Democracies* (Pharr and Putnam 2000), and *Political Disaffection in Contemporary Democracies* (Torcal and Montero 2006). But, once again, the claims of this sort of work were not confirmed by survey research which has failed to find a long-term secular decline in trust in many western democracies. One recent study (Marien 2011) concludes that 'no general declining trend could be found in institutional trust among a wide variety of European countries in the past decade'. Evidence of decline was found in Greece, Hungary and the Ukraine, but decline in some countries in the 1990 and early 2000s was offset by recovery later in the decade. Another study of eight core nations of the EU finds trendless fluctuation rather than a slippery slope of falling trust in government (Roger 2010. See also van de Walle, et al. 2008).

There is also debate about whether low levels of trust are a cause for concern at all. One school of thought, dating back to the classic argument between Citrin and Miller (Citrin 1974: 988; Miller 1974a, 1974b. See also Lenard 2008), argues that a degree of scepticism about government is a good thing that indicates 'vigilant scepticism' and 'realistic cynicism'. Huntington's opinion is that distrust is 'as American as apple pie' (in Orren 1997: 88–89). According to this view, political trust is bad because it indicates political ignorance about the real world and a degree of Panglossian starry-eyed optimism.

Another school agrees that it is unwise to assume the trustworthiness of politicians but that it is precisely for this reason that we should build our system of government with great care. As David Hume (1741: 40) pointed out, every politician must be supposed to be a knave and, therefore, we must build a democratic system with the checks and balances that force a degree of trustworthy behaviour on any knaves who happen to be in power. Consequently, there is nothing strange about setting up an effective system of checks and balances based on a deep distrust of politicians in general, while, at the same time, trusting a particular set of leaders in office because the checks and balances enforce their trustworthy behaviour (Petitt 1998: 295–314). In which case we should distinguish between the idea that there are usually a few bad apples in a barrel, while concluding from experience that most, not all, will be good if care is taken to keep them well in the first place. The most rational strategy in politics is to assume that at least some politicians will not be trustworthy, and so construct a set of democratic institutions designed to keep them in order.

It is no coincidence that developed democracies display comparatively high levels of political trust, while countries with poorer levels of democratic development have substantially lower levels. Confidence in the parliament in Norway, the Netherlands and Sweden in 2000 was above the 50 per cent mark, but in Macedonia, Peru, South Korea and the Dominican Republic it was 12 per cent or less. It does not seem plausible, given what we know about the differences between Denmark and the Dominican Republic, to claim that the Danes are more trusting simply because they are innocent and naïve.

Similarly, levels of social trust between citizens vary considerably across the world's nations, with high scores (more than 50 per cent) in Denmark, Norway, Sweden, the Netherlands and New Zealand, and low scores (less than 15 per cent) in South Africa, Algeria, Columbia, Uganda and Tanzania. The intentional homicide rate in Denmark per 1000,000 population in 2012 was 0.9. In South Africa it was 31.8 (UNODC 2011. See also Messner et al. 2004). This suggests one good reason why Danes trust each other and South Africans do not. It also suggests that social trust is driven, at least in part if not in whole, by objective social conditions because individuals build their sense of trust and distrust on the basis of their daily experience of the world and whether they find that others are trustworthy or untrustworthy. In other words, trust responses in the social surveys are a litmus test of how citizens feel about their social and political circumstances, and how they feel is firmly rooted in their daily experience of real life. As such, low or declining trust should be a source of concern not just for political scientists but for governments, politicians and policy makers.

Even if there is no demonstrable long-term decline in western democracies it is still important to understand why countries display very different levels of trust. If political trust and distrust have a pervasive association with all kinds of good and bad things, then it is important to understand the determinants of trust and the consequences it has for life in general. Why do Denmark, Finland, Norway, the Netherlands and Sweden regularly appear among the countries at the top of the world trust tables, while Brazil, Peru, Turkey, the Philippines and Columbia are often at the bottom? Is trust driven primarily by underlying social factors such as the decline of voluntary associations or watching too much television (Putnam 1995, 2000), or perhaps by economic conditions, or by the performance of politicians and the quality of public services and decisions they make? According to some recent research it is not a decline of voluntary associations, social trust or television viewing that causes a decline in political trust and rising levels of political disenchantment, but the performance of political and economic systems (Rose and Mishler 2011). The social sub-structure of civil society, voluntary associations and citizen attitudes towards one another may remain at the same high level, but political distrust and disenchantment can rise steeply as performance falls. Equally, political confidence can return quickly if performance levels are restored (Newton 2006).

Social services and citizen experience of them may play an important part in the mix of performance indicators that help to drive both trust and disenchantment. Rothstein (1998) and Rothstein and Stolle (2003) argue that a welfare state built on universal benefits, rather than a means tested one, can generate trust between citizens and between citizens and their political leaders and institutions. Universal benefits generate a sense of community and equality, while means tested benefits have a divisive character that sets the 'needy' against others, and creates the false distinction between the 'deserving' and 'undeserving' poor. Kumlin (2004) finds that everyday experience of welfare state services has an effect not only on political trust but on attitudes towards a broader range of issues such as the proper scope of the welfare state, left-right politics, and attitudes towards the system of government. In this case, it may not only be institutions that matter but also performance.

In the same way that it is important to understand how and why states vary in their levels of trust, so it is also important to understand how and why individuals and social groups within states vary. If we want to produce a healthy and happy society with low levels of conflict and high levels of co-operation and efficiency, then it is as well to identify the people who are distrustful and compare them with the trustful in order to find out why they feel this way. Some important factors have been discovered, especially the almost universal role of education as a powerful predictor of trust (Uslaner 2008: 108). But education is usually closely associated with other powerful variables such as income, class, happiness, life satisfaction, health, job satisfaction, unemployment, majority-minority group status and post-materialism. One way of summing up this closely packed set of trust correlates is to see trust as the characteristic of winners in society, and distrust and disenchantment as a feature of the losers. By winners is meant those with money, status, education, good jobs, high job satisfaction, high life satisfaction, happiness, and health. The evidence suggests that the winners in society tend to be trusting, while the losers are distrusting (Zmerli and Newton 2011). This conclusion is not exactly startling but it helps to pull together a great deal of disparate research on the causes of trust and distrust.

Different groups react in different ways to their low trust and disenchantment: some withdraw from political action and participation; some turn out to vote, perhaps for radical and protest parties; some engage in political protest in the form of demonstrations, sit-ins, strikes and boycotts; and some turn to civil disturbance and even violence. It is often the case in social research that similar sorts of people react in rather different ways to similar sorts of circumstances, and trust research is no different in this respect.

Trust research, however, is beset by some thorny problems. First, different types of trust are closely inter-connected with each other and with a large syndrome of other variables. At the individual level, social and political trust are both closely associated with a range of powerful attitudinal variables, including life satisfaction, happiness, job satisfaction, optimism, and a strong sense of public safety. At the individual level they are also closely associated with the objective social characteristics of income, education, class, success in life and being tied into networks of informal social contacts. At the national level trust is associated with democratic development, good government, wealth, social and economic equality, Protestant traditions, and ethnic homogeneity. The problem is that these variables are so entangled with each other that it is exceedingly difficult to isolate one from the others. As a result the independent effect of each variable upon the others is difficult, if not impossible, to estimate. However, it is possible that this is the wrong way of looking at the problem. Perhaps it makes more sense to see this tangled knot of variables as a single and indivisible whole that cannot be taken apart at the seams. In this case, trust may not have a life of its own, separate and independent yet associated with other powerful variables; it exists and operates only as an integral part of a tightly interwoven network of variables.

This raises the further problem that the tangle is so tight and complicated that it is difficult to sort out any given cause from any given effect. For example, social trust is closely correlated with economic equality, but which causes what? It is easy to imagine that citizens find it easier to accept policies that redistribute income when they trust others not to abuse those policies, but equally it may be easier to trust others who have similar economic circumstances to our own, and less easy to trust those who, for whatever reason, are wealthier or poorer. Or perhaps social uniformity is a common underlying cause of both trust and equality because we are more likely to trust people like us and more likely to accept redistribution of income to people like us? Uslaner (2011: 159) describes the close association of inequality, corruption, and poor public service quality in similar ways: 'High levels of corruption may lead to poor services, but poor services lead to less confidence in government...and then to greater levels of tax evasion – and, in turn, to poorer levels of service and more inequality and more corruption – and to the never-ending inequality trap'. Almost all research on trust entails this difficulty of which comes first, the chicken or the egg. It is tempting to conclude that there is a reciprocal relation between the variables of the syndrome, but equally this may also seem to be a way of avoiding the problem.

A third challenge for trust research concerns the approach of top-down theorists of trust contrasted with those who take a bottom-up view of it (Mishler and Rose 2001). For some, trust is a core personality characteristic of individuals that is accompanied by a sense of optimism, the ability to control one's own life and the possibility of co-operation with others (Erikson 1950; Allport 1961; Rosenberg 1956; 1957; Uslaner 1990, 2000–2001, 2002). The distrusting, according to this theory, are misanthropic individuals with a pessimistic opinion of human nature who acquire these attitudes as a result of early childhood socialisation and experiences that tends to stay with them for the rest of their life.

Others see trust as a top-down product of contexts and institutions. Research shows that people report higher levels of trust in countries with an impartial police force, a just legal system that operates under the rule of law, an honest bureaucracy and public policies that have regard for the common good (see, for example, Hooghe and Stolle 2003). In other words, just as systems of democratic government follow Hume's prescription for democracy as a set of institutions designed for knaves, so a wide array of other institutions have been created to enforce trustworthy behaviour on the part of citizens. These include the courts, police and civil service, as well as a broad array of rules and practices enforced by regulatory agencies –ticket inspectors, school inspectors, health inspectors, highways and bridges inspectors, police inspectors, safety inspectors, trading inspectors, livestock inspectors, hospital inspectors, all of whom operate within elaborate codes of conduct designed to ensure that individuals, goods and services live up to minimum standards. For example, one might board a plane with equanimity not because you know the pilot, cabin staff and maintenance crew personally but because you trust the airline to select good people, train them well, regulate their working hours, make sure they are not drugged or drunk on duty, and have procedures to ensure that the plane is serviced and safety-checked correctly. To this extent it is the system that enforces trustworthy behaviour that induces a sense of trust in its passengers.

There is no incompatibility between the individual, bottom-up and the societal, top-down approaches. Individuals can differ because of their personality and up-bringing, and societies can differ according to their histories, cultures and institutional arrangements. The inter-action between individual and contextual effects may also produce what, at first sight, appear to be strange results. For example, low trust individuals in high trust societies might have higher levels of trust than the average in some low trust societies. Conversely, high trust individuals in low trust societies might have a lower level of trust that the average in high trust societies.

Moreover, there is evidence of the 'rainmaker effect', in which individuals with a propensity to distrust because of their own background and life experience are influenced by a general climate of high trust around them and, therefore, have a higher level of trust than might otherwise be expected (Putnam, Pharr and Dalton 2000: 26; Newton and Norris 2000; Van der Meer 2003; Van der Meer and

Dekker 2011). In these circumstances the contextual effect acting on trust is not the performance of government or the economy, nor any set of institutions, but the general level of trust itself. In dealing with both micro and macro considerations it helps if both are taken into account by means of multi-level modelling (see, for example, van der Meer and Dekker 2011, Newton and Zmerli 2011).

It is true that understanding trust is one thing, and social engineering it is quite another. Some of the factors that drive trust are not easily controlled or manipulated and some are not controllable at all. For example, the close relationship between trust and corruption leads to the question 'how is it possible to increase trust so as to lower corruption, or should it be the other way round?' In either case, a solution to the puzzle of corruption and low trust in others is made all the more difficult because they form a vicious circle; to eliminate corruption it is necessary to engender a degree of trust in others, but to increase trust it is necessary to remove the fear that others will be corrupt if they have the chance. To raise trust and reduce corruption requires society to pull itself up by its own bootstraps and, moreover, solutions are likely to run into the intractable dilemma of collective action (Rothstein 2000, 2005). As a result, practical policies to reduce distrust and corruption constitute a social trap that would present even Houdini with the severest difficulty.

It is clear that distrust and disenchantment with government present social scientists and politicians, theorists and practitioners, with important and challenging matters. This is what gives the subject its fascination and its frustrations. The study of trust has gone quite a long way in the past decade or two, but there is still a long way to go.

References

Allport, Gordon W. 1961. *Patterns and Growth in Personality*. New York: Holt Rinehart and Winston.

Brehm, John and Wendy Rahn. 1997. "Individual-Level Evidence for the Causes and Consequences of Social Capital." *American Journal of Political Science* 41: 999–1023.

Citrin, Jack. 1974. "Comment: The Political Relevance of Trust in Government." *American Political Science Review* 68: 973–988.

Crozier, Michael, Huntington, Samuel P. and Joji Watanuki. 1975. *The Crisis of Democracy*. New York: New York University Press.

Delhey, Jan and Kenneth Newton. 2005. "Predicting Cross-National Levels of Social Trust: Global Pattern or Nordic Exceptionalism?." *European Sociological Review* 21: 311–327.

Della Porta, Donatella. 2000. "Social Capital, Beliefs in Government, and Political Corruption." In *Disaffected Democracies* edited by Susan J. Pharr and Robert D. Putnam, 202–228. Princeton, Princeton University Press.

Erikson, Erik H. 1950. *Childhood and Society.* New York, Norton.

Freitag, Markus. 2003. "Social Capital in (Dis)Similar Democracies: The Development of Generalized Trust in Japan and Switzerland." *Comparative Political Studies* 36: 936–966.

Freitag, Markus and Marc Bühlmann. 2009. "Crafting Trust: The Role of Political Institutions in a Comparative Perspective." *Comparative Political Studies* 42: 217–232.

Glanville Jennifer L. and Pamela Paxton. 2007. "How do We Learn Trust? A Confirmatory Tretrad Analysis of the Sources of Generalized Trust." *Social Psychological Quarterly* 70: 230–242.

Helliwell, John F. and Robert D. Putnam. 2004. "The Social Context of Well-being." *Philosophical Transactions of the Royal Society B* 359: 1435–1446.

Hetherington, Marc J. 1999. "The Effect of Political Trust on the Presidential Vote, 1968–96." *American Political Science Review* 93: 311–326.

Hooghe, Marc and Dietlind Stolle (Eds.). 2003. *Generating Social Capital: Civil Society and Institutions in Comparative Perspective.* Basingstoke: Palgrave.

Hume, David. [1741] 1985. "Of the Independency of Parliament." David Hume: Essays Moral, Political, and Literary. Indianapolis: Liberty Classics: 42–46.

Inglehart, Ronald. 1997. *Modernization and Postmodernization: Cultural, Economic, and Political Change in 43 Societies.* Princeton, NJ: Princeton Univ. Press.

Keele, Luke. 2007. "Social Capital and the Dynamics of Trust in Government." *American Journal of Political Science* 52: 241–254.

Knack, Stephen and Philip Keefer. 1997. "Does Social Capital Have an Economic Payoff? A Cross-Country Investigation." *Quarterly Journal of Economics* 112: 1251–1288.

Kumlin, Staffan. 2004. *The Personal and the Political: How Personal Welfare State Experiences Affect Political Trust and Ideology.* Basingstoke, Palgrave.

Lenard, Patti Tamara. 2008. "Trust Your Compatriots but Count Your Change: The Roles of Trust, Mistrust and Distrust in Democracy." *Political Studies* 36: 312–332.

Marien, Sofie. 2011. "Measuring Political Trust across Time and Space." In *Political Trust: Why Context Matters* edited by Sonja Zmerli and Marc Hooghe, 13–45. Colchester: ECPR Press.

Marien, Sofie and Marc Hooghe. 2011. "Does Political Trust Matter? An Empirical Investigation into the Relation between Political Trust and Support for Law Compliance." *European Journal of Political Research* 50: 267–291.

Messner, Steven F., Baumer, Eric P. and Richard Rosenfeld. 2004. "Dimensions of Social Capital and Rates of Criminal Homicide." *American Sociological Review* 69: 882–903.

Miller, Arthur H. 1974a. "Political Issues and Trust in Government, 1964–70." *American Political Science Review* 68: 951–972. (1974a and 1974b is correct).

Miller, Arthur H. 1974b. "Rejoinder to Comment by Jack Citrin: Political Discontent or Ritualism?." *American Political Science Review* 68: 989–1001.

Mishler, William and Richard Rose. 2001. "What Are the Origins of Political Trust? Testing Institutional and Cultural Theories in Post-Communist Societies." *Comparative Political Studies* 34, 30–62.

Newton, Kenneth. 2006. "Political Support, Social Capital, Civil Society and Political and Economic Performance." *Political Studies* 54, 846–864.

Newton, Kenneth and Pippa Norris. 2000. "Confidence in political institutions: faith, culture, or performance?", in Susan Pharr and Robert Putnam, eds., Disaffected Democracies: What's Troubling the Trilateral Countries?, Princeton, Princeton University Press, 2000: 52–73.

Newton, Kenneth and Sonja Zmerli. 2011. "Three Forms of Trust and their Association." *European Political Science Review* 3, 1–32.

Nye, John S., Zelikow, Phillip D. and David C. King (Eds.). 1997. *Why People don't Trust Government*. Cambridge: Harvard University Press.

Orren, Gary. 1997. "Fall From Grace: The Public's Loss of Faith in Government." In *Why People don't Trust Government* edited by John S. Nye, Phillip D. Zelikow and David C. King, 42–87. Cambridge: Harvard University Press.

Petitt, Philip. 1998. "Republican Theory and Political Trust." In *Trust and Governance* edited by Valerie A. Braithwaite and Margaret Levi, 295–314. New York: Russell Sage Foundation.

Pharr, Susan J. and Robert D. Putnam (Eds.). 2000. *Disaffected Democracies: What's Troubling the Trilateral Countries?* Princeton: Princeton University Press.

Putnam, Robert D. 1993. "The Prosperous Community." *The American Prospect* 4: 1–11.

——. 1995. "Tuning in, Tuning Out. The Strange Disappearance of Social Capital in America" *PS: Political Science and Politics* 29: 664–683.

——. 2000. *Bowling Alone: The Collapse and Revival of American Community*. New York: Simon and Schuster.

Putnam, Robert D., Pharr, Susan J. and Russell J. Dalton. 2000. "Introduction: What's Troubling the Trilateral Democracies?." In *Disaffected Democracies: What's Troubling the Trilateral Countries?* edited by Susan J. Pharr and Robert D. Putnam, 3–27. Princeton: Princeton University Press.

Roger, Charles B. 2010. "The Truth about Public Trust in Government." *Open Democracy* http://www.opendemocracy.net/charles-barclay-roger/truth-about-public-trust-in -government, August 13.

Rose, Richard and William Mishler. 2011. "Political Trust and Distrust in Post-Authoritarian Contexts." In *Political Trust: Why Context Matters* edited by Marc Hooghe and Sonja Zmerli, 117–140. Colchester: ECPR Press.

Rosenberg, Morris. 1956. "Misanthropy and Ideology." *American Sociological Review* 26: 690–695.

——. 1957. "Misanthropy and Attitudes towards International Affairs." *The Journal of Conflict Resolution* 1: 340–345.

Rothstein, Bo. 1998. *Just Institutions Matter: the Moral and Political Implications of the Universal Welfare State*. Cambridge: Cambridge University Press.

——. 2000. "Trust, Social Dilemmas and Collective Memories." *Journal of Theoretical Politics* 12: 477–501.

——. 2005. *Social Traps and the Problem of Trust*. Cambridge: Cambridge University Press.

Rothstein, Bo and Dietlind Stolle. 2003. "Social Capital, Impartiality, and the Welfare State: An Institutional Approach." In *Generating Social Capital: Civil Society and Institutions in Comparative Perspective* edited by Marc Hooghe and Dietlind Stolle, 191–209. Basingstoke: Palgrave.

Scholz, John T. and Marc Lubell. 1998. "Trust and Taxpaying: Testing the Heuristic Approach to Collective Action." *American Journal of Political Science* 42: 903–920.

Torcal, Mariano and Montero, José R. (Eds). 2006. *Political Disaffection in Contemporary Democracies: Social Capital, Institutions and Democracy*. London: Routledge.

UNODC. 2011. *2011 Global Study on Homicide*. http://www.unodc.org/unodc/en/data -and-analysis/homicide.html

Uslaner, Eric M. 1990. "Democracy and Social Capital." In *Democracy and Trust* edited by Mark E. Warren, 121–150. Cambridge: Cambridge University Press.

——. 2000–2001. "Producing and Consuming Trust." *Political Science Quarterly* 115: 569–590.

——. 2002. *The Moral Foundations of Trust*. New York: Cambridge University Press.

——. 2008. "Trust as a Moral Value." In *Handbook of Social Capital* edited by Dario Castiglione, Jan W. van Deth and Guglielmo Wolleb, 101–121. Oxford: Oxford University Press.

——. 2011. "Corruption, the Inequality Trap and Trust in Government." In *Political trust: Why Context Matters* edited by Sonja Zmerli and Marc Hooghe, 141–162. Colchester: ECPR Press.

Uslaner Eric M. and Mitchell Brown. 2005. "Inequality, Trust and Civic Engagement." *American Politics Research* 33: 868–894.

Van der Meer, Tom. 2003. "Rain or Fog? An Empirical Analysis of Social Capital's Rainmaker Effects." In *Social Capital: Civil Society and Institutions in Comparative Perspective* edited by Marc Hooghe and Dietlind Stolle, 133–151. Basinstoke: Palgrave.

Van der Meer, Tom and Dekker, Paul. 2011. "Trustworthy States, Trusting Citizens? A Multilevel Study into Objective and Subjective Determinants of Political Trust." In *Political Trust: Why Context Matters* edited by Sonja Zmerli and Marc Hooghe, 95–116. Colchester: ECPR Press.

Van de Walle, Steven, van Roosbroeck, Steven and Bouckaert, Geert. 2008. "Trust in the Public Sector: Is there any Evidence for a Long-term Decline." *International Review of Administrative Science* 72: 47–64.

Zak, Paul. J. and Knack, Stephen. 2001. "Trust and Growth." *Economic Journal* 111: 295–321.

Zmerli, Sonja and Kenneth Newton. 2008. "Social Trust and Attitudes Towards Democracy." *Public Opinion Quarterly* 74: 706–724.

——. 2011. "Winners and Losers and Three Types of Trust." In *Political trust: Why Context Matters* edited by Sonja Zmerli and Marc Hooghe, 67–94. Colchester: ECPR Press.

CHAPTER 2

Trends in Conventional and Unconventional Political Participation in Europe, 1981–2008

Rik Linssen, Hans Schmeets, Peer Scheepers and
Manfred te Grotenhuis

Introduction and Research Questions

The current view in both society and academia suggests that western democracies are suffering the yoke of mass citizen withdrawal from channels of political participation. Connecting citizens to the state by means of participation in the political decision-making process is regarded as a prerequisite for proper democratic performance (Dahl 1971). As the political system in western democracies is equalitarian, in principle these systems are based on universal suffrage where each person should have equal influence (Verba, Nie, and Kim 1978). Consequently, democracies heavily depend on citizen pressure on the political decision-making process. Citizens are expected to engage in collective (political) action and hold political authorities accountable for their actions, which requires a certain level of political trust. This implies that democracy does not only depend on the form of its basic structure (Rawls 1971) but also on the qualities and attitudes of citizens (Kymlicka and Norman 1994).

If democracy's wellbeing depends on actively engaged citizens, a disconnected public threatens to drain the lifeblood out of democracy. Putnam (2000, 2007) argues that democracy's wellbeing is currently threatened by a widespread decline in civic engagement. Civic engagement would be created through day-to-day interactions in for instance voluntary associations or sports clubs. Such associational involvement fosters interpersonal and political trust, which benefits collective action (such as political participation). The social ties created within these associations are the glue of civil society and democracy. In addition, voluntary organisations may act as schools of democracy and nurture core democratic and participatory values (Van der Meer 2009). A decline in civic engagement in general and associational involvement in particular would be detrimental for the democratic qualities and attitudes of citizens. Civic disengagement breeds distrust towards politics, which then would lead to declining political participation. According to Putnam "the most visible symptom" (Putnam 2000, 23) of civic decline is citizen's withdrawal from politics, exemplified by the half-empty ballot box during elections.

Yet, others find empirical evidence for countervailing trends in political participation (Dalton 2008; Inglehart 1997; Norris 2002; Norris 2011). Contrasting to Putnam's (2000) observation of declining civic engagement and participation, Norris (2002, 2011) challenges the notion that low (or declining) political trust unambiguously lead to lower levels of political participation. According to Norris (2011), signs of disenchantment with politics such as falling voter turnout, declines in party membership and low political trust may mobilize people to participate in alternative (unconventional) modes of political participation. Political distrust as well as dissatisfaction with politics might encourage people to protest and challenge political regimes. In the same vein, Dalton (2008) suggests a shift in the repertoire of political activities employed by citizens. Instead of participating in traditional acts such as voting and party membership, citizens are crowding-out from conventional towards new, 'alternative' or 'unconventional' channels of political participation, such as demonstrating, in recent decades.

The bulk of research on political participation originates from the United States (e.g. Brady, Verba and Schlozman 1995; Putnam 2000; Rosenstone and Hansen 1993). However, as the specific culture of the United States and the individualistic values rooted in the constitution set a very specific cultural milieu, there may very well be a case of American exceptionalism (Lipset 1996). Or, as Norris notes: "civic ills do not necessarily creep north over the Canadian border, let alone spread widely like a virus throughout Western political systems" (Norris 2002, XI). Moreover, trends in political participation have rarely been empirically studied cross-nationally in Europe (exceptions are: Kent Jennings and van Deth 1990; Marsh 1990; Norris 2002; Stolle and Hooghe 2011). Therefore, our research question reads: *What have been the main trends in conventional and unconventional political participation in Europe over the past decades?*

We aim to provide a longitudinal and cross-national European perspective, simultaneously comparing trends in both conventional and unconventional means of political participation. The arguments that motivate our research question are fourfold. First, the current literature produces contrasting theoretical expectations with respect to trends in conventional and unconventional means of political participation. These claims center around a widespread decline in participation (Putnam 2000) versus a shifting repertoire from conventional towards unconventional means of participation (Dalton 2008; Norris 2002). Second, apart from a few exceptions (e.g. Kent Jennings and van Deth 1990; Norris 2002; Stolle and Hooghe 2011; Verba et al. 1978), the current body of cross-national research focuses on *either* conventional *or* unconventional political participation separately while these contrasting theoretical expectations call for *simultaneous* comparisons of trends in both forms of political participation. Third, a cross-national longitudinal perspective on political participation focusing on Europe is currently missing. Using both the European Values Studies (EVS) and the European Social Survey (ESS) datasets enables us to re-construct a time-trend ranging from 1981 until 2008. Fourth, the extent to which measurements of political participation are equivalent cannot be taken for granted in cross-national research, but must be assessed empirically. As a first step in accurately describing trends in participation we therefore focus on the equivalence of measurements of political participation before estimating trends thereof.

In the following sections we provide a brief literature review on the definition of political participation as well as previous research on trends in political participation. Next, the data and methodology used to construct a cross-national equivalent index of political participation are introduced to ultimately arrive at descriptions of trends in conventional and unconventional political participation in Europe.

Defining Political Participation

Political participation can broadly be defined as acts employed by private citizens to influence government decision-making, either directly or indirectly (Brady 1999; van Deth 2008). This definition includes a wide variety of activities, ranging from voting and signing petitions to demonstrating and volunteering. Therefore, several sub-dimensions classifying the overarching concept of political participation have been proposed over time.

Early studies on political participation solely focused on voting and campaign activities (Berelson, Lazarsfeld, and McPhee 1954). Almond and Verba (1963) as well as Verba, Nie, and Kim (1978) broadened the concept of political participation by inclusion of activities not directly to be found within the setting of party politics but also communal activities such as attending neighbourhood meetings. Likewise, Dahl (1971) distinguished between campaign and non-campaign participatory activities. Strictly speaking, these activities are all conventional activities taking place via institutionalized routes (Burt 2002; Reeskens, Quintelier, and Billiet, 2009). In the 1960s the range of political activities was broadened further with protesting, petitioning and even violent actions. These activities were classified as 'unconventional' (Barnes and Kaase 1979) or 'elite-challenging' (Marsh 1990) political participation. The classification between conventional and unconventional political participation as proposed and empirically assessed by Barnes and Kaase (1979) became, "the primary focus of attention" (Dekker, Koopmans, and van den Broeck 1997, 225).

Admittedly, the labels 'conventional' and 'unconventional' are controversial and therefore these two dimensions of political participation are often labeled differently. Certain unconventional acts such as petitioning or demonstrating have become generally accepted ways of influencing the political decision-making process, thereby losing their 'unconventional' connotation (Dalton 2008; Norris, Walgrave, and Van Aelst 2005). Therefore Marien, Hooghe and Quintelier (2010) label these dimensions 'institutionalized forms' and 'non-institutionalized' forms of political participation. Similarly, Stolle and Hooghe (2011) note that unconventional means of participation have become increasingly accepted and label unconventional acts as 'emerging' acts of political participation. Although these two dimensions are labeled differently they still reflect the difference between conventional and unconventional political participation, both theoretically as well as in terms of the items included in the operationalization of these two dimensions.

Accordingly, conventional political participation consists of legally embedded activities aimed at influencing public officials. Conventional political participation therefore includes contacting politicians and government officials, party membership and working for political parties, and all activities directly related to the electoral process such as voting and campaigning (Barnes and Kaase 1979). Next to these conventional activities, citizens can urge political authorities to represent their interests via unconventional means of participation. These actions are not structurally embedded in the political system and may be illegal. Unconventional political participation includes boycotting, signing petitions, attending (un-) lawful demonstrations, occupying buildings, and political violence (Barnes and Kaase 1979). This distinction between conventional and unconventional political participation is (although labeled slightly different) reflected in a wide array of studies (Barnes and Kaase 1979; Brady 1999; Dalton 2008; Hooghe and Dejaeghere 2007; Inglehart 1997; Marien et al. 2010; Stolle and Hooghe 2011).

Previous Research

The existing body of literature provides an abundance of single-country empirical studies on conventional political participation, mostly focusing on the United States (e.g. Brady et al. 1995; Rosenstone and Hansen 1993; Schlozman, Verba, and Brady 1995). In many cases, shortly after each election, within-country trends are assessed on the basis of a wide variety of election studies (e.g. Bousetta 1997; Castenmiller and Kriesi 1987; Parry and Moyser 1990). Longitudinal research on conventional political participation is often limited to separate acts of participation such as voting (Blais, Gidengil, Nevitte, and Nadeau 2004; Franklin 2004; Geys 2006) or party membership (Mair and van Biezen 2001). Regarding unconventional participation most studies take *either* a cross-national perspective (Marien et al. 2010) *or* a longitudinal perspective on unconventional political participation (Inglehart 1997). Moreover, they analyse unconventional acts of participation separately, irrespective of relevant developments in conventional participation.

In the rather scarce studies taking a longitudinal perspective and simultaneously analysing conventional as well as unconventional political participation, the scope is either rather small in the number of countries studied (Kent Jennings and van Deth 1990; Stolle and Hooghe 2011; Verba et al. 1978) or in the number of unconventional political activities analysed (Norris 2002). Verba, Nie, and Kim (1978) for instance, compare merely seven countries and include solely three western democracies (the Netherlands, Austria and the United States). Similarly, Kent Jennings and van Deth (1990) analyse trends in unconventional political participation but restrict their analyses to trends in West-Germany, the United States and the Netherlands. Stolle and Hooghe (2011) analyse Germany, the United Kingdom (UK), the Netherlands, Italy, Switzerland, and Finland. Despite the extensive scope of countries studied by Norris (2002), the analyses focus on two unconventional activities (petition signing and demonstrating) and two conventional activities (voter turnout and party membership). However, none of these studies systematically compared trends in both conventional and unconventional participation. Moreover, they did not address the issue of equivalent measurements for political participation across countries and over time.

Equivalence

In order to reach meaningful insights in trends in political participation, the modus operandi is to compare different phenomena in similar contexts or, to compare similar phenomena across different contexts. In this case, we compare similar phenomena, political participation, across different contexts, 22 European countries. Before we can make such a comparison, it needs to be assured that similar political phenomena are being measured (Przeworski and Teune 2008) or, put differently, that measurements are equivalent.

Although Almond and Verba (1963) as well as more recently van Deth (1986, 1998, 2009) drew attention to the problem of limited equivalence, van Deth concluded: "yet, despite the striking consensus about the problem, the number of proposals to deal with it are rather limited, and attempts to handle equivalent indicators in comparative research are the exceptions, not the rule" (van Deth 1998, 2). These exceptions include, van Deth (1986) and Reeskens,

Quintelier and Billiet (2009). Van Deth (1986) assessed equivalence of a scale consisting of items ranging from discussing politics to painting slogans on walls in the UK, Germany, Austria, United States, Italy, Switzerland, and Finland. Based on the 2006 ESS, Reeskens, Quintelier, and Billiet (2009) assessed cross-national equivalence of items referring to conventional and unconventional political participation at one point in time. In all longitudinal studies on political participation, equivalence of measurements is left unaddressed and taken for granted (Kent Jennings and van Deth 1990; Norris et al. 2005; Stolle and Hooghe 2011; Verba et al. 1978). In this contribution, aimed at charting trends in political participation in Europe, we include assessments of equivalence within countries as well as equivalence of measurements over time focusing on the most recent data available.

Data and Measurements

Data

To assess trends in conventional and unconventional participation in Europe we rely on survey-data from the European Values Study (EVS, 1981, 1990, 1999, 2008) and the European Social Survey (ESS, 2002, 2004, 2006, 2008). The EVS is an on-going project to assess socio-cultural change and to monitor changes in values and norms across different cultures, using face-to-face interviews. It is funded by a wide variety of national level research and academic foundations and other sponsors. We will use the EVS-waves covering the time span 1981–1999, and 2008 for comparisons with ESS. The ESS is a cross-nationally comparable survey aimed to chart and explain the interaction between Europe's changing institutions and the social and political beliefs and behaviour of European citizens. The European Commission and the European Science Foundation fund the ESS.

For conventional political participation we solely use ESS data. We cannot combine both since measurement of conventional political participation in the EVS is incomparable over time. This holds for the question-wording concerning voting behaviour, which is inconsistent over time in the EVS. In 1981 the respondents were asked whether they considered themselves as close to a particular political party. In 1990 and 1999 respondents were asked which political party they would vote for if there were general elections tomorrow.

In the ESS respondents were asked to indicate which political party they had voted for in the most recent parliamentary elections in all waves, which is comparable over time. For unconventional political participation we are able to estimate a longer trend. Thus, using both the EVS and the ESS data enables us to describe trends in unconventional political participation from 1981 onwards while trends in conventional political participation can be studied from 2002 onwards, in 22 European countries. A comparison of trends in conventional and unconventional political participation is made for the period after the turn of the millennium. An overview of sample sizes and participating countries is provided in Table 1.

TABLE 1   *Participating countries and sample size in EVS and ESS surveys, by year*

	EVS			ESS				
	1981	1990	1999	2002	2004	2006	2008	Total
Austria	[a]	1,295	1,454	2,135	2,034	2,185	[a]	9,103
Belgium	927	2,427	1,779	1,709	1,686	1,688	1,669	11,885
Czech republic	[a]	1,692	1,669	1,279	2,733	[a]	1,894	9,267
Denmark	968	967	955	1,452	1,410	1,453	1,537	8,742
Estonia	[a]	1,638	819	[a]	1,858	1,433	1,576	7,324
Finland	[a]	413	929	1,886	1,919	1,811	2,096	9,054
France	1,091	889	1,466	1,450	1,752	1,920	2,000	10,568
Germany[b]	1,091	2,837	1,803	2,740	2,658	2,763	2,646	16,538
Greece	[a]	[a]	1,031	2,461	2,338	[a]	1,991	7,821
Hungary	[a]	905	937	1,603	1,413	1,453	1,475	7,786
Ireland	1,074	964	953	1,892	2,138	1,585	[a]	8,606
Netherlands	1,074	982	999	2,288	1,823	1,841	1,729	10,736
Norway	962	1,125	[a]	2,004	1,688	1,663	1,479	8,921
Poland	[a]	829	1,079	1,944	1,603	1,615	1,533	8,603
Portugal	[a]	978	936	1,430	1,987	2,153	2,281	9,765
Slovakia	[a]	802	1,083	[a]	1,327	1,616	1,748	6,576
Slovenia	[a]	[a]	909	1,426	1,334	1,382	1,232	6,283
Spain	1,847	1,930	946	1,617	1,569	1,790	2,476	12,175
Sweden	877	967	986	1,882	1,852	1,827	1,722	10,113
Switzerland	[a]	[a]	[a]	1,944	2,059	1,749	1,760	7,512
UK	1,091	1,404	940	1,986	1,818	2,307	2,267	11,813
Ukraine	[a]	[a]	989	[a]	1,916	1,919	1,748	6,572
Total	11,002	23,044	22,662	35,128	40,915	36,153	36,859	205,763

SOURCE: ESS, EVS
[a]   No data.
[b]   Only West-Germany in 1981.

Measurements

Concerning political participation the EVS and ESS included the items displayed in Table 2 in their core modules, which are implemented in every wave. For conventional participation we use the items about voting in most recent parliamentary elections, membership of political parties, and working in a political party or action group. Unconventional political participation is measured using the items demonstrating, boycotting and signing petitions. Note that one can easily imagine other newer forms of political participation,

TABLE 2   *Question-wording and answer categories for items conventional and unconventional political participation in EVS and ESS*

Data	Years	Unconventional political participation (1981–2008)	Answer categories
EVS	1981–1999	I'm going to read out some different forms of political action that people can take:	
		Signing a petition	Have done/Might do/Would never do
		Joining in boycotts	Have done/Might do/Would never do
		Attending lawful demonstrations	Have done/Might do/Would never do
ESS	2002–2008	During the last 12 months, have you done any of the following?	
		signed a petition?	Yes/No
		taken part in a lawful public demonstration?	Yes/No
		boycotted certain products?	Yes/No
Data	*Years*	*Conventional political participation (2002–2008)*	*Answer categories*
ESS	2002–2008	Some people don't vote nowadays for one reason or another. Did you vote in the last [country] national election in [month/year]?	Yes/No
ESS	2002–2008	During the last 12 months, have you done any of the following: worked in a political party or action group?	Yes/No
		Are you a member of any political party?	Yes/No

especially in the context of the rise of the Internet. However, due to the longitudinal nature of the paper we focus on forms of political participation prevalent throughout the whole time-period studied.

For unconventional political participation, the exact question-wording differs over the various datasets, as shown in Table 2. First, in the EVS respondents were asked to indicate whether they *ever* engaged in a certain type of political action. In the ESS the respondents were asked to mention political activities in which they engaged within a time-constraint of the past 12 months. Since the ESS-items pose a time-wise constraint of twelve months, it is likely that this will result in lower proportions of people engaging in a certain act compared to EVS-items. If asked whether people *ever* engaged in an unconventional act (EVS) it does not unambiguously capture participation at the time of survey but might include political participation in the past. Second, for unconventional participation the EVS inquires about "joining in boycotts" whereas the ESS specifically asks whether people boycotted certain products. Joining in boycotts may be interpreted in a different way than boycotting certain products. We suspect that joining in boycotts may be interpreted as a more activist act referring to blocking buildings and roads whereas "boycotting certain products" refers to refraining from buying certain products driven by political motives. Besides, the EVS includes a "might do" category on items referring to unconventional political participation. Respondents who indicate that they "might engage" in a certain act are combined with respondents who would never do a certain act in order to measure actual participation as is done in the ESS.

As a result of these differences in question-wording, we split our data and analyses in two separate parts. Unconventional political participation can be studied before and after the turn of the millennium based on EVS and ESS data. Conventional political participation can be studied from the turn of the millennium onwards. Hence, the trends displayed in this article are based on the EVS data for the period 1981–1999 and trends from 2002 to 2008 are based on the ESS data.

Methods

Mokken Scale Analyses

We employ Mokken scale analyses (Mokken 1971; van Schuur 2003) to arrive at a cross-nationally and longitudinally comparable model of political participation. By doing this we aim to compare similar concepts (modes of political participation) across different contexts (various European countries at different points in time).

Mokken scale analyses builds on the classic Guttman scaling approach. Consider a mathematics test consisting of problems ranging from easy (e.g. subtracting) to more complicated problems (e.g. calculus). The response on these problems can be identified as a simple dichotomy, namely correct versus incorrect. The result (correct/incorrect) corresponds with a perfect deterministic Guttman scale when all those who answered problems that are more difficult correctly (calculus) also found correct solutions to less difficult problems (subtracting). The 'difficulty' or 'popularity' of the items is expressed in the proportion of correct responses; the larger the proportion of incorrect response the more 'difficult' the question. Conversely, the larger the proportion of correct responses, the more easy or 'popular' the question.

Mokken scale analysis is the probabilistic version of the Guttman scale. Mokken scale analysis uses a set of dichotomous indicators (i.e. voting yes/ no, boycotting yes/no, etc.). Some items (e.g. voting) may be easier -popular-activities compared to others (e.g. being a member of a political party). Here, the difficulty of the items is expressed as the proportion of respondents who engage in a particular political activity. The decisive notion is that those who engage in more difficult activities (members of political parties) will probably (not *necessarily*, like in the deterministic Gutman scaling) also engage in easier or more popular activities (voting). We will investigate to what extent these response-patterns are similar across countries and over time.

Mokken scale analysis has numerous advantages over more mainstream scaling methods and ways to establish cross-national equivalence, such as factor analyses and measurement models specified in structural equation modeling. These methods are based on the decomposition of covariance and assume that frequency distributions of the items can be regarded as 'parallel' and the items have more or less the same mean and standard deviation. Thus, all items need to be equally 'popular' to be adequately used for scaling (van Schuur 2003). The frequency distributions of the items for political participation clearly demonstrate that this is not the case, e.g. the proportion of people voting is considerably larger compared to the proportion of members of political parties.

The cumulative nature of the response on the items for political participation also has important theoretical implications which are neglected when analysing these items using scaling methods such as factor analyses It is theoretically implicitly or explicitly assumed that people specialize within either conventional or unconventional modes of participation and that participation is cumulative (c.f. Millbrath 1965; Verba et al. 1978; Zukin et al. 2006). Mokken scale analyses incorporates the respective 'difficulty' of certain acts of political participation (e.g. being a member of a political party) vis-à-vis other, easier or more mainstream acts of political participation (e.g. voting at national elections). By assessing the respective difficulty of acts of political participation using Mokken scaling, we acknowledge this cumulative nature of participation.

We also take into account the scalability of our measures. The Mokken procedure provides the following scalability coefficients. The so-called Loevinger's-Hi- parameter refers to the scalability of one particular item. For each item separately, the ratio between the 'incorrect' answers (Guttmann errors) in the observed data and the expected number of 'incorrect' answers under the null hypothesis (non-cumulative independent items), results in Loevinger's- Hi. The scalability of the entire scale is expressed in the parameter scale-H. Scale-H is defined as the ratio of the total sum of all observed errors versus the sum of all expected errors. Scale-H parameters between 0.3 and 0.4 indicate weak scales. Scale-H parameters higher than 0.4 and lower than 0.5 indicate moderate scales. Finally, scale-H parameters higher than 0.5 indicate strong scales (Sijtsma and Molenaar 2002). By using probabilistic scale modeling techniques one is able to test the assumption of monotone homogeneity. Following Item Response Theory, this means that the probability of a positive response to an item increases in concordance with the value of a subject's latent trait. Applied to political participation this means we can test whether an individual engaging in a more difficult (less popular) activity (being a member of a political party), thereby having a higher score on the latent trait 'political participation', also engages in an easier (more popular) activity (voting).

In terms of comparability of measurements, or equivalence, we analyse the extent to which the ordering in terms of difficulty of the items are similar across countries and over time. Do those who engage in less popular or difficult activities (e.g. members of political parties) also engage in easier or more popular activities (e.g. voting) and is this pattern comparable across countries? In case these patterns are similar, we can estimate trends based on equivalent measures of political participation. If they turn out to be non-equivalent we exclude these measurements from our analyses.

Assessing Equivalence

To assess the extent to which the scales for conventional and unconventional political participation are equivalent we use the following three-step analytical strategy. First, to assess the *cross-national* equivalence of scales we compare the pattern in item ordering over all countries taken together (as shown in the row totals on p.A.12 in the Appendix) with the item-ordering in each separate country. Countries that deviate from this general pattern are considered non-equivalent. Second, to assess *cross-national* and *longitudinal* equivalence, we check the consistency in item ordering across all country-year combinations. Thus, if a given country-year combination reflects the same general pattern observed in all other country-year combinations, the measurement is considered cross-nationally and longitudinally equivalent. Third, we assess the quality of the scales based on scalability parameters Loevinger's- Hi and scale-H. If scale-H is smaller than 0.3 the country is excluded from analyses. Hence, based on the three conditions of item-ordering across counties, item-ordering across country-year combinations, and scalability parameters we determine which countries are non-equivalent. The relevant parameters (i.c. exceptions to the general pattern and/or low scalability parameters) are highlighted in the Appendix A,Table A.1.[1]

Additionally, to determine to what extent conventional political participation is associated with unconventional political participation and to assess whether there is a negative or a positive relationship, Spearman rank correlation coefficients between the (ordinal) scales for conventional and unconventional political participation are also displayed in the Appendix.

Equivalence of Scales Over Time and Across Countries: Unconventional Political Participation

Let us first look at the general behavioural pattern, as shown in the row total at the bottom of the Table A.1[2] in the Appendix. Petitioning turns out to be the most popular political activity. On average, 30 percent of the respondents indicated that they had signed a petition. Boycotting is a more difficult/less popular activity since 14 percent of the respondents indicated they had used boycotting as a means of political participation. The least popular activity is demonstrating. On average, 11 percent of the respondents attended a demonstration.

However, the ordering of items is different before and after the year 2000. Before the turn of the millennium, the item ordering is petitioning, demonstrating, and boycotting, respectively. After 2000, the item ordering is petitioning, boycotting, and demonstrating. So demonstrating and boycotting switched places in the ordering. This pattern is found in the majority of countries and is graphically displayed in Figure 1. The switch in demonstrating and boycotting may be due to the aforementioned difference in question-wording between EVS and ESS regarding the time-interval and differences in interpretation.

---

1   Please refer to the online appendix: http://dx.doi.org/10.1163/9789004276062_004.
2   See footnote 1.

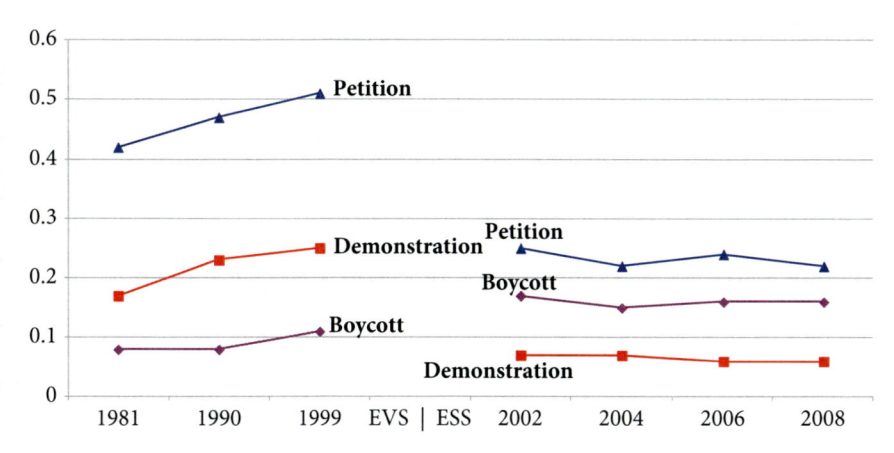

FIGURE 1   *Change in item ordering before and after the turn of the millennium: Average item difficulties by year.*[a]

[a] Note that the question wording changes after the turn of the millenium.

Notable exceptions to this pattern are Portugal, Spain, Greece, and Ukraine. In Portugal, the ordering of items is consistent over time (no switch) but inconsistent compared to other countries because the ordering is petitioning, demonstrating, boycotting. So, for Portugal the scale is equivalent over time but incomparable to other countries. A similar interpretation holds for Ukraine, where the ordering of items is also consistent over time but inconsistent compared to other countries; demonstrating is more popular than petitioning and boycotting, whereas in other countries petitioning is the most popular activity. However, this is due to very close inter-item difficulties in Ukraine. In 2008 the popularity of demonstrating (0.4) is equal to the popularity of petitioning (0.4). In Spain and Greece the item ordering switches continuously after the turn of the millennium.

Since the order of demonstrating and boycotting changes consistently in most countries, we split our dataset and separately calculate scalability parameters before and after the turn of the millennium. All in all, we find that the EVS-waves provide good scales (scale-H = 0.64) whereas the ESS-waves provide moderate scales (scale-H = 0.41), as shown in the bottom rows of Table A.1[3] in the Appendix.

The proportion of people demonstrating, petitioning and boycotting are smaller in the ESS compared to the EVS. Likewise, the difference in popularity between demonstrating, petitioning and boycotting is also smaller in the ESS

---

3   For the online appendix's url see footnote 1.

compared to the EVS. As a result, small deviations from the general item-ordering pattern may have a stronger influence on overall scalability parameters for the ESS compared to the EVS. Nonetheless, we find that the overall picture indicates moderate to strong scales for most countries. However, we find very weak scales (scale-H < 0.3) for Denmark, Estonia, Greece and Poland, as demonstrated in Table A.1 in the Appendix.[4] Consequently, we will treat these countries separately in further analyses.

Summarizing, concerning unconventional political participation we find that demonstrating is less popular after the turn of the millennium. Instead, boycotting products is a more prevalent unconventional political activity from 2000 onwards. On the basis of item ordering, Spain, Portugal, Ukraine, and Greece are non-equivalent since they deviate from the general behavioural pattern. On the basis of scalability parameters Denmark and Estonia are non-equivalent as scalability coefficients are weak. Greece is non-equivalent due to both distinctive item ordering and low scalability coefficients.

Equivalence of Scales Over Time and Across Countries: Conventional Political Participation

For conventional political participation, we find that the general ordering of items from most popular to least popular is voting (0.8), membership of a political party (0.5), and working for a political party (0.4), see Figure 2 for details.

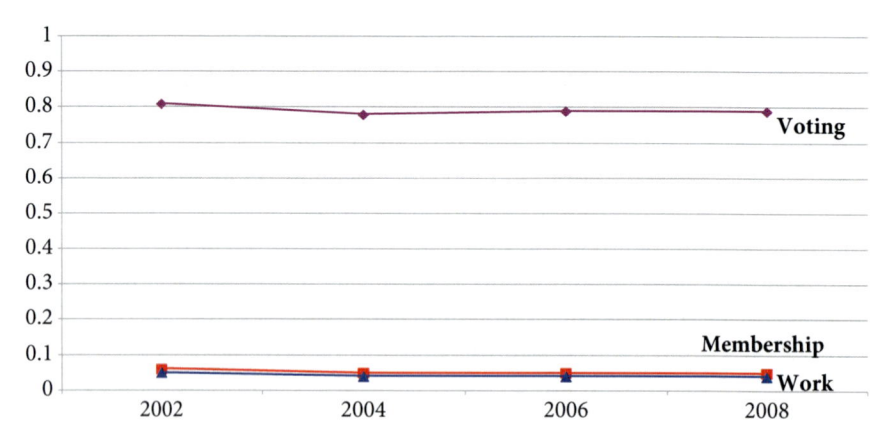

FIGURE 2   *Difference in item popularity for voting vs. membership of and working for political parties*

---

4 For the online appendix's url see footnote 1.

The ordering voting, membership, and working for political parties, exists in the vast majority of countries. The notable exceptions to this item ordering are Germany, Hungary, Estonia, Spain, Slovakia, and Poland. In Spain, Slovakia and Poland working for political parties is consistently more popular compared to being a member of a political party. Estonia, Hungary and Germany show inconsistent anomalies to the general ordering of voting, working for and membership of political parties. As shown in the Appendix Table A.1,[5] in Estonia, Germany and Hungary the item ordering is inconsistent with the general pattern in 2004 and 2006. However, the popularities for working for a political party and membership are very close in these cases.

Overall scalability-parameter scale-H indicates a good scale for conventional political participation (scale-H = 0.60). None of scale-H parameters in the country-year combinations studied is below the 0.3 threshold.

Summarizing, concerning conventional political participation we argue that Germany, Hungary, Estonia, Spain, Slovakia, and Poland are non-equivalent as the item ordering deviates from the generally observed pattern.

Analyses of Trends

On the basis of assessment of equivalence, we now turn to the analyses of trends in political participation in Europe. For unconventional political participation we analyse the trend before and after the turn of the millennium. The scale for unconventional political participation is constructed using the average score on the items, petitioning, boycotting, and demonstrating so that the country-level aggregates represent the proportion of people engaging in unconventional political participation.

For conventional political participation it is to be noted that voting is by far the most popular activity (see Figure 2). Although the scale for the items voting, membership, and working for political parties is equivalent, we choose to analyse voting separately for the following reasons. First, a scale that includes voting will be disproportionally influenced by (volatility in) the proportion of people who vote compared to the proportion of membership and working for political parties. Second, voting can theoretically be considered as a truly different activity compared to membership and working for political parties. Voting is only possible once every few years whereas membership and working for political parties involve more prolonged commitment. Thus, voting is analysed separately. For membership of political parties and working for political parties a scale using the average score on both items is used. Analogous to unconventional political participation, the country-level

---

5   For the online appendix's url see footnote 1.

aggregates of these scales represent the proportion of people engaging in conventional political acts.

Results

Based on the assessment of equivalence in the previous sections, a division is made between those countries being classified as equivalent and as non-equivalent. The analyses of trends in conventional and unconventional political participation in Europe are presented in Table 3 and Table 4, which display the average scale values by country and year.

Since we are primarily interested in the trajectory of political participation over time we employ analysis of variance (ANOVA). Levels of political participation may demonstrate a clear linear increase or decrease. Alternatively, participation may simply fluctuate over time. Therefore, we do not want to impose a -rather strict- linear trend of political participation but also allow for the possibility of non-linear fluctuation over time. In contrast to other techniques, ANOVA allows us to model this non-linear fluctuation and test the validity of the linearity assumption, by conducting tests for linearity. If non-linear trends over time occur, we report the Eta-coefficient per country (see column Eta in Table 3 and Table 4). If levels of political participation increase or decrease linearly over time, we present the linear measure of association R, which is equal to Eta in case there is no deviation from linearity. As demonstrated in Table 3 and Table 4, the data demonstrate linear trends over time for most countries (e.g. all equivalent countries before the turn of the millennium) while some countries show non-linear fluctuation.

In addition to measuring variance over time, we can also measure variance between countries. Therefore Eta is reported in a separate row (below the row with total). The estimate of Eta in the row tests the extent to which political participation varies over countries. Since some countries did not participate in some EVS or ESS waves, Eta is only calculated for countries that participated in all EVS or ESS waves. Because of limited data availability in certain countries and non-equivalence, some other measures of association cannot be calculated as well (see footnotes for Table 3 and Table 4).

As demonstrated in Table 3, unconventional participation increases before the turn of the millennium. Overall, we find an increase in unconventional political participation (ranging from 0.22 in 1981 to 0.38 in 1999 overall). Unconventional political participation heavily increased in Belgium, where the proportion of active people tripled, as well as in Sweden and in the Netherlands, where the proportion doubled between 1981 and 1999. Sweden is the most active country studied; in 1999 a majority of the Swedish population reported that they engaged in a boycott, demonstration or petition. The French, Irish, and Britons also demonstrate increased unconventional political activism between 1981 and 1999. This is however a less sharp increase compared to Belgium, Sweden, and the Netherlands. Germany, Finland, Norway, Slovakia, and Austria demonstrated rather weak (the difference in proportion between 1981 and 1998 does not exceed 0.06), though significant, increased levels of unconventional participation before the turn of the millennium.

Although unconventional political participation increases before the turn of the millennium, after the turn levels of unconventional political participation are characterized by stability. The total proportion of active people ranges from 0.19 in 2002 to 0.20 in 2008. This is also reflected in the measures of association. Although parameters Eta and R are significant, Table 3 does not show a pronounced increase or decrease in unconventional participation. For unconventional political participation, our analyses reveal that the trend remains clearly stable as all parameters are not significant.

Looking at unconventional political participation both before and after the turn of the millennium, the most striking finding is that differences between countries are larger than differences over time. For example, in 2008, one in every four French respondents engaged in unconventional acts against one in every twenty Slovenian respondents. After the year 2000 this is also shown in the differences between countries as measured by Eta. The variation between countries (Eta ranges between 0.26 and 0.29) is much larger compared to the variation within countries (Eta ranges between 0.02 and 0.11).

We already mentioned the differences in question-wording between ESS and EVS when it comes to the time-interval and the interpretation of boycotting. This effect is apparent in Figure 3 where the trend for unconventional political participation is plotted for the equivalent countries and measurements. For 2008, we are able to compare the ESS (with the 12 months interval of unconventional participation) with the EVS measurement (ever participated in unconventional participation) since both surveys are carried out in 2008. As demonstrated in Figure 3 the EVS-measurement yields consistently higher values compared to the ESS measurement. This supports our claim that the EVS-measurement is an overestimation of actual participation rates since it might, and probably does, include participation in the more distant past. However, we acknowledge that the difference in question-wording does not fully explain the (upward) trend in political participation before the turn of the millennium.

For conventional political participation, we find that membership and working for political parties is also stable over time. There is some minor

TABLE 3 *ANOVA unconventional political participation: Proportion active respondents before and after the turn of the millennium, equivalent and non-equivalent countries.*

Equivalent countries — EVS (before turn of millennium)

Year	1981	1990	1999	Eta		R	
Belgium	0.13	0.26	0.41	0.32	**	0.32	**
France	0.28	0.33	0.40	0.15	**	0.15	**
Germany	0.27	0.34	0.32	0.09	**	0.05	**
Ireland	0.16	0.22	0.31	0.20	**	0.20	**
Netherlands	0.18	0.29	0.39	0.26	**	0.26	**
Sweden	0.26	0.37	0.53	0.34	**	0.34	**
UK	0.27	0.34	0.37	0.15	**	0.15	**
Total	0.22	0.31	0.38				
Eta	0.20 **	0.15 **	0.20 **				
Finland	a	0.24	0.27	0.06	*	b	
Hungary	a	0.08	0.08	0.00		b	
Norway	0.27	0.31	a	0.08	**	b	
Slovenia	a	a	0.17	b		b	
Switzerland	a	a	a	b		b	

ESS (after turn of millennium)

	2002	2004	2006	2008	Eta		R	
Belgium	0.18	0.13	0.16	0.16	0.08	**	-0.02	*
France	0.26	0.24	0.25	0.25	0.02		0.00	
Germany	0.23	0.21	0.20	0.23	0.05	**	-0.01	
Netherlands	0.12	0.12	0.11	0.12	0.02		-0.01	
Sweden	0.27	0.31	0.27	0.30	0.07	**	0.03	**
UK	0.24	0.20	0.24	0.22	0.05	**	-0.01	
Finland	0.18	0.19	0.21	0.22	0.07	**	0.06	**
Hungary	0.04	0.04	0.04	0.05	0.03	*	0.02	*
Norway	0.22	0.24	0.24	0.23	0.03	*	0.01	
Slovenia	0.07	0.03	0.08	0.05	0.11	**	0.00	
Switzerland	0.28	0.24	0.24	0.24	0.05	**	-0.04	**
Total	0.19	0.19	0.19	0.20				
Eta	0.27 **	0.29 **	0.26 **	0.27 **				
Austria	0.20	0.17	0.15	a	0.08	**	-0.08	**

Austria	a		0.21	0.27	0.11	**	b		Czech Republic	0.10	0.08	a	0.09	0.05	**	0.00
Czech Republic	a		0.30	0.31	0.01		b		Slovakia	a	0.13	0.11	0.09	0.09 **		-0.09 **
Slovakia	a		0.23	0.25	0.05	*	b		Ireland	0.16	0.13	0.14	a	0.05 **		-0.03 *

Non-equivalent countries[c]							*ESS*				
Denmark	0.24	0.30	0.37				Denmark	0.20	0.21	0.23	0.22
Estonia	a	0.23	0.11				Estonia	a	0.03	0.05	0.05
Greece	a	a	0.33				Greece	0.06	0.04	a	0.09
Poland	a	0.15	0.11				Poland	0.04	0.06	0.04	0.05
Portugal	a	0.18	0.16				Portugal	0.05	0.03	0.04	0.04
Spain	0.20	0.17	0.20				Spain	0.15	0.24	0.17	0.14
Ukraine	a	a	0.12				Ukraine	a	0.10	0.05	0.03

SOURCE: ESS, EVS

[a] No data.

[b] could not be estimated due to small number of measurements (number of waves < 3).

[c] Eta and R are not calculated since measurements are not equivalent for these countries.

* $p < 0.05$ ** $p < 0.01$.

TABLE 4   *ANOVA membership and working for political parties and voting: Proportion of active respondents after the turn of the millennium, equivalent and non-equivalent countries*

Equivalent countries	Membership and working for political parties						Voting					
Year	**2002**	**2004**	**2006**	**2008**	**Eta**	**R**	**2002**	**2004**	**2006**	**2008**	**Eta**	**R**
Belgium	0.07	0.06	0.07	0.05	0.04 **	−0.03 **	0.87	0.93	0.93	0.92	0.08 **	0.06 **
Denmark	0.05	0.06	0.06	0.07	0.03 *	0.03 **	0.94	0.92	0.93	0.95	0.04 *	0.02
Finland	0.06	0.06	0.06	0.06	0.02	0.00	0.82	0.79	0.84	0.83	0.05 **	0.03 *
France	0.03	0.03	0.03	0.03	0.01	−0.01	0.75	0.77	0.78	0.78	0.03	0.02 *
Netherlands	0.04	0.05	0.04	0.04	0.01	0.00	0.87	0.81	0.84	0.86	0.06 **	0.00
Norway	0.09	0.09	0.08	0.07	0.04 **	−0.04 **	0.85	0.86	0.86	0.86	0.01	0.01
Portugal	0.04	0.02	0.03	0.02	0.05 **	−0.04 **	0.74	0.71	0.76	0.73	0.04 **	0.00
Slovenia	0.04	0.03	0.05	0.04	0.03	0.00	0.81	0.70	0.78	0.73	0.10	−0.04 **
Sweden	0.07	0.05	0.06	0.06	0.03	−0.01	0.87	0.89	0.89	0.91	0.04 **	0.04 **
Switzerland	0.08	0.07	0.07	0.06	0.04 **	−0.04 **	0.69	0.66	0.66	0.64	0.04 **	−0.04 **
UK	0.03	0.03	0.03	0.03	0.02	−0.01	0.73	0.69	0.73	0.71	0.03 *	0.00
Total	0.06	0.05	0.05	0.05			0.81	0.79	0.81	0.81		
Eta	0.10 **	0.10 **	0.10 **	0.09 **			0.18 **	0.22 **	0.21 **	0.24 **		

Austria	0.12	0.11	0.12		0.02 **	0.01	0.88	0.80	0.87		0.10 **	−0.01
Czech Republic	0.04	0.03	a	0.04	0.02 **	0.00 *	0.64	0.56	a	0.58	0.07 **	−0.02 *
Greece	0.05	0.07	a	0.06	0.04 **	0.01 **	0.91	0.91	a	0.88	0.05 **	−0.04 **
Ireland	0.05	0.05	0.05		0.02 **	−0.01 **	0.81	0.82	0.77		0.05 **	−0.03 **
Ukraine		0.04	0.04	0.03	0.02 **	−0.01 *		0.85	0.88	0.83	0.06 **	−0.02 *
Non-equivalent countries[b]												
Estonia	a	0.02	0.03	0.04			a	0.61	0.59	0.66		
Germany	0.04	0.03	0.04	0.03			0.86	0.81	0.79	0.83		
Hungary	0.02	0.01	0.02	0.01			0.83	0.80	0.77	0.80		
Poland	0.02	0.02	0.01	0.02			0.68	0.66	0.67	0.73		
Slovakia	a	0.03	0.03	0.02			a	0.76	0.69	0.77		
Spain	0.04	0.06	0.04	0.02			0.79	0.83	0.80	0.81		

SOURCE: ESS, EVS

[a] no data

[b] Eta and R are not calculated since measurements are not equivalent for these countries. * $p < 0.05$ ** $p < 0.01$

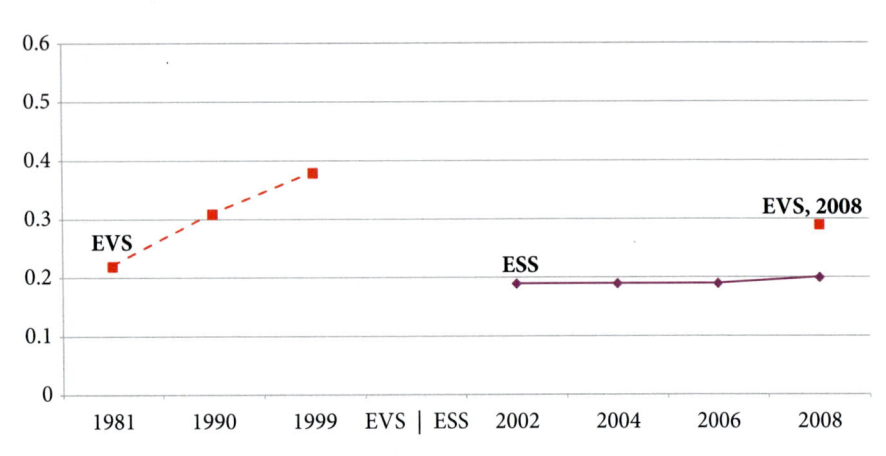

FIGURE 3   *Trends in unconventional political participation, 1981–2008 for equivalent countries*

fluctuation, ranging from 0.06 in 2002, via 0.05 in 2004 and 2006 to 0.04 in 2008. The results for separate countries underline the stability in membership and working for political parties. In Finland, France, the Netherlands, Slovenia, Sweden and, the UK we find no significant variation over time. Although the variation over time is significant in Belgium, Denmark, Norway, Portugal, Switzerland, Austria, Switzerland, Czech Republic, Greece, Ireland and Ukraine, it is very small. The differences in proportions over time do not exceed 0.02. Overall, working for political parties and membership is a relatively marginal phenomenon, especially compared to voting, as previously demonstrated by the large differences in item popularities. For conventional political participation the differences between countries are larger than differences over time, which corresponds with our findings regarding unconventional political participation, where variance over time is also limited compared to differences between countries.

Reported voting is also stable between 2002 and 2008. Overall, we find the proportion of respondents indicated that they voted fluctuates around 0.80 (0.81 in 2002 to 0.80 in 2008, with a very small uptick in 2006 to 0.82). Looking at the individual countries underlines the notion of stability as reflected in very low values of Eta and R. Also concerning voting, the most striking finding is that differences between countries are larger than differences over time. Eta for differences between countries ranges between 0.18 and 0.24, whereas Eta for differences over time ranges between 0.01 and 0.10.

Note that when using ANOVA, the dependent variable is assumed to be interval scaled. For voting, which is dichotomous, this is unproblematic. However, membership and working for political parties, and unconventional political participation are strictly speaking ordinal scaled. To check for robustness of our findings and take into account the ordinal nature of the scale, we also plotted the median instead of the mean over time. Visual inspection of these plots leads us to the same conclusions as drawn from Table 3 and Table 4.

Additionally, the association between conventional and unconventional political participation is positive in all countries (see Appendix Table A.1[6]). This is not in line with the claim of a crowding-out effect. If there were a crowding-out effect from conventional to unconventional modes, we would expect (increasingly) negative associations between conventional and unconventional political participation. Moreover, aggregate levels of unconventional political participation remain stable, after the turn of the millennium, which also speaks against the notion of a crowding-out effect.

Conclusion and Discussion

In this contribution we started off with the debate between an alleged decline in political participation in general (Putnam 2000) and a shift in the repertoire of political activities from conventional to unconventional political participation (Dalton 2008; Inglehart 1997; Norris 2002; Norris et al. 2005). These contradictory assumptions have not been addressed empirically. This holds especially for the European case; trends in political participation have rarely been studied outside the United States and seldom in a cross-national perspective. We used a theoretically motivated division between conventional and unconventional forms of political participation.

The current body of literature focused on conventional or unconventional political participation separately, while the notion of a shifting repertoire calls for a systematic comparison of trends in conventional as well as unconventional political participation. In short, the aforementioned contrasting theoretical expectations call for a cross-national and longitudinal perspective on both conventional and unconventional political participation incorporating a large set of European countries. However, to accurately describe trends in political participation we first needed to overcome the -often overlooked-methodological hurdle of constructing cross-nationally equivalent measurements of participation (van Deth 1998, 2009). By using Mokken scale analysis (Mokken 1971; van Schuur 2003), which incorporates the cumulative pattern of various forms of political participation, and compares this across countries, we were able to assess cross-national as well as longitudinal equivalence of these

---

6   For the online appendix's url see footnote 1.

scales. With a few exceptions, the measurements for conventional and unconventional political participation were found equivalent across countries and over time.

Our results demonstrate an upward trend in unconventional political participation before the turn of the millennium and stable levels of unconventional political participation after the turn of the millennium. The increase in unconventional political participation before the turn of the millennium may be due to measuring whether respondents 'ever' participated in unconventional acts, which leads to estimates of higher aggregate levels of participation and inflates the measurement of unconventional political participation over time. When measuring actual participation (the past 12 months), as is done after the millennium, we find low and stable levels of unconventional political participation.

Conventional political participation remained stable after the turn of the millennium. Voting is the most common political activity. On average about 80 percent of the respondents reported that they voted in the most recent parliamentary elections. Membership of, and working for political parties is a marginal phenomenon; on average roughly 5 percent reports to either working for or membership of a political party.

Contrary to Putnam's (2000) finding of a widespread decline in civic engagement in the United States where decreasing voter turnout would be the most emblematic phenomenon, for Europe we find stability in conventional political participation. The notion that Western democracies suffer the yoke of mass citizen withdrawal from conventional channels of participation in recent decades seems therefore overstated for the European case. Additionally, since conventional political participation is stable, our results are at odds with the alternative claim, as put forward by Norris (2002) and Dalton (2008). They argue that disenchantment with politics could mobilize individuals towards unconventional political action (Norris 2011). Thus, there would be a shift from conventional to unconventional political participation. If this would be the case, one would expect decreasing levels of conventional political participation and an increase of unconventional political participation.

Yet, there are large cross-national differences. In short, differences between countries are larger than differences within countries over time for both conventional and unconventional political participation. As political participation is embedded in the nation state, which determines legal conditions, political actors and the strength of political institutions (Newton and Giebler 2008; van der Meer 2009), country-specific characteristics seem to be more important in shaping political participation than changes over time. Szreter (2002) notes that the institutional setting has a "critical facilitating" role in the opportunity to participate. Similarly, Kriesi (2008) claims that political participation research underestimates the impact of institutions. These mixed findings of trends in political participation indicatively support the claim that the institutional setting has a critical facilitating role in channelling participation and that more attention needs to be paid to the effects of the institutional setting and other country-specific factors. Explaining cross-national differences in conventional and unconventional political participation involves formulating and testing hypotheses concerning this institutional setting.

Ideally, we would have included an even longer time trend. However, data availability hampers this approach. Moreover, also the need to maintain data comparability – demonstrated by the assessments of equivalence over time – might have resulted in excluding more countries from further analyses. Still, the trends depicted here are, to our knowledge, among the most extensive in terms of time-span as well as the variety of countries. Furthermore, the rate of recurrence of certain modes of political participation is not taken into account. Unfortunately, the measurements used do not contain information on the frequency or recurrence of for instance demonstrating or petitioning. Additionally, one can imagine that newer methods of political participation are on the rise, especially in the context of the emergence of the Internet. Further research needs to address these issues.

References

Almond, Gabriel A., and Sidney Verba. 1963. *The Civic Culture: Political Attitudes and Democracy in five Nations.* Princeton: Princeton University Press.

Barnes, Samuel H., and Max Kaase. 1979. *Political Action: Mass Participation in five Western Democracies.* Beverly Hills: Sage.

Berelson, Bernard R., Paul F. Lazarsfeld, and William M. McPhee. 1954. *Voting: A Study of Opinion Formation in a Presidential Campaign.* Chicago: University of Chicago Press.

Blais, André, Elisabeth Gidengil, Niel Nevitte, and Richard Nadeau. 2004. Where Does Turnout Decline Come From? *European Journal of Political Research* 43: 221–236.

Bousetta, Hassan. 1997. Citizenship and Political Participation in France and the Netherlands: Reflections on two local cases. *New Community* 23: 215–231.

Brady, Henry E. 1999. Political Participation. In *Measures of Political Attitudes*, edited by John P. Robinson, Philip R. Shaver, and Lawrence S. Wrightsman, 737–801. San Diego: Academic Press.

Brady, Henry E., Sidney Verba, and Kay L. Schlozman. 1995. Beyond Ses – a Resource Model of Political-Participation. *American Political Science Review* 89: 271–294.

Burt, Sandra. 2002. The Concept of Political Participation. In *Citizen Politics: Research and Theory in Canadian Political Behavior*, edited by Joanna M. Everitt, and Brenda L. O'Neill, 232–246. Oxford: Oxford University Press.

Castenmiller, Peter, and Hanspeter Kriesi. 1987. De Ontwikkeling van Politiek Protest in Nederland Sinds de Jaren zeventig. *Acta politica* 22:61.

Dahl, Robert A. 1971. *Polyarchy; Participation and Opposition*. New Haven: Yale University Press.

Dalton, Russell J. 2008. Citizenship Norms and the Expansion of Political Participation. *Political Studies* 56: 76–98.

Dekker, Paul, Ruud Koopmans, and Andries van den Broeck. 1997. Voluntary Associations, Social Movements and Individual Political Behaviour in Western Europe. In *Private Groups and Public Life: Social Participation, Voluntary Associations and Political Involvement in Representative Democracies,* edited by Jan W. Van Deth, 224–243. London: Routledge.

ESS. *European Social Survey Round 1 Data.* 2002. Data file edition 6.2. Norwegian Social Science Data Services. Norway : Data Archive and distributor of ESS data.

———. *European Social Survey Round 2 Data.* 2004. Data file edition 3.2. Norwegian Social Science Data Services. Norway : Data Archive and distributor of ESS data.

———. *European Social Survey Round 3 Data* .2006. Data file edition 3.3. Norwegian Social Science Data Services. Norway : Data Archive and distributor of ESS data.

———. *European Social Survey Round 4 Data.* 2008. Data file edition 4.0. Norwegian Social Science Data Services. Norway : Data Archive and distributor of ESS data.

EVS. *European Values Study 1981 Integrated Dataset.* 1981. Surveys designed and executed by the European Values Study Group and World Values Survey Association. File Producers: ASEP/JDS, Madrid, Spain and Tilburg University, Tilburg, the Netherlands. File Distributors: ASEP/JDS and GESIS, Cologne, Germany.

———. *European Values Study 1990 Integrated Dataset.* 1990. Surveys designed and executed by the European Values Study Group and World Values Survey Association. File Producers: ASEP/JDS, Madrid, Spain and Tilburg University, Tilburg, the Netherlands. File Distributors: ASEP/JDS and GESIS, Cologne, Germany.

———. *European Values Study 1999 Integrated Dataset.* 1999. Surveys designed and executed by the European Values Study Group and World Values Survey Association. File Producers: ASEP/JDS, Madrid, Spain and Tilburg University, Tilburg, the Netherlands. File Distributors: ASEP/JDS and GESIS, Cologne, Germany.

———. *European Values Study 2008 Integrated Dataset.* 2008. Surveys designed and executed by the European Values Study Group and World Values Survey Association. File Producers: ASEP/JDS, Madrid, Spain and Tilburg University, Tilburg, the Netherlands. File Distributors: ASEP/JDS and GESIS, Cologne, Germany.

Franklin, Mark N. 2004. *Voter turnout and the dynamics of Electoral Competition in Established Democracies since 1945.* Cambridge: Cambridge University Press.

Geys, Benny. 2006. Explaining Voter Turnout: A Review of Aggregate-level Research. *Electoral Studies* 25: 637–663.

Hooghe, Marc., and Yves Dejaeghere. 2007. Does the 'Monitorial Citizen' Exist? An Empirical Investigation into the Occurrence of Postmodern Forms of Citizenship in the Nordic Countries. *Scandinavian Political Studies* 30: 249–271.

Inglehart, Ronald. 1997. *Modernization and Postmodernization: Cultural,Economic, and Political Change in 43 Societies.* Princeton: Princeton University Press.

Kent Jennings, M., and Jan W van Deth. 1990. *Continuities in Political Action: a Longitudinal Study of Political Orientations in three Western Democracies.* Berlin: Walter de Gruyter.

Kriesi, Hanspeter. 2008. Political Mobilisation, Political Participation and the Power of the Vote. *West European Politics* 31:147–168.

Kymlicka, Will, and Wayne Norman. 1994. Return of the Citizen – a Survey of Recent Work on Citizenship Theory. *Ethics* 104: 352–381.

Lipset, Seymour M. 1996. *American Exceptionalism : A Double-edged Sword.* New York: W.W. Norton.

Mair, Peter, and Ingrid van Biezen. 2001. Party Membership in twenty European Democracies, 1980–2000. *Party Politics* 7: 5–21.

Marien, Sofie, Marc Hooghe, and Ellen Quintelier. 2010. Inequalities in Non-institutionalised Forms of Political Participation: A Multi-level Analysis of 25 countries. *Political Studies* 58: 187–213.

Marsh, Alan. 1990. *Political Action in Europe and the USA.* London: MacMillan.

Millbrath, Lester W. 1965. *Political Participation: How and Why do People Get Involved in Politics?* Chicago: Rand McNally.

Mokken, Rob J. 1971. *A Theory and Procedure of Scale Analysis with Applications in Political Research.* The Hague: Mouton & Co.

Newton, Kenneth, and Heiko Giebler. 2008. *Patterns of Participation: Political and Social Participation in 22 nations.* Berlin: WZB

Norris, Pippa. 2002. *Democratic Phoenix : Reinventing Political Activism.* Cambridge: Cambridge University Press.

——. 2011. *Democratic Deficit: Critical Citizens Revisited.* Cambridge: Cambridge University Press.

Norris, Pippa, Stefaan Walgrave, and Peter Van Aelst. 2005. Who Demonstrates? Antistate rebels, Conventional Participants, or Everyone? *Comparative Politics* 37: 189–205.

Parry, Geriant, and George Moyser. 1990. A Map of Political-Participation in Britain. *Government and Opposition* 25: 147–169.

Przeworski, Adam, and Henry Teune. 2008. Equivalence in Cross-National Research. In *Attitude Measurement Volume 4: Expanding Measurement Horizons*, edited by Caroline Roberts, and Roger Jowell. Los Angeles: Sage.

Putnam, R.D. 2000. *Bowling Alone: The Collapse and Revival of American Community*. New York: Simon & Schuster.

———. 2007. E Pluribus Unum: Diversity and Community in the twenty-first Century the 2006 Johan Skytte Prize Lecture. *Scandinavian Political Studies* 30: 137–174.

Rawls, John. 1971. *A Theory of Justice*. Cambridge, MA: Belknap Press of Harvard University Press.

Reeskens, Tim, Ellen Quintelier, and Jaak Billiet. 2009. "Assesing the Cross-cultural Equivalence of Political Participation in the European Social Survey." Paper presented at the Cinefogo WP 11 Workshop: Methodological challenges in cross-national participation research, the Hague, the Netherlands, Januari 16–17, 2009.

Rosenstone, Steven J., and John M. Hansen. 1993. *Mobilization, Participation, and Democracy in America*. New York: Maxwell Macmillan International.

Schlozman, Kay. L., Sidney Verba, and Henry E. Brady. 1995. Participation is Not a Paradox – the View from American Activists. *British Journal of Political Science* 25: 1–36.

Sijtsma, Klaas, and Ivo W. Molenaar. 2002. *Introduction to Nonparametric Item Response Theory*. Thousand Oaks: Sage.

Stolle, Dietlind, and Marc Hooghe. 2011. Shifting Inequalities? Patterns of Exclusion and Inclusion in Emerging Forms of Political Participation. *European Societies* 13: 119–142.

Szreter, Simon. 2002. The State of Social Capital: Bringing Back Power, Politics, and History. *Theory and Society* 31: 573–621.

van der Meer, Tom. 2009. "States of Freely Associating Citizens." PhD diss., Radboud University Nijmegen, Nijmegen.

van Deth, Jan W. 1986. A Note on Measuring Political Participation in Comparative Research. *Quality and Quantity* 20: 261–272.

———. 1998. *Comparative Politics: The Problem of Equivalence*. London: Routledge.

———. 2008. Political Participation. In *Encyclopedia of Political Communication*, edited by Linda L. Kaid, and Chriztina Holtz-Bacha, London: Sage.

———. 2009. Estabilishing Equivalence. In *The Sage Handbook of Comparative Politics*, edited by Todd Landman, and Neil Robinson, 84–100. London: Sage.

van Schuur, Wijbrant. H. 2003. Mokken Scale Analysis: Between the Guttman Scale and Parametric Item Response Theory. *Political Analysis* 11: 139–163.

Verba, Sidney, Norman H. Nie, and Jae-on Kim. 1978. *Participation and Political Equality: A seven-nation Comparison*. Cambridge: Cambridge University Press.

Zukin, Cliff, Scott Keeter, Molly Andolina, Krista Jenkins, and Michael X. Delli Carpini. 2006. *A New Engagement? Political Participation, Civic Life, and the Changing American Citizen*. Oxford: Oxford University Press.

CHAPTER 3

Rethinking the Meaning and Measurement of Political Trust

Suzanne L. Parker, Glenn R. Parker and Terri L. Towner

Introduction

Few areas in the study of political attitudes are as rife with controversy as the analysis of political trust. The issues touch upon measurement, conceptualization, and theory, and empirical analyses have resulted in contradictory findings. Despite a growing literature, there are lingering, fundamental questions about political trust that remain unanswered. Even basic questions such as what is being measured by the most popular indicators of political trust in the U.S., the American National Election Studies (ANES) questions, are under contention.[1] In this analysis, questions that remain about political trust are examined using new measures of trust in political incumbents.

Specifically, a number of research questions are addressed: First, do citizens distinguish between trust in the government, and trust in individual politicians? Second, to what extent is trust in government an all-embracing concept—that is, do the trust-in-government questions represent system support (or regime support), or trust in only the national (federal) government? Third, since presidents, due to their recognizable influence over public policy, represent government in the minds of many citizens, do citizens differentiate between their trust in government and their evaluations of incumbent presidents? Fourth, are there theoretical and causal linkages

---

1 The ANES trust questions are: (1) How much of the time do you think you can trust the government in Washington to do what is right—just about always, most of the time, or only some of the time? (2) Would you say the government is pretty much run by a few big interests looking out for themselves or that it is run for the benefit of all the people? (3) Do you think that people in government waste a lot of money we pay in taxes, waste some of it, or don't waste very much of it? (4) Do you think that quite a few of the people running the government are a little crooked, not very many are, or do you think hardly any of them are crooked at all? (5) Do you feel that almost all of the people running the government are smart people who usually know what they are doing, or do you think that quite a few of them don't seem to know what they are doing?

between the concepts trust in government, trust in incumbent presidents, and presidential job evaluations? These issues revolve around two lingering questions regarding trusting attitudes: Are the conceptual distinctions between incumbent trust, presidential evaluation, and trust in government meaningful empirically, and if they are distinctive concepts, how are they interrelated?

To answer these issues, we use survey data appropriate for disentangling the various interpretations of trust; these data include conventional trust-in-government items, measures of trust in several incumbent political leaders and trust in different levels of government, as well as multiple-indicators of presidential performance evaluations. The availability of multiple indicators of different concepts, and a variety of survey items explicitly designed to address these questions, places this analysis in the rare position to investigate these issues and the contrasting hypotheses surrounding them.

Measurement of Trust

Numerous scholars have examined political trust; however, a debate remains on what is actually being measured. Among the many controversies surrounding this literature, the most prominent is: Do the trust-in-government indicators measure diffuse support for the political system (Miller 1974a, 1974b), specific support for elected officials (Citrin 1974), or satisfaction with the performance of incumbent presidents (Citrin and Green 1986)? David Easton (1965, 1975) was one of the earliest scholars to distinguish between the two types of trust by defining the referents of each: Trust in authorities (specific support) is directed at elected officials, such as the u.s. Congress, whereas trust in the regime (diffuse support) is directed toward the form and structure of government. Following Easton's argument that trust reflects support for the political regime, a battery of questions regarding trust in the regime were developed and included in ANES studies. The results from the ANES's trust-in-government index, however, have generated numerous debates regarding what the conventional political trust indicators actually measure. Citrin (1974) initially raised this issue in his critique of Miller's (1974a) analysis; he contended that the "trust-in-government" questions measured support for the political incumbents and not the political system. In contrast with Miller's prediction of persisting public cynicism, Citrin contended that trust could be restored by simply voting the rascals out of office. That is, if trust in government reflected trust in incumbents, the implications were not as dire as Miller contended; from Citrin's (1974) perspective, lower trust in incumbents did not pose an immediate threat to the political system.

Since the initial exchange about the meaning of the ANES trust measures between Miller (1974a) and Citrin (1974), there have been subsequent attempts to clarify the relationship between support for the political system, trust in incumbent public officials, and presidential evaluations by including measures specifically designed to reflect specific support in the ANES surveys (see for example Abramson and Finifter 1981; Craig, Niemi and Silver 1990; Erber and Lau 1990; Muller and Jukam 1977; Muller, Jukam and Seligson 1982; Seligson 1982; for a review see Citrin and Muste 1999; Levi and Stoker 2000). These attempts did little to resolve the question about the meaning of the ANES indicators, in part because it proved difficult to disentangle specific and diffuse support with the questions that were designed for those surveys. Despite the extensive study of political trust, there remains no consensus on how to measure the underlying concept.

Explaining Political Trust
Subsequent research has shown that many factors cause changes in political trust but here too there is no dominant consensus as to what are the most important forces. For instance, political trust can depend on citizens' satisfaction with policy (King 1997; Miller 1974a), national economic evaluations (Chanley, Rudolph and Rahn 2000; Citrin and Green 1986; Citrin and Luks 2001; Feldman 1983; Hetherington 1998; Keele 2007; Lawrence 1997; Miller and Borrelli 1991; Weatherford 1984), evaluations of incumbents and institutions (Citrin and Green 1986; Citrin and Luks 2001; Craig 1993, 1996; Erber and Lau 1990; Feldman 1983; Hetherington 1998; Lipset and Schneider 1983, 1987; Miller and Borrelli 1991; Williams 1985), political scandals and corruption (Chanley, Rudolph, and Rahn 2000; Orren 1997; Weatherford 1984), crime, poverty, and family decline (Chanley, Rudolph, and Rahn 2000; Craig 1993; Hetherington 1998; Mansbridge 1997; Pew Research Center 1998), war and foreign policy concerns (Chanley 2002; Damico, Conway and Damico 2000; Nye 1997; Parker 1995), macro- and micropartisanship (Chanley, Rudolph and Rahn 2000; Keele 2005), and social capital (Keele 2007). All in all, the underlying assumption is that the public is more trusting when they are satisfied with policy outcomes, the economy is booming, citizens are pleased with incumbents and institutions, political scandals are nonexistent, crime is low, a war is popular, the country is threatened, and social capital is high.

Given the extensiveness of literature, it is not easy to summarize the determinants of trust. In addition, many analyses raise questions about what the conventional political trust indicators measure (e.g., Citrin 1974; Miller 1974a). Feldman (1983) suggested that trust-in-government measured evaluations of

Congress more than any other institution. Feldman's findings also are criticized for being derived from a misspecified model, which when corrected, supplied evidence that trust in government actually reflected institutional more than congressional evaluations (Williams 1985). Furthermore, in a study of racial policy preferences, Hetherington and Globetti (2002) hinted that trust in government is particular to the federal government, but few studies have empirically tested what trust is really measuring.

This analysis attempts to clarify the meaning of "trust in government" by empirically disentangling it from the many competing interpretations—that is, we distinguish trust in government from system-wide trust, trust in politicians, and evaluations of job performance. We expect these concepts to form separate, identifiable dimensions. Specifically, we contend that trust in government reflects trust in the federal or national government, which can be distinguished from trust in incumbent political leaders, trust in state government, and presidential job evaluations. Once these distinguishable dimensions of trust are established, we then model the causal relationships between trust and political attitudes and behaviors.

The Consequences of Trust

A second leading area of political-trust research has been the question of the consequences of political trust on other attitudes and behaviors. The relationship of presidential evaluations to trust remains perhaps the most controversial of all the issues, with many models characterizing evaluations of presidents as causing trust. For example, several studies have found that evaluations of the president's performance had a direct effect on trust, so that higher dissatisfaction with presidential performance is associated with higher levels of public distrust (Erber and Lau, 1990; Citrin 1974; Damico, Conway and Damico 2000; Miller 1974b; Feldman 1983). Conversely, Hetherington (1999) found that respondents with low levels of trust were more likely to vote for the non-incumbent or third party candidate (see also Peterson and Wrighton 1998), and that trust influences evaluations of the president and the u.s. Congress (Hetherington 1998, 2005). He also uncovered a reciprocal relationship between presidential performance and trust, although the causal path from trust to presidential evaluation was the stronger of the two paths. Thus, another unresolved question in the trust literature is the direction of influence between presidential evaluations and trust, if one indeed exists. We anticipate that trust in the federal government influences trust in incumbent politicians, and that a reciprocal relationship between the two does not exist.

Data and Measures

The data were collected by means of random sampling and telephone interviewing with adult (18 years and older), Florida residents[2] as part of an annual policy survey conducted by the Survey Research Laboratory at Florida State University in the u.s. Even though these data were collected from Florida residents, it would be unwise to interpret the findings as limited to a single state. Florida has a heterogeneous population reflecting the cultures of several regions in the u.s. in addition to the South, in particular the Midwest and Northeast—only about one-fifth of the population is native to the state. Further, the candidate-centered politics that have come to characterize national politics in the last two decades (see, for instance, Wattenberg 1990, 1991) have been widespread in Florida since the 1940s (Key 1949). Arguably, then, our findings could be generalized to other u.s. states as well as states in federated systems; as this analysis unfolds it will be evident why state surveys may actually be most useful in exploring questions involving trust in political leaders. That is, in order to query people about their trust in politicians, respondents need to recognize and evaluate a common group of incumbent officials. State surveys provide that opportunity because all respondents are asked to evaluate the same state officials, as well as their state government.

Trust in Government
Three of the five original indicators of trust in government typically included in the ANES surveys are used here: trust in the government in Washington to do what is right; is government run by a few big interests looking out for themselves or for the benefit of all people; and perceived degree of waste of tax money in government. (See Appendix A for the wording for all questions used in this analysis; the frequencies for the questions are available in Supplemental Material A.[3]) In measuring trust in government, the original ANES questions that asked whether most people in government were (1) "honest" and (2) "knew what they were doing" were omitted, because these questions appear to be directed at incumbent political leaders; hence, including them would surely bias the analysis toward finding that trust reflects support for incumbent. At the very least, it might confound the effects of trust in incumbent politicians with trust in government.

---

2 The data were collected using a list-assisted random sample, and with a sample size of 1083, the sampling error is +/- 5%. The response rate for this survey was 60%. The interviewing was conducted from January-April, 1997.

3 Please refer to the online appendix: http://dx.doi.org/10.1163/9789004276062_005.

To ensure this key latent concept continues to retain a high degree of reliability, a question about the quality of representation provided by the federal government was substituted. A preliminary factor analysis showed that this variable occupied the same dimension as the three ANES indicators of trust in government, thereby enhancing the reliability of the trust-in-government measure. At a later point, we demonstrate that this indicator behaves properly in terms of the measurement of trust in government.

Trust in State Government

In addition to trust in the federal government, respondents were queried about trust in Florida's state government. Four questionnaire items served this objective. Two questions duplicate the format and wording of the questions about the federal government: trust in state government to do what is right and the extent of tax waste in state government. Similar to the national-level questions, the third question asks if respondents are well represented by state government. The final indicator of trust in state government is the degree of attention given to Florida public opinion.

The trust in state government measure does more than simply permit an examination of whether people distinguish between levels of government in making their trust-in-government evaluations. More importantly, it allows us to test whether the trust-in-government measure is capturing general system support, or only orientations directed at the national/federal government. That is, do the trust-in-government items record levels of trust in the entire political system, or basically just the federal government, as the wording of some of the items contained in the measure imply?

Trust in Political Leaders

Central to an understanding of the meaning of political trust, as well as addressing the long-standing Miller-Citrin debate, is whether voters are thinking about *individual* incumbents when responding to the trust-in-government questions; hence, it is imperative to in some way differentiate between attitudes toward government, and those directed at incumbent officeholders, in measuring trust. Previous efforts to develop measures of incumbent trust in order to empirically test for differences between the two concepts have encountered difficulties. For instance, a noteworthy effort in the 1978 ANES study used questions measuring trust in then U.S. President Jimmy Carter to this end, but analysis of these measures with the trust-in-government questions found them closely aligned with the trust-in-government questions. Consequently, the authors concluded that the new measures did a poor job measuring trust in the incumbent president (Abramson and Finifter 1981). On the other hand, questions included in the

1987 ANES pilot survey were able to distinguish between regime-based and incumbent-based trust (Craig, Niemi, and Silver 1990), but regrettably, these items were not repeated in subsequent surveys, so the conceptualization is of limited value. Nor have a sufficient number of questionnaire items been included in past studies to allow for the development of measurement models that could disentangle the relationships among the latent concepts underlying trust in the regime and trust in the political authorities.

We address this issue by measuring both types of trust: trust in political leaders captures the attitudes of voters toward incumbent politicians, whereas trust-in-government captures constituents' attitudes toward the broader political system, or merely the national government. In this analysis, trust in political leaders is linked to constituents' perceptions that the official is taking advantage of his or her position as a public servant, and exploiting the office for personal benefit. It incorporates four survey items eliciting respondents' views of the extent to which political leaders: (1) kept their campaign promises, (2) used their position for personal gain, (3) appeared to be honest, and (4) generally could be trusted to do the right thing. To ensure that respondents' attention was clearly directed at incumbent politicians, and to enhance the generalizability of our findings, well-known incumbent political leaders, at both the national and local levels (elected state-wide), were used as the reference points for these trust items—specifically, then U.S. President Bill Clinton (D), and Florida's two U.S. Senators at the time, Bob Graham (D) and Connie Mack III (R).[4] We believe that this helps to clarify the referent of the trust measures and as noted earlier renders national surveys typically lacking such reference points less useful.

U.S. Presidential Performance

Individual and aggregate-level analyses of trust have done little to alleviate the uncertainty about whether evaluations of presidential job performance are structured by trust in government, or vice versa. Performance evaluations frequently serve as snapshots of how presidents are "doing," and these ratings have been shown to be responsive to short-term conditions and events, like rallying events and economic "slump" (Mueller 1973; Parker 1995); nonetheless,

---

4 Clinton had just been elected to his second presidential term, while Graham had served as Senator for 10 years, and Mack had served for 8 years. Prior to serving as Senator, Graham was a two-term governor and Mack was a two-term U.S. representative. The three incumbents investigated here, then, had ample time in office and sufficient prominence for citizens to have formed some estimation of their trustworthiness. It is important to note that the 1997 Florida survey did not elicit respondents' views on trust in the incumbent Florida governor, Lawton Chiles. Thus, we are limited to comparing the two Florida Senators and the U.S. President.

there may be a more enduring component to U.S. presidential popularity that resides in peoples' trust in government and, perhaps, assessments of individual presidents. Alternatively, poor presidential performance can sour individuals on the national government, or even the entire political system.[5]

Three indicators of job performance are used to measure evaluations of President Clinton. Job evaluation questions asked respondents to evaluate Clinton's performance over "the last four years" in the following areas: the economy, foreign policy, and overall performance. His performance was ranked on a four-point scale that ranged from excellent to poor.[6]

Dimensionality of Trust Measures

The first question examined is whether "trust in government," "trust in political leaders," and "evaluations of presidential performance" can be distinguished from one another. Simply put, can one differentiate trust in government from support for authorities and the political system, and do citizens do the same? Thus, we clarify the meaning of political trust by empirically testing a series of alternative conceptual specifications. Next, the causal relationships between trust and job evaluations of incumbent officials are modeled.

Tests for the distinctiveness of the concepts were conducted by examining the dimensionality of these measures when subjected to a Confirmatory Factor Analysis (COFAMM); this statistical technique allows one to specify and test the fit of a theoretically-specified dimensional measurement model. The goodness-of-fit of the models is determined by the significance of a Chi-squared statistic, which measures the difference between the correlation matrix produced by the specified (hypothesized) measurement model, and the actual (observed) correlation matrix among the indicators. If the hypothesized measurement model provides a good fit to these data (the dimensional nature underlying the correlation matrix is correctly specified) a nonsignificant Chi-squared statistic results, thereby indicating no significant difference between the observed and hypothesized correlation matrices.

---

5   Both possibilities are tested (see footnote 9).

6   The initial step in modeling the causal relationship between trust in government, trust in authorities, and evaluations of incumbent performance is to build a measurement model for the three latent concepts and their indicators. Confirmatory Factor Analysis (COFAMM) is used to test if these measures form three distinct dimensions, and therefore if citizens distinguish between their trust in a leader and their evaluations of his or her performance.

Levels of Government

If trust in government primarily captures attitudes toward the entire political system, then citizens will not distinguish between their trust in the federal and state governments. Still, there is reason to imagine that citizens differentiate between their trust in federal and state governments. For instance, Jennings and Zeigler (1970) find that American citizens readily distinguish between different levels of government affairs. In fact, Jennings (1998, 241) finds that Americans expressed greater confidence in local than national-level government (see also, Conlan 1993). In addition, in the u.s., the system of government is a federal one, where policy responsibilities lie with the state rather than the national government. Citizens are aware that these levels of government have different functions and responsibilities. While citizens differentiate between their trust in various levels of government, one might also imagine a positive relationship between the two. Simply put, either citizens trust the government, both at the national and state levels, or they do not trust government. They do not form distinct trust levels for each level of government. Indeed, trust in state government is usually higher than federal government, but states are not the reservoir of trust and confidence among citizens. Hetherington and Nugent (2001) find that trust at the state level of government is generally dependent on trust in other levels of government. Other scholars also show that state trust is simply influenced by the same variables, such as the status of the economy, that influence trust in federal government (Uslaner 2001; Wolak and Palus 2010). In sum, our arguments lead to the expectation that trust in the state and federal government will form separate dimensions, with a positive relationship between the two.

As expected, we find two latent dimensions: the Chi-squared (20.6, df = 15) for the two-dimensional solution is insignificant (see Figure 1). The largest correlated errors between the indicators of the two underlying concepts are for the correlation between how well represented people feel in both levels (r = 0.41) and between indicators of the degree of waste at each level (r = 0.30).[7] Two points are worth noting about this model. First, the signs of the indicators of each unmeasured concept are in the same direction. Second, the correlation between trust in the federal government and trust in the state government is positive. Both of these findings support the contention that people differentiate in terms of their trust between these two levels of government, and the relationship between them is highly positive (r = 0.75): People who are trusting of the federal government tend to also trust state government. Thus, trust in

---

7 This may result from the similarity in the format and wording of these two questions. Abramson and Finifter (1981) and Feldman (1983), for example, find wording effects for the trust-in-government questions, but they find them for different questions than we do.

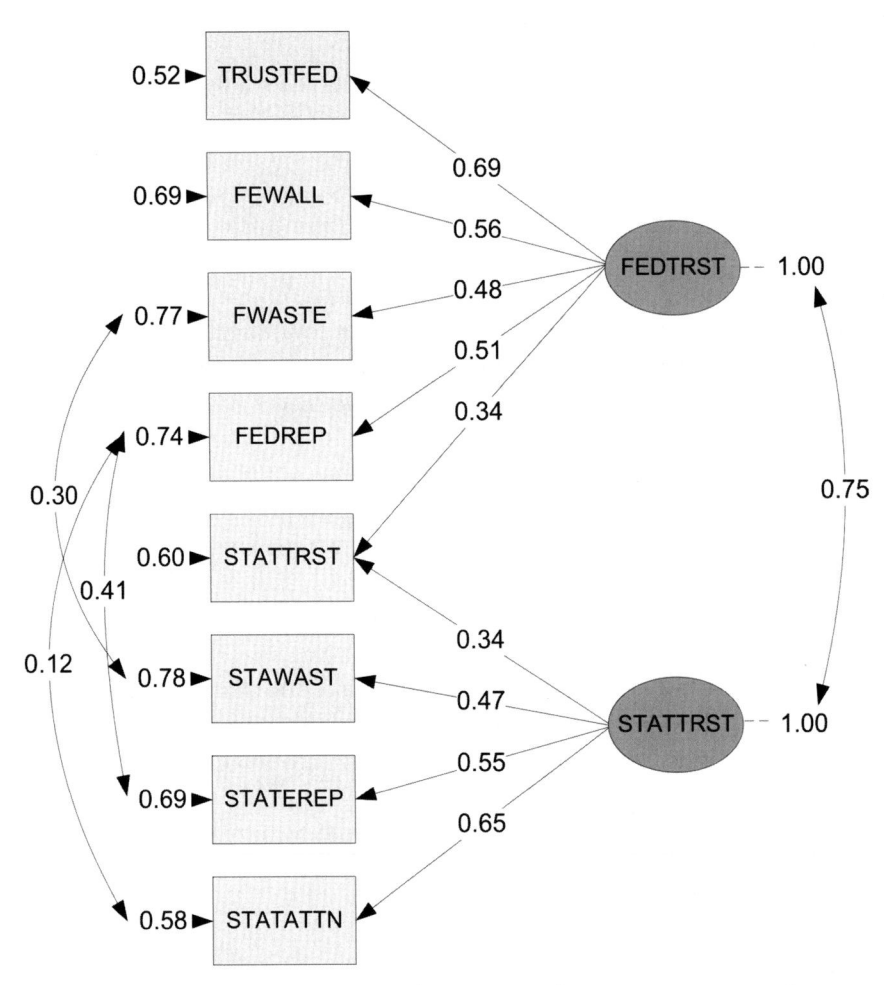

FIGURE 1   *Trust in the government in Washington, D.C. and trust in state government in*
Florida: A measurement model. Chi-Square = 20.6, df = 15, P = 0.15, RMSEA = 0.02,
Adjusted Goodness of Fit Index = 0.99, N = 832.

government is directed at trust in the federal or national government, rather than trust in the political system or in all levels of government, as demonstrated by peoples' distinctions between state and federal governments. Although we are reluctant to generalize this finding to all federated systems, the relationship is certainly worthy of investigation in such settings.

Political Leaders and Government

Having established that trust in government reflects feelings toward the national government, the next step is to examine whether citizens distinguish between their trust in the national government and in incumbent politicians.

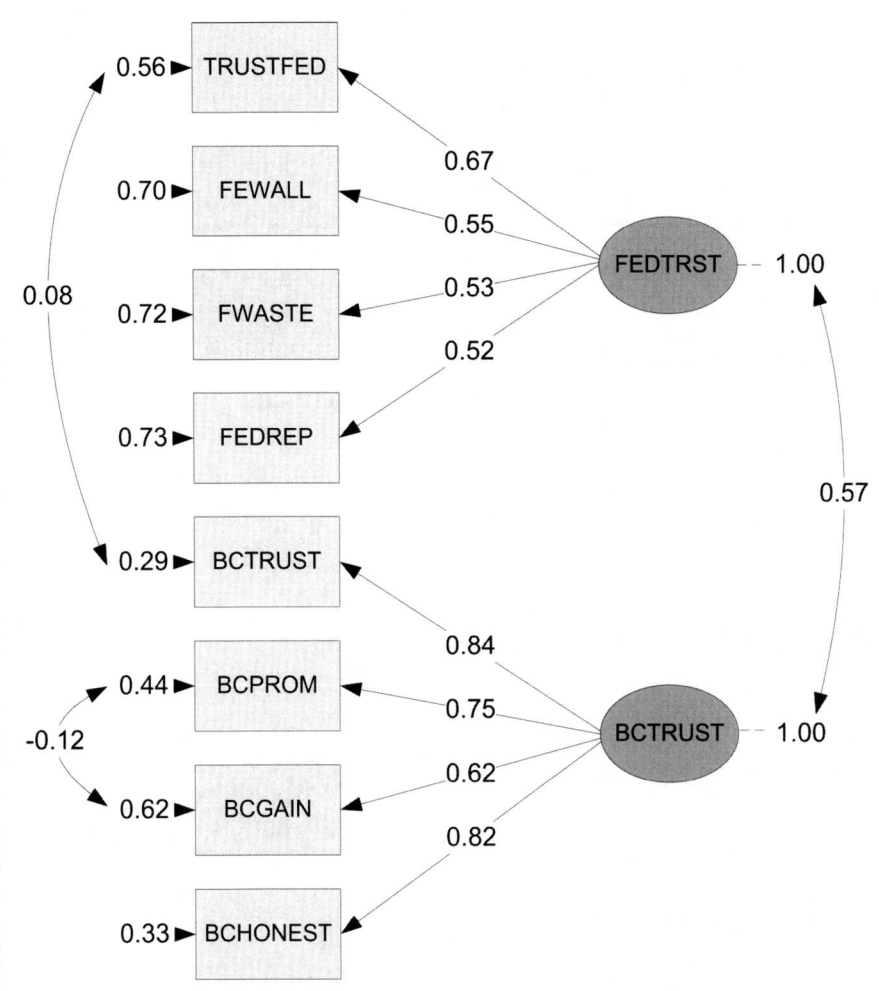

FIGURE 2   *Trust in government and trust in incumbent political leaders: Measurement models.*
(a) Trust in Bill Clinton: Chi-square = 22.97, df = 17, P = 0.19, RMSEA = 0.02, Adjusted
Goodness of Fit Index = 0.99, N = 856, (b) Trust in Bob Graham: Chi-Square = 26,
df = 19, P = 0.12, RMSEA = 0.03, Adjusted Goodness of Fit Index = 0.98, N = 563, (c)
Trust in Connie Mack: Chi-Square = 26, df = 19, P = 0.73, RMSEA = 0.00, Adjusted
Goodness of Fit Index = 0.99, N = 495.

Once again, the fit of these data to COFAMM models stipulating a two-dimensional solution between trust in the federal government, and trust in each of the (three) specific politicians, is used to test these relationships.

All three models (incumbent politicians and trust in government) matched these data quite well, with insignificant Chi-squares associated with each (Figure 2). Few of the error terms for the indicators are correlated, and the two

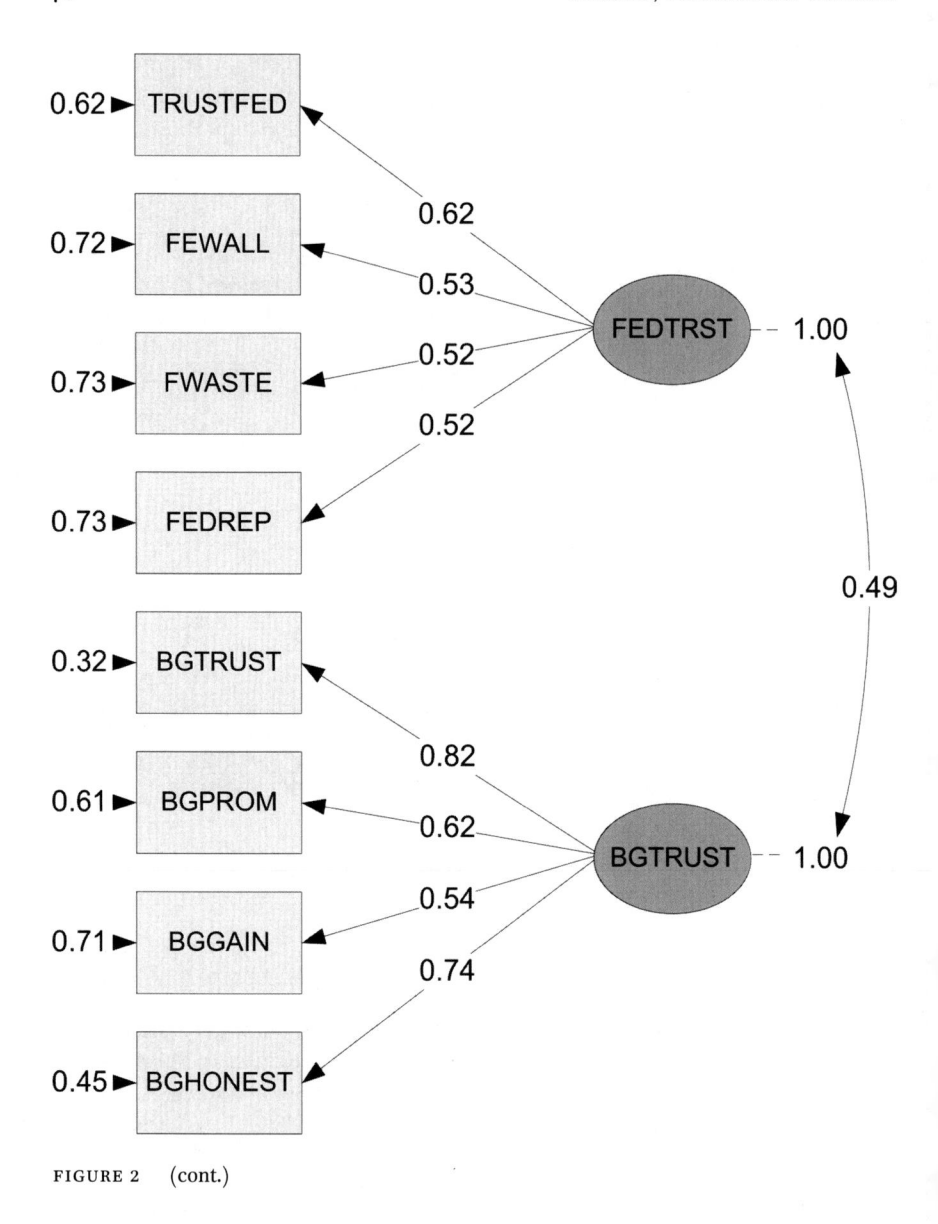

FIGURE 2   (cont.)

that are correlated in the model (for Clinton) are small. Clearly, trust in government and individual politicians are distinctive concepts; they are, as expected,
also positively correlated—that is, higher trust in government is associated
with higher trust in incumbent political leaders. The correlations are moderate
in size, with trust in government more strongly associated with trust in national
leaders—i.e., Clinton (r = 0.57)—than more local ones—Graham (r = 0.49)
and Mack (r = 0.37). In short, people distinguish between "government" and

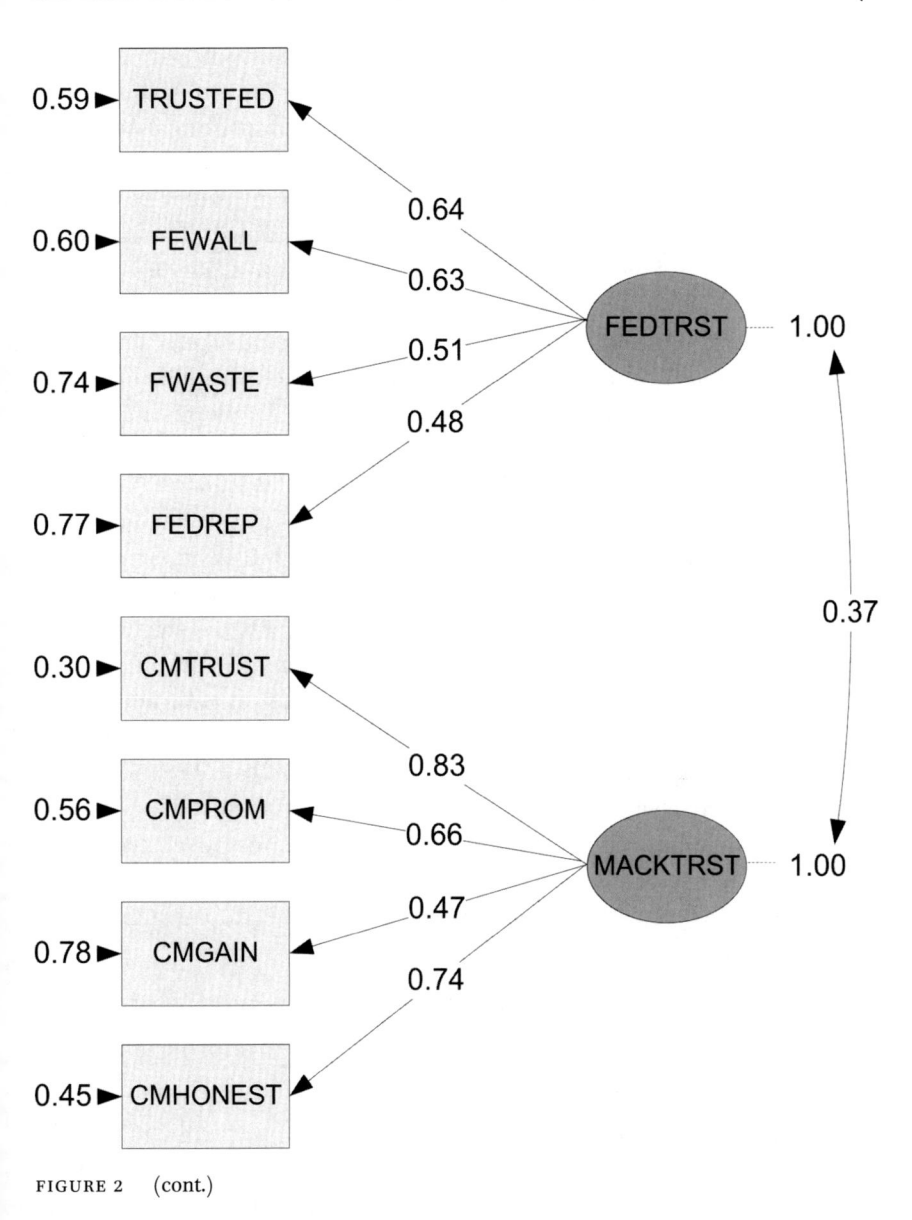

FIGURE 2   (cont.)

incumbent political leaders; still, those who are more trusting of government are also more trusting of incumbent political leaders. Yet, the concepts are clearly distinctive.

Trust and Evaluations of Job Performance

Now that a difference between trust in government and trust in politicians has been established, the next task is to demonstrate that these trust measures can be differentiated from citizen assessments of incumbent job performance. Some scholars have suggested that the trust-in-government questions reflect little more than satisfaction/dissatisfaction with the job performance of the current administration (Citrin 1974; Citrin and Green 1986)—simply put, trust in government and incumbent evaluations are interchangeable; we believe otherwise. By following the same testing procedures—namely, formulating a COFAMM model and testing for a three-dimensional fit to the data—we find that Clinton's performance ratings can be differentiated from both trust in government and trust in Clinton. As the model in Figure 3 indicates, Clinton job evaluations (i.e., evaluation of his last four years in office, evaluation of his job performance on the economy, and evaluation of his job performance on foreign policy) form a dimension separate from both trust in Clinton and trust in the federal government (Figure 3). In short, there are three identifiable dimensions underlying these trust and evaluation variables—i.e., trust in the federal government, trust in Clinton, and performance ratings of Clinton.

The three dimensions also are related to one another: The strongest correlation is between Clinton trust and Clinton evaluations ($r = 0.86$)—higher levels of Clinton trust are associated with higher evaluations of Clinton's performance. The next strongest relationship is between trust in government and trust in Clinton ($r = 0.57$), and the weakest of the three is between trust in government and Clinton's job evaluation ($r = 0.46$). Once again, higher levels of trust are associated with higher job evaluations. In sum, the results of the confirmatory factory analyses indicate that trust in government reflects attitudes about the federal government, which can be distinguished from trust in incumbent political leaders, trust in state government, and presidential job evaluations.

Structural-Equation Models

We have now demonstrated that these concepts—trust in incumbents, trust in the political system, and satisfaction/dissatisfaction with presidential performance—are not interchangeable with trust in government, but this should not be construed to mean that these distinctive latent concepts are unrelated. It is expected that theoretically-based causal connections underlie these concepts. Blindness to the causal dynamics among these concepts may be one reason why studies have largely ignored the face validity of the trust-in-government questions with their reference to the federal government firmly embedded within the survey items. Hence, the next question is whether these distinctive concepts relate to each other, and if so, how they are related. For this purpose,

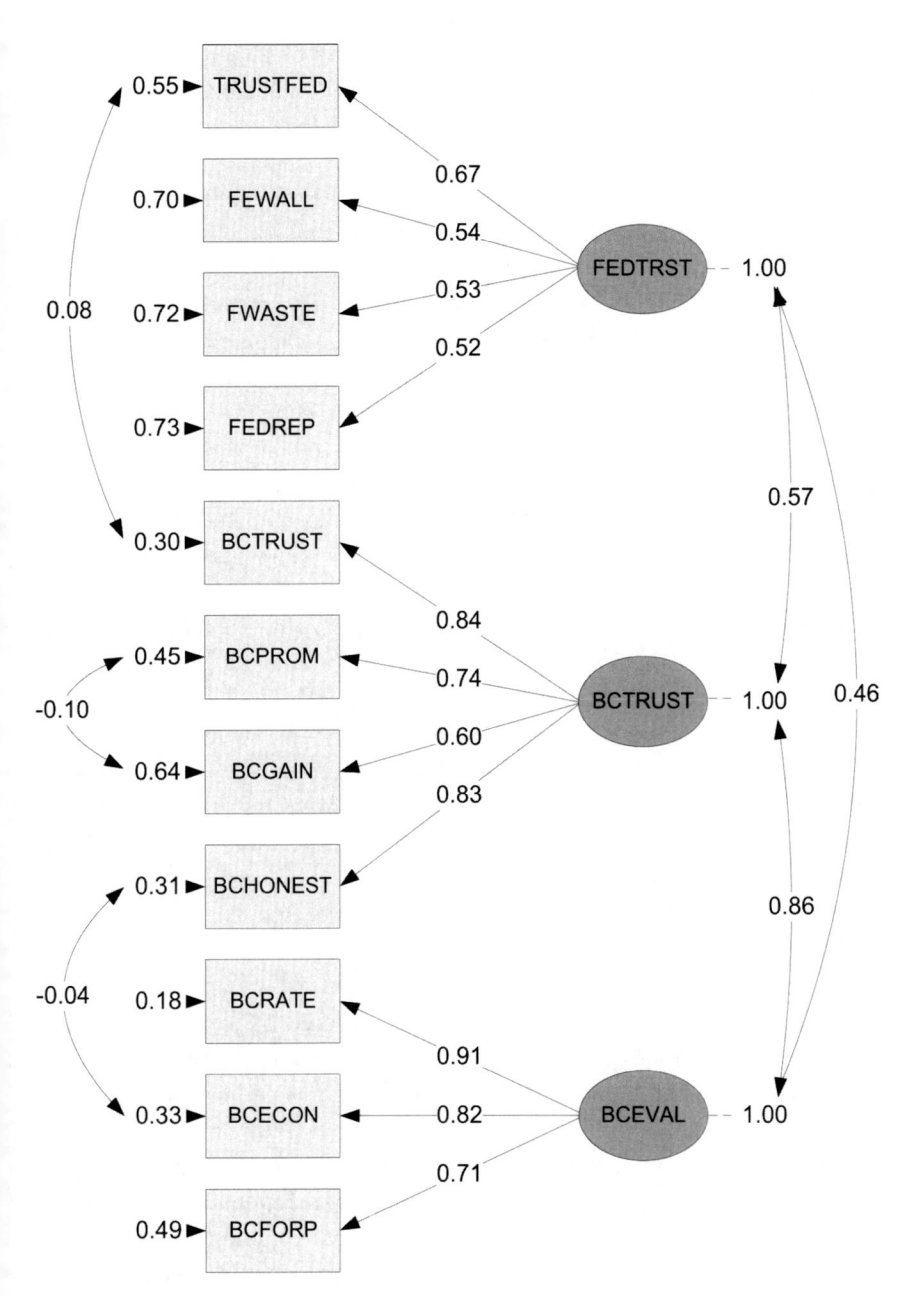

FIGURE 3 *Trust in government, trust in Clinton, and Clinton job evaluations: A measurement model. Chi-Square = 49, df =38, P = 0.12, RMSEA = 0.02, Adjusted Goodness of Fit Index= 0.98, N=818.*

structural-equation models of the relationships among these variables are developed and tested. This section of the analysis tests the aforementioned causal relationships using Structural Equation Modeling (SEM) and maximum likelihood estimates in LISREL.[8]

This statistical technique is particularly well suited for situations in which modeling the measurement error is important and multiple measures of the latent concepts are available. A modeling process is followed where COFAMM measurement models are initially built, and then path analyses using maximum likelihood estimation are performed. Although the possibility exists that important variables are omitted from the models, this is not a critical problem for the following reasons: the chi-squared statistics were reduced to insignificance in every instance, which indicates that the model is a good representation of the observed correlations among indicators of the latent concepts; the goodness-of-fit statistics (AGFI, goodness-of-fit index adjusted for degrees of freedom) are large, and well beyond the acceptable range; and there are not even modest correlations between the error terms for the indicators of the dependent and independent variables (concepts), the existence of which might suggest some third variable, excluded from the analysis, but nonetheless related to both the independent and dependent variables.

Consistent with other studies, in particular Williams (1985) and Hetherington (1999), we hypothesize that trust in the federal government *causes* trust in incumbent politicians. Since the analysis reveals that trust in government taps attitudes toward the federal government, it is reasonable to expect that trust in national leaders would be affected by trust in the national government. However, we do *not* hypothesize that the influence between these two latent concepts also flows in the opposite direction—i.e., trust in government is affected by trust in political elites—because untrustworthy or unresponsive political leaders can be removed from office before their actions critically damage levels of governmental trust (Citrin 1974; Easton 1965). Indeed, a study of the relationship between system trust and trust in U.S. Representatives found no evidence of a causal linkage extending from trust in the U.S. Representative to system trust, although a causal linkage in the opposite direction was clearly evident (Parker and Parker 1993).

Further, we expect that *trust in the president is a far better predictor of evaluations of job performance than trust in government*. Presidential evaluations tend to focus on individuals, which makes it far easier for citizens to link that performance to how much they trust the incumbent Chief Executive, than to their more amorphous views of government. In their haste to uncover the

---

8 Readers seeking a more in-depth discussion of LISREL modeling are directed to Joreskog and Sorbom (1993).

roots and effects of trust in government, scholars may have, regrettably, ignored the relevance of citizen trust in incumbent office holders. Simply put, trust in presidents, rather than the larger national government, structures citizen evaluations of presidential job performance. In fact, a spurious relationship between trust in government and evaluations of presidential performance is suspected, contrary to Citrin's (1974) contention.

The first model includes both direct and indirect relationships between trust in government and Clinton evaluations, with the indirect path operating through trust in Clinton (Figure 4, Model 1). While the direct relationship between trust in government and Clinton's evaluations is not significant (Beta = −0.04), the direct relationship between trust in Clinton and Clinton evaluations is strong and positive (Beta = 0.88); thus, trust in Clinton leads to higher evaluations of his job performance. The important conclusion that can be drawn from this model is that trust in government has only an indirect effect on Clinton evaluations with trust in Clinton mediating the relationship.

In Model 2 (Figure 4) the direct path between trust in government and Clinton evaluations has been eliminated and the model is reestimated. Once again, the model provides a good fit to these data with an insignificant Chi-square value. The relationship between trust in Clinton and job evaluations remains significant (Beta = 0.86), as does the path between trust in the federal government and trust in Clinton (Beta = 0.57). The modification index, which specifies whether further adjustments to the model are warranted, indicated that there were no significant paths left out of the model and, more importantly, that a reciprocal relationship between trust in government and trust in incumbents was needless.[9] Thus, all the evidence points to a causal link from trust in government to trust in incumbent political leaders, and from trust in leaders to job evaluations. Although these findings are limited to the u.s., there is no reason to believe that the job performance of chief executives in general is immune to such effects.[10]

---

9   A model was tested that included a reciprocal relationship between trust in the political system and trust in Bill Clinton. The path from Bill Clinton trust to system trust was not statistically significant. A model was also tested with a reciprocal relationship between Clinton trust and Clinton evaluations, but the path from Clinton evaluations to Clinton trust was not statistically significant.

10 Models were tested to examine if personal characteristics, particularly partisanship, drive trust in government. To test the latter, we estimated the causal model in Figure 4, Model 2, separately for Republicans and Democrats. The models show that the patterns for Republicans and Democrats are the same. The latter is not surprising, as previous scholars show that trust in government is weakly explained by personal differences (Stokes 1962; Uslaner 2001). See Supplemental Material B for the partisan models (Please refer to http://www.brill.com/products/book/political-trust-disenchantment-politics).

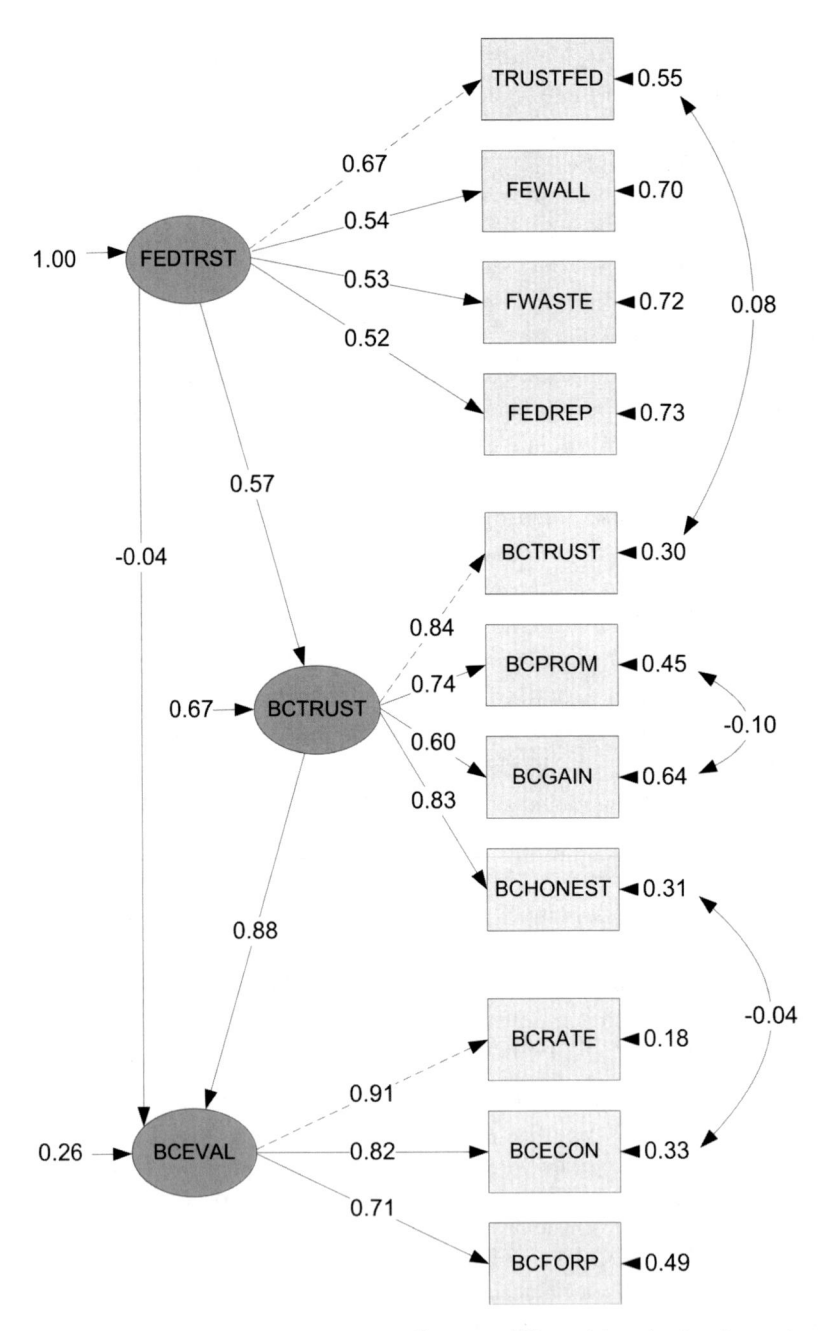

Trust in government, trust in Clinton, and Clinton job evaluation: A causal
model (standardized solution). (a) Model 1: Chi-Square = 49, df = 38,
P = 0.12, RMSEA = 0.02, Adjusted Goodness of Fit Index = 0.98, N = 818,
(b) Model 2: Chi-Square = 50, df = 39, P = 0.12, RMSEA = 0.02, Adjusted
Goodness of Fit Index = 0.98, N = 818.

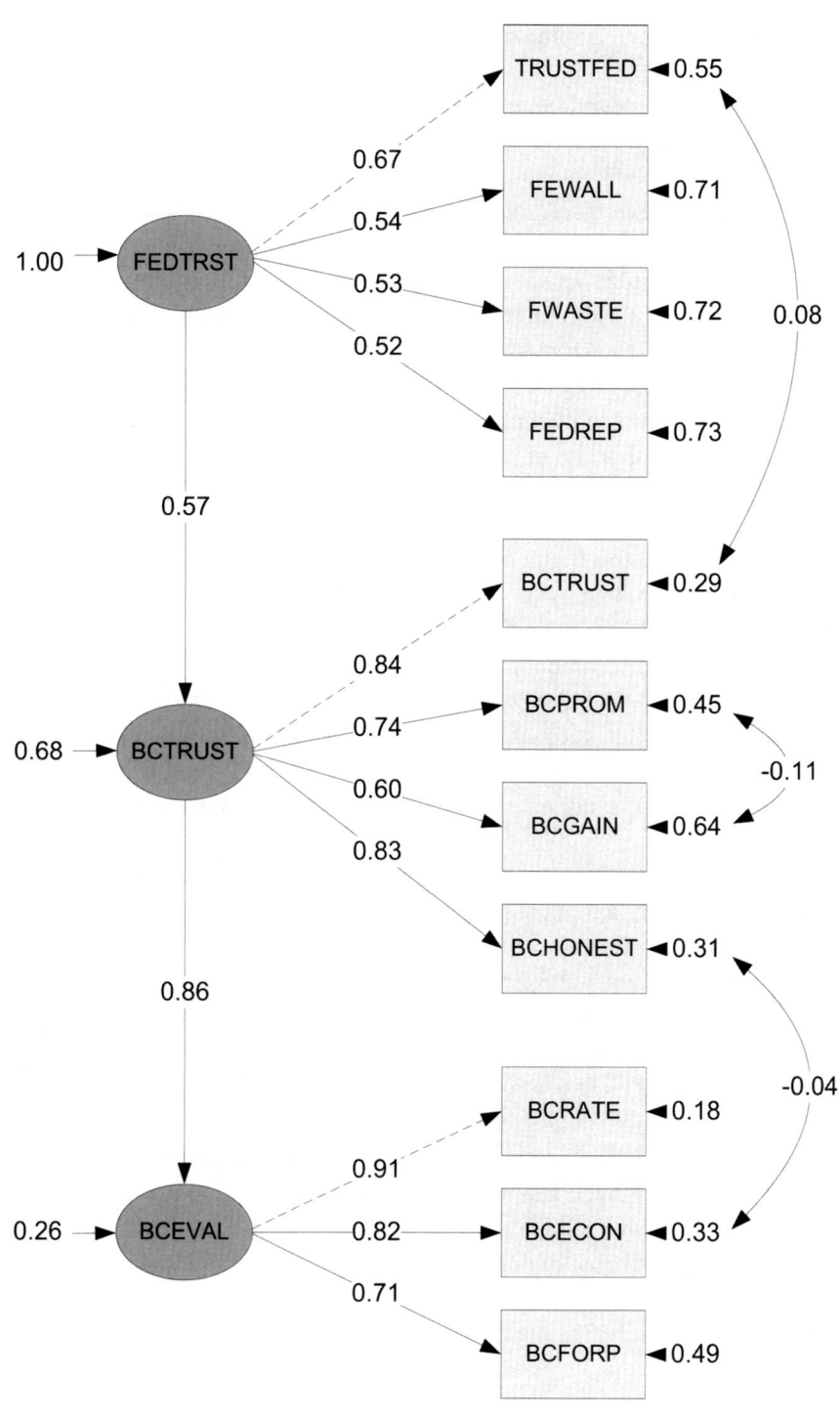

FIGURE 4   (cont.)

Summary and Implications

To summarize, the measurement and causal models presented here support the contention that the trust-in-government measures refer to attitudes directed at the federal government. Although there is a strong relationship between trust in government and trust in incumbent authorities, it is not so strong as to suggest that they are measuring the same thing. In short, we have been able to distinguish between incumbent and federal government support.

Then, how do the above findings fit with previous research about trust in government? As to the disagreement between Citrin and Miller, we would suggest that Citrin (1974) was right to point to the distinction between trust in government and trust in incumbent politicians; Miller (1974a, 1974b) was correct in contending that the measures reflected more than trust in incumbent officials. Our research shows that citizens differentiate between trust in government and their trust and evaluation of public officials (at least the u.s. president and senators). Our findings show three distinct dimensions of trust—trust in the federal government, trust in the state government, and trust in incumbent officials. Finally, Citrin (1974) was also correct in suggesting that declining trust in government did not necessarily mean that people were dissatisfied with the political regime, principles, norms or institutions. It is not the case, however, that voting the incumbents out would restore trust in government. Given that trust in the federal government is distinct from trust in officials, throwing the rascals out does not necessarily increase trust in the government.

The missing variable in the Citrin (1974) and Miller (1974a, 1974b) analyses that permits us to disentangle the meaning of trust is "trust in the state government." This variable allows us to uncover the true focus of the trust-in-government variables—the *federal* government. Using state trust, we show that those who trust the federal government tend to also trust the state government. While Americans distinguish between the two levels of government, the way they feel about one level of government depends on the other level. In other words, the degree to which trust varies at the state level is in part a reflection of sentiments about the national government. This means that state and local governments have limited ability to promote public trust. The implications of this finding are: declining trust in government may denote declining distrust of democracy or support for radical changes in the constitutional system.

Citrin and Green (1986) suggest that the rise in trust in government during the Reagan presidency (1981–89) reflects the effects of presidential performance on people's trust in government. In contrast, we find that trust in government indirectly affects presidential evaluations, and presidential evaluations do not cause trust in government. Yet, it is possible levels of trust in the federal government increased because Republicans believed that President Reagan was successfully restraining the power and size of the federal government. That is, Republicans began to trust the federal government because Reagan was finally able to rein it in after Democratic control. He restrained busing; he reduced social spending and increased military spending; and he was outwardly sympathetic toward citizens' distrust of the federal government. On the other hand, it can be argued that Democrats naturally have a higher regard for the federal government because of their strong belief in using the federal government to solve national problems. In general, Republicans' belief that the federal government was reduced in size and power relative to the state government restored trust in the 1980s in the U.S. This is a reoccurring theme in American politics, and may be endemic to its federal structure.

It is also not surprising to see trust in the federal government responsive to performance of the national economy (Chanley, Rudolph and Rahn 2000), to international events, and to military actions (Parker 1995), as these are legitimate areas within the federal government's purview. Further, given that trust in government reflects the belief by many that the federal government had overstepped constitutional bounds and grown too powerful, finding that those who displayed reduced trust were less supportive of expanded social programs and spending (see Hetherington 2005) is not surprising.

Our research suggests that it might be fruitful to investigate government trust in other countries, particularly within other federated systems. This is particularly important as trust in government has declined in numerous industrial democracies across the globe (Dalton 2004). For example, in Europe, trust in the European Union is very important, as the EU is currently increasing its political authority over the member states. One might expect that citizens in these federations might not like to see the role of the federal government expanded relative to the role of state governments. As a result, antipathy for the European government may increase among citizens in member states. Drawing on our research, we would argue that growing distrust at the state level is linked to the increasing distrust toward the EU. To re-establish trust, the EU must rebuild confidence at the national level rather than member states seeking to restore trust at home. Turning to trust in political actors, Dalton (2004) reports that distrust in politicians is evident in the U.S. as well as Sweden and Canada. Our study suggests that even if Swedes and Canadians removed those incumbents—trust would not be restored—as trust in the federal government is distinct from trust in politicians.

References

Abramson, Paul R. and Ada Finifter. 1981. "On the Meaning of Political Trust: New Evidence from Items Introduced in 1978." *American Journal of Political Science* 25(2):297–307.

Chanley, Virginia. 2002. "Trust in Government in the Aftermath of 9/11: Determinants and Consequences." *Political Psychology* 23(3):469–483.

Chanley, Virginia, Thomas Rudolph and Wendy Rahn. 2000. "The Origins and Consequences of Public Trust in Government: A Time Series Analysis." *Public Opinion Quarterly.* 64(3):239–256.

Citrin, Jack. 1974. "Comment: The Political Relevance of Trust in Government." *American Political Science Review* 68(3):973–988.

Citrin, Jack and Donald P. Green. 1986. "Presidential Leadership and the Resurgence of Trust in Government." *British Journal of Political Science* 16(4):431–453.

Citrin, Jack and C. Muste 1999. "Trust in Government." In *Measures of Political Attitudes,* edited by John P. Robinson, Philip R. Shaver and Lawrence S. Wrightsman, 465–532. San Diego, CA: Academic Press.

Citrin, Jack and Samantha Luks. 2001. "Political Trust Revisited: D'ej'a Vu All Over Again?" In *What Is It about Government That Americans Dislike?,* edited by John R. Hibbing and Elizabeth Theiss-Morse, 9–27. New York: Cambridge University Press.

Conlan, Timothy J. 1993. "Federal, State, or Local? Trends in the Public's Judgment." *The Public Perspective* 4:3–10.

Craig, Stephen C. 1993. *The Malevolent Leaders.* Boulder, CO: Westview.

———. 1996. *Broken Contract.* Boulder, CO: Westview.

Craig, Stephen C, Richard G. Niemi and Glenn E. Silver. 1990. "Political Efficacy and Trust: A Report on the NEW Pilot Study Items." *Political Behavior* 12(3):289–314.

Dalton, Russell. 2004. *Democratic Challenges, Democratic Choices.* Oxford University Press, Oxford.

Damico, Alfonso, M. Margaret Conway and Sandra Bowman Damico. 2000. "Patterns of Political Trust and Mistrust: Three Moments in the Lives of Democratic Citizens." *Polity* 32(3):377–400.

Easton, David. 1965. *A System Analysis of Political Life.* New York: Wiley.

———. 1975. "A Re-assessment of the Concept of Political Support." *British Journal of Political Science* 5(4):435–457.

Erber, Ralph and Richard Lau. 1990. "Political Cynicism Revisited: An Information Processing Reconciliation of Policy-Based and Incumbency-Based Interpretations of Changes in Trust in Government." *American Journal of Political Science* 34(1):236–253.

Feldman, Stanley. 1983. "The Measurement and Meaning of Trust in Government." *Political Methodology* 9(3):341–354.

Hetherington, Marc J. 1998. "The Political Relevance of Political Trust." *American Political Science Review* 92(4):791–808.

_____. 1999. "The Effect of Political Trust on the Presidential Vote: 1968–1996." *American Political Science Review* 93(2):311–326.

_____. 2005. *Why Trust Matters*. Princeton: Princeton University Press.

Hetherington, Marc J. and John D. Nugent. 2001. "Explaining Public Support for Devolution: The Role of Political Trust." In *What is it About Government that Americans Dislike?*, edited by John R. Hibbing and Elizabeth Theiss-Morse, 134–155. Cambridge, UK: Cambridge University Press.

Hetherington, Marc J. and Suzanne Globetti. 2002. "Political Trust and Racial Policy Preferences." *American Journal of Political Science* 46(2):253–275.

Jennings, M. Kent. 1998. "Political Trust and the Roots of Devolution." In *Trust and Governance*, edited by Victoria Braithwaite and Margaret Levi, 218–244. New York: Russell Sage.

Jennings, M. Kent and Harmon Zeigler. 1970. "The Salience of American State Politics." American Political Science Review 64(2):523–535.

Joreskog, Karl G. and Dag Sorbom. 1993. *LISREL 8 User's Reference Guide*. Chicago: Scientific Software International.

Keele, Luke. 2005. "The Authorities Really Do Matter: Party Control and Trust in Government." *Journal of Politics* 67(3):973–886.

_____. 2007. "Social Capital and the Dynamic of Trust in Government." *American Journal of Political Science* 51(2):241–254.

Key, V.O. 1949. Southern Politics in State and Nation. New York: Knopf.

King, David. 1997. "The Polarization of American Parties and Mistrust of Government." In *Why People don't Trust Government*, edited by Joseph S. Nye, Jr., Philip D. Zelikow and David C. King, 155–178. Cambridge, MA: Harvard University Press.

Lawrence, Robert Z. 1997. "Is it Really the Economy, Stupid?" In *Why People don't Trust Government*, edited by Joseph S. Nye, Jr., Philip D. Zelikow and David C. King, 111–132. Cambridge, MA: Harvard University Press.

Levi, Margaret and Laura Stoker. 2000. "Political Trust and Trustworthiness." *Annual Review of Political Science* 3:475–507.

Lipset, Seymour Martin and William Schneider. 1983. "The Decline of Confidence in American Institutions." *Political Science Quarterly* 98(3):379–402

_____. 1987. "The Confidence Gap during the Reagan Years, 1981–1987." *Political Science Quarterly* 102(1):1–23.

Mansbridge, Jane. 1997. "Social and Cultural Causes of Dissatisfaction with U.S. Government." In *Why People don't Trust Government*, edited by Joseph S. Nye, Jr., Philip D. Zelikow and David C. King, 133–154. Cambridge, MA: Harvard University Press.

Miller, Arthur H. 1974a. "Political Issues and Trust in Government: 1964–1970." *American Political Science Review* 68(3):951–972.

_____. 1974b. "Rejoinder to 'Comment' by Jack Citrin: Political Discontent or Ritualism?" *American Political Science Review* 68(3): 989–1001.

Miller, Arthur H. and Stephen A. Borrelli. 1991. "Confidence in Government during the 1980s." American Politics Quarterly 19:147–173.

Mueller, John. 1973. *War, Presidents, and Public Opinion.* New York: Wiley & Sons.

Muller, Edward N. and Thomas O. Juckam. 1977. "On the Meaning of Political Support." *American Political Science Review* 71(4):1651–1595.

Muller, Edward N., Thomas O. Jukam and Mitchell A. Seligson. 1982. "Diffuse Political Support and Anti-System Political Behavior: A Comparative Analysis." *American Journal of Political Science* 26(2):240–264.

NyeJoseph S. Jr. 1997. "Introduction: The Decline of Confidence in Government." In *Why People don't Trust Government,* edited by Joseph S. Nye, Jr., Philip D. Zelikow and David C. King, 1–18. Cambridge, MA: Harvard University Press.

Orren, Gary. 1997. "Fall from Grace: The Public's Loss of Faith in Government." In *Why People don't Trust Government,* edited by Joseph S. Nye, Jr., Philip D. Zelikow and David C. King, 77–108. Cambridge, MA: Harvard University Press.

Parker, Suzanne L. 1995. "Toward an Understanding of 'Rally' Effects: Public Opinion in the Persian Gulf War." *Public Opinion Quarterly* 59(4):526–546.

_____ and Glenn R. Parker. 1993. "Why Do We Trust Our Congressman?" *Journal of Politics* 55(2):442–453.

Peterson, Geoff and J. Mark Wrighton. 1998. "Expression of Distrust: Third-Party Voting and Cynicism in Government." *Political Behavior* 20(1):17–34.

Pew Research Center. 1998. Deconstructing Trust: How Americans View Government. Washington, D.C.: Pew Research Center for the People and the Press.

Seligson, Mitchell A. 1982. "On the Measurement of Diffuse Support: some Evidence from Mexico." *Social Indicators Research* 12(1):1–24.

Stokes, Donald E. 1962. "Popular Evaluations of Government: An Empirical Assessment." In *Ethics and Business: Scientific, Academic, Religious, Political, and Military*, edited by Harlan Cleveland and Harold D. Laswell. New York, NY: Harper & Brothers.

Uslaner, Eric M. 2001. "Is Washington Really the problem?" In *What is it about Government that Americans Dislike?,* edited by John R. Hibbing and Elizabeth Theiss-Morse, 118–133. Cambridge, MA: Cambridge University Press.

Wattenberg, Martin P. 1990. *The Decline of American Political Parties.* Cambridge: Harvard University Press.

_____. 1991. *The Rise of Candidate-Centered Politics.* Cambridge: Harvard University Press.

Weatherford, M. Stephen. 1984. "Economic 'Stagflation' and Public Support for the Political System." *British Journal of Political Science* 14(2):187–205.

Williams, John T. 1985. "Systemic Influences on Political Trust: The Importance of Perceived Institutional Performance." *Political Methodology* 11(1–2):125–142.

Wolak, Jennifer and Christine Kelleher Palus. 2010. "The Dynamics of Public Confidence in U.S. State and Local Government." *State Politics & Policy Quarterly* 10(4):421–445.

CHAPTER 4

When Citizens Lose Faith
Political Trust and Political Participation

Christina Eder and Alexia Katsanidou

Introduction[1]

For months, the same pictures appeared on TV and in newspapers almost every day: Thousands of Europeans protesting against their governments. In Greece and Iceland, they voiced their anger with the actions government took to tackle the financial crises. In Spain and Portugal, they demanded jobs for the young. In Germany, they marched for a nuclear phase-out and against the reconstruction of a main railway station. In Italy, resistance against budget cuts and the Berlusconi-administration rose as well. In traditionally peaceful Britain, we experienced the outbreak of riots as a result of police misconduct. Without even touching upon the 'Arab Spring', mass demonstrations and uprisings in the Middle East against authoritarian regimes, the examples listed above point towards a general tension between citizens and institutions, representatives and represented – in Europe, the cradle of democracy.

When studying news features or public discussions, recent European developments are often characterized by the term '(political) disenchantment'. The concept is rather vague, but essentially means that there is a growing distance between the people and their politicians, that voters feel unrepresented, unheard and increasingly frustrated, even alienated. At this point, several authors establish a link between increasing disenchantment and decreasing levels of trust in politicians and political institutions (cf. Dalton 2004; Norris 2011, 8; Nye, 1997) which is said to ultimately result in lower levels of participation, most often decreasing turnout rates on Election Day. But is there a relationship between political trust and political participation? And if so, are different means of participation influenced in the same way?

To answer these questions, we analyze EU- and EFTA-countries using the 4th wave of the European Values Study (EVS) that was conducted from 2008 to 2010. From the manifold literature on political trust and political participation,

---

1   We thank Nathalie Giger and Malina Voicu as well as the two anonymous reviewers for their invaluable comments and suggestions. All remaining mistakes are ours.

we derive several hypotheses that are tested employing multilevel modeling. This method is appropriate for our nested data structure of individuals living in nation states and accounts for the fact that, according to previous research, levels of political trust as well as the individual willingness to participate can be influenced by micro- and macro-level effects.

The novelty of this article lies in its innovative combination of (a) multilevel analysis which has gained importance in this research area only in the last few years with the incorporation of systemic variables to account for differences in context and (b) the operationalization of participation as different ways of engagement – institutionalized and non-institutionalized – thus refocusing from voting in elections only to get a broader and more accurate picture of the state of European democracy.

The discussion is structured as follows: theoretical underpinnings for political participation and political trust are presented in the next section followed by the hypotheses. The research design is outlined in section three where we also describe the data used in more detail. Section four shows the results of our analyses; the final section summarizes the findings with some concluding remarks.

Theoretical Background and Hypotheses

Political Participation

The aim of this paper is to examine how different means of political participation are affected by individual and national characteristics, in particular levels of political trust. In contemporary democracies, there are numerous ways for every citizen to become active in the political sphere: from wearing a button supporting a candidate or party, writing a letter to a representative, becoming a member of a political party or even founding new one one, to standing as a candidate oneself, just to name a few, the list of possibilities is almost endless. The means can be differentiated by the effort an individual has to invest when using them, by the kind of commitment necessary or by the degree of conventionality assigned to them. Applying the last criterion, voting in an election is the most conventional and widespread form of involvement (Perea Anduiza 2002, 644 ff.). More than that, it is a democratic citizen's most fundamental right, a duty even in some countries and can thus be termed an institutionalized form of participation (Marien et al. 2010). Elections give people a say in politics, they provide opportunities to evaluate government's performance and 'throw the rascals out' if needed. The commitment is relatively low; the costs of turning out are a matter of the individual's characteristics and the overall situation.[2] Yet, authors like Norris (2011, 221) demonstrate a clear downward trend of average aggregate turnout percentages in twenty-four Western European countries, dropping as low as 70 percent in the most recent years. Many studies confirm this decrease in turnout (cf. Gray and Caul 2000).

Other traditional, conventional and institutionalized forms of participation are party membership and party engagement. As today's democracies are largely run by parties (cf. Dalton et al. 2012; Kriesi 2008, 149) and those organizations fulfill numerous tasks such as channeling, aggregating and mediating interests as well as candidate selection and nomination, it is vitally important that citizens work for them, be it paid or unpaid. Yet, studies discussing challenges of modern democracy have established a declining trend of traditional political engagement, in particular party membership (van Biezen et al. 2012; Whiteley 2011). There is rich evidence that most Western European parties experience long-term erosion in their loyalties as party identification and party membership rates fall across the continent (Mair and van Biezen 2001).[3] Regardless of the reasons of this decline, in what counts as traditional or institutionalized political participation we can see a direct effect of decreasing party membership on the eroding basis of unpaid grassroots party work. Less and less people engage voluntarily with canvassing and other types of party supporting voluntary work (Scarrow 2001).

Given this situation, citizens find new ways of political expression. These new ways lack the institutionalized form of traditional political engagement, are sporadic, issue-specific, abrupt, occasionally extremely proactive and requiring a lot of engagement from the citizen (Stoker 2006). These actions are sometimes referred to as "unconventional" (Barnes and Kaase 1979; van Deth 1986) and are important political actions connected to specific issues people feel strongly about. Some can be used by one individual alone, like writing a letter to a Member of Parliament, but other forms like boycotting a product, organizing a demonstration or occupying a building require more energy and investment and potentially an attachment to a network.[4]

---

2   There are numerous ways of determining the costs and benefits of voting. One is Downs' "Economic Theory of Democracy" (1957) that explains why it is (ir)rational to participate in an election.

3   Several studies show that the support for democratic principles nevertheless remains stable (Inglehart 1999, Mishler and Rose 1999, 75).

4   As Kriesi (2008, 156f.) and others note, the former unconventional forms of participation have become increasingly normal, as more and more people seem to use them. This is particularly true for buying or boycotting products, donating money and signing petitions.

From this point on and following Marien et al. (2010), we refer to voting and party engagement as traditional or institutionalized political engagement as they are the classic forms of political participation. Thus, we distinguish them from our two indicators of more innovative or non-institutionalized modes of political engagement, petitioning and protesting. Each of the four items will serve as dependent variable in the multilevel models below.

Political Trust

Although there is no general theory of trust and the notions and explanations vary,[5] scholars agree that without a certain level of trust in others as well as in central political institutions, neither society, nor democracy can function (Dalton 2004; Easton 1965; Freitag and Bühlmann 2009; Keele 2007; Kumlin and Rothstein 2005; Lenard 2008; Miller 1974; Mishler and Rose 1997; Newton 2001; Nooteboom 2007, Nye, 1997; Paxton 2007). We base our work on the definition by Delhey and Newton (2005, 311) who understand trust as the

> belief that others will not deliberately or knowingly do us harm, if they can avoid it, and will look after our interest, if this is possible.

From this, we can deduct two different notions of the concept: *particularized trust* in well-known persons we interact regularly with and *generalized trust* in strangers and groups (Freitag and Bühlmann 2009, 1540).[6] Scholars like Newton (2001) summarize these two as *social trust* and distinguish them from *political trust*. The latter represents the "basic evaluative or affective orientation towards government" (Miller 1974, 952).

This article draws more on the political and less on the social aspect of the trust concept as it deals with the relation between trust and participation, both directed more at the political and less at the social sphere, although we are aware of the fact that it is not easy to separate the two and that society is the foundation the political builds on. As Nannestad (2008, 422) observes, the enormous and often interlinked amount of explanations and effects of trust is like "bowls of well-tossed spaghetti," and the same applies for the relation between social and political trust. We therefore decided to take only a spoon full and analyze it in greater detail. In short, political trust will serve as the main independent variable of our study.

---

5 For an overview of different definitions see for instance Nannestad (2008).
6 See Freitag and Traunmüller (2009) for more terms and definitions and an analysis of how particularized and generalized trust are related.

The concept of political trust includes trust in the system as a whole, trust in the institutions and trust in the political actors. Even from its definition we can see why declining levels of political trust raise concerns with politicians and scholars alike. Looking at the system as a whole, the main elements of modern democracies are fair and free elections that let citizens choose their representatives for the next legislative period. These representatives are then assigned with the mission to govern the state while acting in the best interest of the represented. Otherwise, the next election may bring defeat at the ballot box. Thus, elections are not only means to select political personnel but also a way to hold politicians accountable. These are the mechanisms that need to hold in order for the system to function well. Trust in these mechanisms is the basis of political trust. Turning our attention to the actors within a political system we see that if people do not trust their politicians, for instance because they feel that members of government or parliament pursue their own individual rather than the public interest, then the support for political institutions diminishes, and "legitimacy is called into question" (Hetherington 1998, 792). For the representatives, losing support implies that governing becomes more difficult as people are less willing to follow the politicians' lead (Scholz and Lubell 1998). This, in turn, means that the political system is even less able to deliver what it promised resulting in even lower satisfaction and trust – a vicious circle that may end in "consequences short of government collapse" (Chanley et al. 2000, 239).

What encapsulates the good functioning of polity mechanisms and the good conduct of actors, are political institutions. They are the core of a well-functioning representative democracy and they reflect the true qualities of the system without the short-lived influence of specific events or politicians. Thus, in order to understand the impact of trust on attitudes towards and behaviors within the political system we should consider trust in "core institutions of representative democracy" according to Norris (2011, 10): political parties, parliament, and government. Trust in institutions can be influenced by trust in politicians but it represents the "bigger picture." At the same time it is a result of trust in democratic mechanisms and the political system as a whole. For that reason it is the core of the puzzle.

Trust in these institutions is very important as there is evidence that it is directly related to the willingness of people to comply with existing rules and laws and to the acceptance of government policies (Dalton 2004, 12; Marien and Hooghe 2011: Rudolph and Evans 2005). Furthermore, declining political trust is associated with changes in voting behavior, namely, in gains for protest parties and parties representing particular interests. Levi and Stoker (2000, 490) list several studies that link the success of the US-tax revolt in the 1970s as well as successful popular votes on term limits to decreasing political trust. In sum, the importance of political trust for the political system cannot be over-estimated. As van der Meer (2010, 518) puts it:

> Trust in the political system is crucial to warrant the legitimacy of the system: political trust functions as the glue that keeps the system together and as the oil that lubricates the policy machine.

Hypotheses

Building on the presented insights into political participation and political trust, we can formulate several hypotheses that state a direct relation between levels of trust and political engagement. Traditional political participation shows a deep trust in the functioning of democratic mechanisms, the responsiveness of the system and the functioning of the core political institutions. Citizens feel that they are part of the system, that they influence decision making and that their preferences are taken into consideration. Dissatisfaction or disenchantment ultimately expressed as lower political trust cut the direct link between represented and representatives, citizens and elites (Dalton 2004). Thus, we formally hypothesize:

$H1a$: *The higher the level of trust in political institutions, the higher reported voting.*

$H1b$: *The higher the level of trust in political institutions, the higher party engagement.*

$H1c$: *The lower the level of trust in political institutions, the higher the incentive to petition.*

$H1d$: *The lower the level of trust in political institutions, the higher the incentive to protest.*

If confidence in the central institutions of democratic systems vanes, this should have an effect on the means of engagement. In other words, we expect to see that traditional political engagement in the two forms we have developed above corresponds with higher levels of political trust, while non-institutionalized forms should covariate with lower levels of trust.

The logic of Hypotheses 1a to 1d operates on the individual level or level 1 of our multilevel design. In the literature, we find a number of other factors that are believed to influence political participation on that level of analysis (cf. Brady et al. 1995; Dalton et al. 2009; Marien et al. 2010; Nevitte et al. 2009; Norris 2011, 222 ff.; Norris et al. 2005; Nyckowiak 2009; Perea Anduiza 2002;

Van Aelst and Walgrave, 2001; Verba et al. 1993a; Verba et al. 1993b).[7] We draw on these publications, when we incorporate *interest in politics, satisfaction with democracy, the belief that politics are important, left-right self-assessment, evaluation of government, education, age* and *gender* into our models. Following Verba et al. (1995, 1993 a, b), the last three variables are incorporated to account for the individual's abilities and opportunities to participate. Education plays a critical role here. The assumption is that better educated citizens find it easier to engage because first, they better understand what the decision is about and are better able to collect and process the required information. Second, they most often possess the necessary resources, most notably time, money and social contacts, to become active.[8] The better educated and better-off are also said to profit more from participation. Women are often believed to engage less, particularly in non-traditional forms of participation. For age, results are mixed.

The EVS does not contain information on the assessment of the respondents' own economic situation and the development of it, which is often used as proxy for the evaluation of government performance. Neither does it feature questions on political efficacy or party identification. Both indicators proved to be influential in previous studies.

As we assume context to matter for the incentive to participate, the national state level forms the second level of our multilevel design. The first two indicators stem from the Lijphart-school of measuring democracy: *electoral system* and *federalism* (Lijphart 1999). The idea is that a more consensual democratic system, that is a federal system with proportional representation, provides more access points to the decision-making process and thus a more favorable opportunity structure than more majoritarian systems. For electoral systems, research shows for instance that turnout under proportional representation is higher because fewer votes are 'lost' when distributing seats in parliament (Geys 2006; Klingemann 2009). Proportional systems are thus more inclusive than their counterparts and as a consequence often characterized as producing fewer 'electoral losers' (Norris 2011, 222). A higher chance of being a 'winner' should further citizens' willingness to participate. A higher chance of

---

7 There are many other studies delving into the reasons for why people turn out or abstain in elections. As we are not only interested in electoral participation, we did not list them here.

8 The level of education is always highly correlated with income. As respondents often have problems with or are unwilling to answer questions concerning their financial situation and as we want to avoid problems of multicollinearity in our models while at the same time include as many cases into our analyses as possible, we chose the former indicator over the latter.

being a 'loser' should, in contrast, heighten citizens' readiness to use unconventional forms of participation to have their voice heard in the decision-making process, also on non-Election-Day. In a federal system, political decisions are taken on several levels of state which means that the political sphere is closer to the voter and offers considerably more opportunities for participation than unitary states. We consequently assume that traditional forms of political participation profit more from this willingness to participate than non-institutionalized forms and thus formulate two alternative hypotheses:

H2a: The more proportional an electoral system and the more access points provided, the more institutionalized forms of participation are used.

H2b: The less proportional an electoral system and the less access points provided, the more non-institutionalized forms of participation are used.

Following the work of Vatter and Bernauer (2009) and Vatter (2009), who find that *direct democracy* supplements Lijphart's concept, we include that indicator into our analyses presuming a negative, that is substituting, effect on more innovative forms of participation. Direct democratic instruments provide voters with an unmediated and temporary access to the political process and decisions taken at the ballot booth are often legally and politically binding. Thus, we assume that direct democracy as a political opportunity structure "eats up" the need to protest and petition, as initiatives and referenda provide a more direct and effective way of influencing political decision-making (Fatke and Freitag 2012).[9]

H3a: The more direct democratic instruments are provided, the lower the incentive to use innovative forms of participation.

Whether direct democracy has a positive or negative effect on turnout is still a matter of debate (Baglioni 2007; Budge 2006; Freitag and Stadelmann-Steffen 2010; Möckli 2007; Parry et al. 2012; Tolbert et al. 2001; Tolbert et al. 2003; Tolbert and Smith 2006). In contrast to this article, these studies usually focus on the actual use of initiatives and referenda and not so much on the very existence of the instruments. If one assumes that the provision of a variety of direct democratic instruments in the constitution can serve as a proxy for their importance in law-making and that more direct democracy diminishes the importance of elections, then one can create a hypothesis that reads:

---

9 "When authorities offer a given constituency routine and meaningful avenues for access, few of its members protest because less costly, more direct routes to influence are available" (Meyer 2004, 128).

H3b: The more direct democratic instruments are provided, the lower the incentive to vote in the coming election.

In order to incorporate the financial and economic situation of the analyzed countries, we use two variables: change in unemployment between 2005 and 2007, and public deficit for the year 2007. Unemployment is an indicator that directly affects citizens' general resources to engage in politics and, it is a crucial aspect of the public's evaluation of government performance and public mood. This element is important as it captures the changes in trust in institutions that are not due to system pathologies but rather indicators of public dissatisfaction with specific policy outcomes. The change of this indicator over the two years prior to the conduction of the EVS captures the effects of the beginning of the financial crisis on the general public better than a static unemployment rate. Recent events in Greece, London or Paris show that economic slump can quite quickly lead to violent protests even in established democracies. We therefore formulate that:

H4: The higher the increase of the unemployment rate, the higher the use of non-institutionalized means of participation.

The public deficit on the other hand is an indicator of economic performance and government policy choices. Considering that the financial crisis first hit the countries with high public deficit and accumulating public debt we can hypothesize that:

H5: The lower the public deficit the higher the use of institutionalized means of participation.

Data sources, operationalizations and expected direction of influence are presented in the annotations. The next section describes the dataset used and the methods employed before we present the results of our analyses in section 4.

Data and Research Design

To test our hypotheses, we use the integrated dataset of the 4th wave of the European Values Study (EVS 2010) that was conducted from 2008 to 2010,[10] and deleted all countries that are neither part of the European Union (EU) nor of

---

10   For more information on the EVS see http://www.europeanvaluesstudy.eu/.

the European Free Trade Association (EFTA)[11] to obtain a Most-Similar-Systems-Design. We also had to exclude Italy due to very low numbers of respondents on the participation variables. The result is a database comprising 29 West, Central and East European countries and about 38 100 interviews.[12]

Multilevel modeling seems appropriate due to several reasons: First, we examine how individual *and* national characteristics affect political participation. Second, the graphs in Figure 1a below point towards considerable between-nation variation on all four dependent variables. Third, we face a nested data structure of individuals living in nation states. By ignoring this data structure, we would run the risk of committing Type I errors. Therefore, we decided for generalized hierarchical models. As each of our four dependent variables is coded binary, a logistic link function is employed.

We use a bottom-up strategy to build our models; that is we work from simple to more complex. Consequently, the first model will be the empty model or null-model that does not contain any explanatory factors.[13] The second step is to include independent variables from the micro-level, in our case the individual level information stemming from the EVS and afterwards our macro-level variables, and then random coefficients until we obtain our full model that is given in equation 1:

$$(1)\ \eta_{ij}=\text{logit}(\pi)_{ij}=\ln\left(\frac{\pi ij}{1-\pi ij}\right)=\text{logistic}(\gamma_{00}+\gamma_{10}X_{ij}+\gamma_{01}Z_{j}+u_{oj}+u_{1j}X_{ij})$$

where i $(=1,...,N_j)$ denotes the micro-level unit and j $(=1,..., J)$ the macro-level unit, with γ_{00} being the regression intercept, X and Z representing the variables at the individual- and group-level, u_{oj} the residual at the country level and $u_{1j}X_{ij}$ a random slope. U_{oj} is assumed to be a normally distributed independent random variable with a mean of zero and a variance of τ^2_0 (Snijders and Bosker 1999, 213). In contrast to linear multilevel regression models, no individual level residual is given as "the variance is completely determined by the mean, and thus is not a separate term to be estimated" (Luke 2004, 55).

The 4th wave of the EVS contains items covering membership and unpaid work for several organizations, including political parties, as well as other

---

11   We had to exclude Northern Ireland although it is a case of its own in the EVS as we were unable to collect the necessary level 2 information.

12   Due to missings on independent level-1 variables, the number of interviews is later reduced to 22.758.

13   Equations and notations taken from Hox (2010, 112ff.). Empty model: $\eta_j=\text{logit}(\pi_j)$

$$=\ln\left(\frac{\pi ij}{1-\pi ij}\right)=\gamma_{00}+u_{oj}.$$

means of action like signing petitions, boycotting products or participating in demonstrations and strikes. In the first step, we performed factor analyses to determine which items load on the same factors. Combining these results with theoretical explanations, we then constructed two single variables and two additive indices that cover different forms of political engagement. *Voting* in the coming election empirically is an own dimension. As one can argue that participating in an election stands for a different quality of engagement and commitment than being a party member or volunteer for parties, we incorporate the item as a variable of its own.

Our first additive measure is *party engagement*. It captures two basic functions: party membership and volunteer work for political parties. Both are dummy variables indicating whether an individual is currently a member of a political party and/or has ever done voluntary work for a political party. If an individual reports to have done neither he is assigned a value of 0, if at least one measure was taken she receives a value of 1.

The second single variable is *petitioning*. This dummy variable shows whether an individual has never signed a petition before or might do that (value = 0) or whether she has actually performed this action (value = 1).

Another index was constructed for active *protesting*. A value of 1 is assigned if a person reported to have done at least one of the following: joined a boycott, attended a lawful demonstration, joined an unofficial strike, or occupied a building or factory. Zero is given otherwise.

Figures 1a and 1b show the distribution of the four modes of participation across the 29 countries in our sample. In all four graphs, we can observe considerable between-nation variation. The top left picture shows the percentage of people stating that they would vote in the coming election which is relatively high in all countries. The levels of party engagement in the top right graph are much lower, with Denmark being an extreme outlier. We observe that newer democracies including Southern European countries show lower levels of petitioning than more established democracies. For protesting, no clear patterns can be identified.

Levels of trust can be measured using survey questions. For political trust, people are asked about the confidence they have in certain institutions and politicians. We picked the 4th wave of the EVS and built an additive index of political trust using respondents' level of confidence in the "core institutions of representative democracy": political parties, parliament, and government (Norris 2011, 10). Factor analyses confirmed that these three items load heavily on the same factor,[14] therefore we added up the answers given by the

---

14   The output shows only one factor. All three item load on that factor with at least 0.85. The
      KMO-test result is 0.72 (non-rotated principal component analysis).

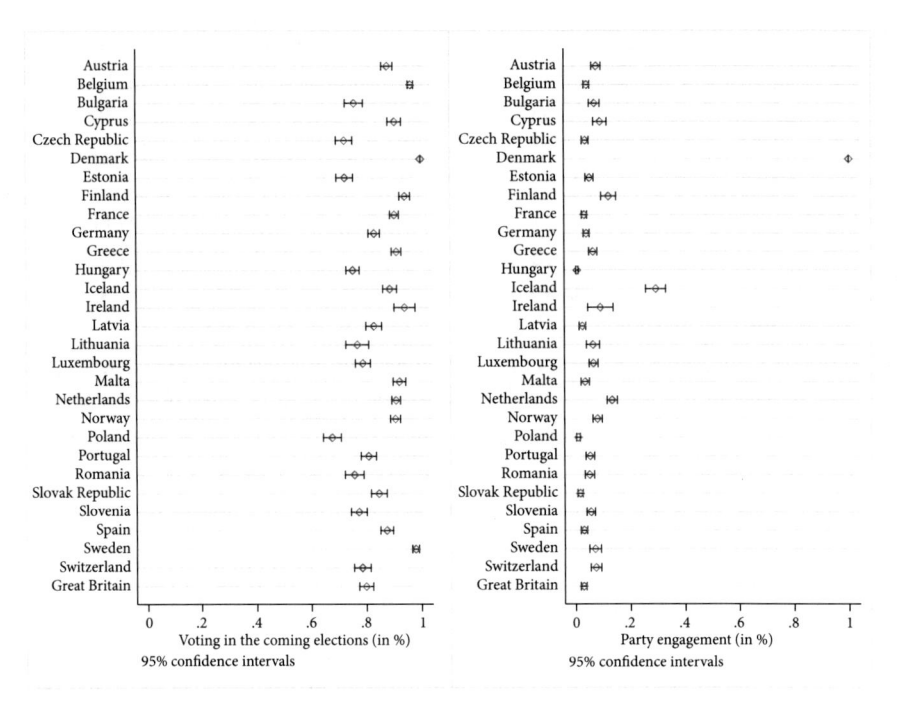

FIGURE 1A *Traditional political participation (mean and confidence intervals)*
SOURCE: OWN GRAPHIC BASED ON EVS 4TH WAVE

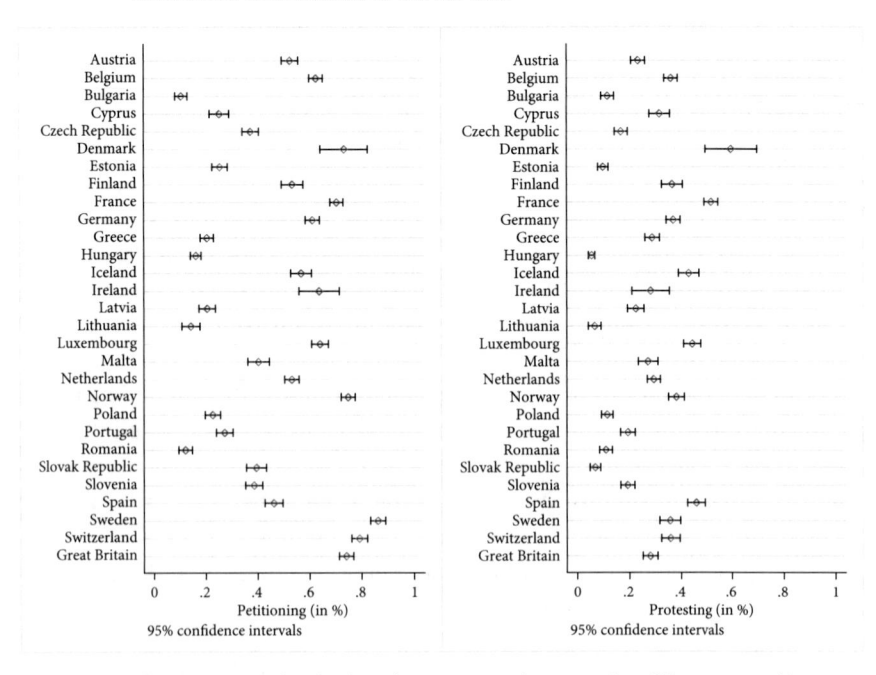

FIGURE 1B *Non-institutionalized political participation (mean and confidence intervals)*
SOURCE: OWN GRAPHIC BASED ON EVS 4TH WAVE

participants on these three questions and rescaled them. The result is an index that ranges from 0 to 9 with 0 indicating that the respondent has no confidence in any of the three institutions and 9 meaning that she has a great deal of trust in all three of them. The numbers show that trust in the core institutions government, parliament and political parties varies considerably across countries. The lowest mean values can be found in Bulgaria (2.09), Hungary (2.40), Lithuania (3.05), Poland (2.51) and Latvia (2.45), the highest values in Norway (4.41), Cyprus (4.59), Malta (4.66), Luxemburg (4.79) and Denmark (5.25) with the latter leading the charts. The varying levels of trust show that we do not only have a considerable amount of between- but also of within-nation variation on our main independent variable.

Empirical Findings

The first models given in Tables 1–4 are the null-models for each dependent variable. They are also called 'empty models', because they do not contain explanatory variables and inform "about the basic partition of the variability in the data between the two levels" (Snijders and Bosker 1999, 46). Thus, it is possible to determine whether multilevel modeling is necessary in the first place. One measure is the (residual) Intraclass Correlation or ICC that can be found in the second last row of each table.[15] It is "the variance in the dependent variable that is accounted for by groups" (Luke 2004, 15) and in our case for the null-models varies between 16% and 38%. This provides us with the first observation that the influence of our four dependent variables by systemic factors varies significantly. The next models, Model 1, always include two sets of individual-level variables: political engagement variables and actual explanatory variables. For Model 2, the national level variables are added. Model 3 relaxes the assumption of all country-specific slopes to be parallel and allows for random slopes for our main independent variable political trust.

For voting (Table 1), we see a positive influence of all political engagement variables, and all political variables as well as education and age. From the other forms of engagement the most influential one on voting is party engagement, while protesting has no influence. Models calculated disentangling the influence of the different variable values (not reported) show that being very interested in politics has a strong positive influence on the likelihood of participating in the next election. The same is true for tertiary education and

---

15   The ICC is computed as $\rho_I = \tau^2{}_0/(\tau^2{}_0 + \pi^2/3)$ with the individual-level variance assumed to equal $\pi^2/3$ in logistic multilevel models (Snijders and Bosker 1999, 224).

TABLE 1   *Voting*

	Model 0	Model 1	Model 2	Model 3
Constant	1.89 (0.15)***	−0.96 (0.16)***	−0.96 (0.43)**	−0.94 (0.44)**
Alternative engagement				
Party engagement		1.02 (0.16)***	1.02 (0.16)***	1.02 (0.16)***
Petition		0.35 (0.05)***	0.35 (0.05)***	0.35 (0.05)***
Protest		0.02 (0.06)	0.02 (0.06)	0.02 (0.05)
Individual level				
Political trust		0.10 (0.01)***	0.10 (0.01)***	0.11 (0.02)***
Political interest		0.53 (0.03)***	0.53 (0.03)***	0.54 (0.03)***
Politics important		0.24 (0.03)***	0.24 (0.03)***	0.24 (0.03)***
Self-placement left		0.19 (0.05)***	0.19 (0.05)***	0.19 (0.05)***
Government good		0.08 (0.01)***	0.08 (0.01)***	0.08 (0.01)***
Education		0.16 (0.04)***	0.16 (0.04)***	0.16 (0.04)***
Age		0.01 (0.00)***	0.01 (0.00)***	0.01 (0.00)***
Gender		0.03 (0.04)	0.03 (0.04)	0.03 (0.04)
Country level				
Electoral system			0.11 (0.13)	0.10 (0.13)
Federalism			−0.07 (0.34)	−0.04 (0.34)
Direct democracy			−0.11 (0.11)	−0.11 (0.11)
Change in unemployment			0.11 (0.07)*	0.11 (0.07)*
Public deficit			0.01 (0.04)	0.01 (0.04)
Random terms				
Variance (Country)	0.62 (0.18)	0.45 (0.13)	0.37 (0.10)	0.53 (0.16)
Variance (Pol. trust)				0.01 (0.00)
Covariance				−0.05 (0.02)
N (Individuals)	22758	22758	22758	22758
N (Countries)	29	29	29	29
Test vs. linear reg. (p)	0.00	0.00	0.00	0.00
(Residual) ICC	0.16			
Wald χ^2 (df)		1696 (11)	1702 (16)	1401 (16)
Log likelihood	−9469	−8443	−8441	−8409

Annotations: ICC – Intraclass Correlation. * $p < 0.1$, ** $p < 0.05$, *** $p < 0.01$. Standard errors in parantheses. All models calculated using xtmelogit routine in STATA which approximates the log likelihood by adaptive Gaussian quadrature with seven integration points (default). Logit coefficients reported. All values rounded to two decimals. df – degrees of freedom. Likelihood ratio test of model 2 and model 3 point towards model 3 being superior.

believing politics to be quite important. Gender does not seem to have an effect here. Decreasing unemployment over the 2005–2007 period seems to increase the likelihood of participating in the next election, the other macro-level variables are of minor influence.

With party engagement (Table 2), the picture looks somewhat different. Voting is less influential on party engagement than vice versa and the other forms of engagement have even less influence. Political interest has considerable influence on party engagement. The effects of political trust, and the belief of politics to be important are also positive. Level of education and age do not seem to make a difference, nor does the evaluation of government performance. Gender, on the other hand, has a clear impact: the chances for party engagement are considerably lower if the respondent is female. At the country level, public deficit has a relatively strong effect: The lower the deficit, the higher the odds of someone being a party member or volunteer. Setting the slope for political trust to random does little to change the effect of the deficit; all other coefficients remain without significant influence.

Turning to more innovative ways of political participation, we see that for petitioning (Table 3), the most influential type of political engagement is protest. Additionally, the level of education and political interest clearly make a difference. Placing oneself on the left side of the political continuum increases the probability of petitioning as does stating that politics is important. Higher levels of political trust apparently diminish the chance. Women appear to use the instrument more often than men. On the country level, a federalist system, lower unemployment and low public deficit have positive effects on the chances of petitioning. The other factors do not turn out significant. Introducing random slopes for political trust increases the impact of federalism, unemployment change and the deficit, and points towards a more majoritarian electoral system diminishing the chances for petitioning.

Protesting (Table 4) is apparently influenced by all variables included on the micro-level apart from voting. A placement on the left part of the left-right-axis, higher levels of education and political interest increase the chance of protesting of at least one form. The belief of politics to be important further helps while higher level of political trust, a positive evaluation of government and being female decrease the odds. On the country level, all variables turn out insignificant. These relations hold if the assumption of parallel slopes across all countries is relaxed, with just one exemption: lower unemployment heightens the chance for protesting.

Let us now relate back to our hypotheses. The results just presented indicate that our hypotheses H1a-d regarding the effect of political trust on the four ways of participation can be accepted for the moment. Higher levels of political trust point to higher chances of voting in the coming election, and the same

TABLE 2   *Party engagement*

	Model 0	Model 1	Model 2	Model 3
Constant	$-2.70\,(0.27)^{***}$	$-6.74\,(0.32)^{***}$	$-6.85\,(0.80)^{***}$	$-7.10\,(0.77)^{***}$
Alternative engagement				
Voting		$0.96\,(0.16)^{***}$	$0.96\,(0.16)^{***}$	$0.96\,(0.16)^{***}$
Protest		$0.35\,(0.07)^{***}$	$0.35\,(0.07)^{***}$	$0.35\,(0.07)^{***}$
Petition		$0.36\,(0.07)^{***}$	$0.36\,(0.07)^{***}$	$0.36\,(0.07)^{***}$
Individual level				
Political trust		$0.12\,(0.02)^{***}$	$0.13\,(0.02)^{***}$	$0.13\,(0.02)^{***}$
Political interest		$0.84\,(0.05)^{***}$	$0.84\,(0.05)^{***}$	$0.84\,(0.05)^{***}$
Politics important		$0.35\,(0.04)^{***}$	$0.35\,(0.04)^{***}$	$0.35\,(0.04)^{***}$
Self-placement left		$0.02\,(0.06)$	$0.02\,(0.06)$	$0.03\,(0.06)$
Government good		$-0.02\,(0.01)$	$-0.02\,(0.01)$	$-0.01\,(0.01)$
Education		$-0.13\,(0.05)$	$-0.01\,(0.05)$	$-0.01\,(0.05)$
Age		$0.01\,(0.00)^{***}$	$0.01\,(0.06)^{***}$	$0.01\,(0.00)^{***}$
Gender		$-0.29\,(0.06)^{***}$	$-0.29\,(0.06)^{***}$	$-0.29\,(0.06)^{***}$
Country level				
Electoral system			$-0.07\,(0.24)$	$0.01\,(0.24)$
Federalism			$-0.63\,(0.62)$	$-0.81\,(0.60)$
Direct democracy			$0.23\,(0.20)$	$0.18\,(0.19)$
Change in unemployment			$0.11\,(0.12)$	$0.08\,(0.12)$
Public deficit			$0.15\,(0.07)^{**}$	$0.14\,(0.07)^{**}$
Random terms				
Variance (Country)	$2.05\,(0.62)$	$1.51\,(0.46)$	$1.25\,(0.39)$	$1.01\,(0.00)$
Variance (Pol. trust)				$0.01\,(0.00)$
Covariance				$0.01\,(0.03)$
N (Individuals)	22758	22758	22758	22758
N (Countries)	29	29	29	29
Test vs. linear reg. (p)	0.00	0.00	0.00	0.00
(Residual) ICC	0.38			
Wald χ^2 (df)		1073 (11)	1078 (16)	1009 (16)
Log likelihood	-4896	-4193	-4190	-4186

Annotations: See Table 1.

TABLE 3   *Petitioning*

	Model 0	Model 1	Model 2	Model 3
Constant	−0.23 (0.20)	−1.86 (0.21)***	−1.09 (0.57)*	−0.95 (0.51)*
Alternative engagement				
Voting		0.36 (0.05)***	0.36 (0.05)***	0.36 (0.05)***
Party engagement		0.40 (0.07)***	0.40 (0.07)***	0.39 (0.07)***
Protest		1.88 (0.04)***	1.88 (0.04)***	1.88 (0.01)***
Individual level				
Political trust		−0.04 (0.01)***	−0.04 (0.01)***	−0.04 (0.01)***
Political interest		0.31 (0.02)***	0.31 (0.02)***	0.31 (0.02)***
Politics important		0.02 (0.02)	0.02 (0.02)	0.02 (0.02)
Self-placement left		0.11 (0.04)***	0.11 (0.04)***	0.10 (0.04)***
Government good		0.00 (0.01)	0.00 (0.01)	0.00 (0.01)
Education		0.52 (0.03)***	0.52 (0.03)***	0.52 (0.03)***
Age		−0.01 (0.00)***	−0.01 (0.00)***	−0.01 (0.00)***
Gender		0.21 (0.03)***	0.21 (0.03)***	0.21 (0.03)***
Country level				
Electoral system			−0.27 (0.17)	−0.36 (0.15)**
Federalism			0.92 (0.45)**	1.33 (0.39)***
Direct democracy			0.00 (0.14)	0.09 (0.12)
Change in unemployment			0.17 (0.09)*	0.20 (0.08)***
Public deficit			0.10 (0.05)**	0.11 (0.04)**
Random terms				
Variance (Country)	1.11 (0.29)	1.04 (0.28)	0.67 (0.18)	0.98 (0.29)
Variance (Pol. trust)				0.00 (0.00)
Covariance				−0.04 (0.02)
N (Individuals)	22758	22758	22758	22758
N (Countries)	29	29	29	29
Test vs. linear reg. (p)	0.00	0.00	0.00	0.00
(Residual) ICC	0.25			
Wald χ^2 (df)		3220 (11)	3231 (16)	3235 (16)
Log likelihood	−13460	−11351	−11345	−11338

Annotations: See Table 1.

TABLE 4   *Protest*

	Model 0	Model 1	Model 2	Model 3
Constant	$-1.11\,(0.15)^{***}$	$-2.95\,(0.15)^{***}$	$-2.64\,(0.39)^{***}$	$-2.57\,(0.40)^{***}$
Alternative engagement				
Voting		$-0.00\,(0.06)$	$-0.00\,(0.06)$	$-0.00\,(0.06)$
Party engagement		$0.37\,(0.07)^{***}$	$0.37\,(0.07)^{***}$	$0.37\,(0.07)^{***}$
Petition		$1.87\,(0.04)^{***}$	$1.86\,(0.04)^{***}$	$1.86\,(0.04)^{***}$
Individual level				
Political trust		$-0.04\,(0.01)^{***}$	$-0.04\,(0.01)^{***}$	$-0.04\,(0.01)^{***}$
Political interest		$0.30\,(0.03)^{***}$	$0.30\,(0.03)^{***}$	$0.30\,(0.03)^{***}$
Politics important		$0.14\,(0.02)^{***}$	$0.14\,(0.02)^{***}$	$0.13\,(0.02)^{***}$
Self-placement left		$0.70\,(0.04)^{***}$	$0.70\,(0.04)^{***}$	$0.69\,(0.04)^{***}$
Government good		$-0.02\,(0.01)^{**}$	$-0.02\,(0.01)^{**}$	$-0.02\,(0.01)^{**}$
Education		$0.32\,(0.03)^{***}$	$0.32\,(0.03)^{***}$	$0.32\,(0.03)^{***}$
Age		$-0.00\,(0.00)^{*}$	$-0.00\,(0.00)^{*}$	$-0.00\,(0.00)^{*}$
Gender		$-0.28\,(0.03)^{***}$	$-0.28\,(0.03)^{***}$	$-0.28\,(0.03)^{***}$
Country level				
Electoral system			$-0.01\,(0.12)$	$-0.04\,(0.12)$
Federalism			$-0.03\,(0.31)$	$-0.02\,(0.31)$
Direct democracy			$-0.10\,(0.10)$	$-0.10\,(0.10)$
Change in			$0.11\,(0.06)$	$0.12\,(0.06)^{*}$
unemployment				
Public deficit			$0.05\,(0.03)$	$0.05\,(0.03)$
Random terms				
Variance (Country)	$0.67\,(0.18)$	$0.41\,(0.11)$	$0.30\,(0.08)$	$0.00\,(0.00)$
Variance (Pol. trust)				$0.37\,(0.11)$
Covariance				$-0.01\,(0.01)$
N (Individuals)	22758	22758	22758	22758
N (Countries)	29	29	29	29
Test vs. linear reg. (p)	0.00	0.00	0.00	0.00
(Residual) ICC	0.17			
Wald χ^2 (df)		3332 (11)	3345 (16)	3322 (16)
Log likelihood	-12379	-10181	-10176	-10174

Annotations: See Table 1.

is true for being a member or volunteer for a party. The chances to petition or protest are negatively influenced. Electoral system and federalism have no effect on institutionalized forms of participation here, therefore H2a is rejected. H2b has to be rejected, too. Yet, federalism shows a positive effect on petitioning which could indicate that this way of participation is used on subnational rather than the national level. Direct democracy has no influence on any of the dependent variables. Therefore, H3a and H3b can be rejected altogether. We have to reject H4 as it seems that decreasing unemployment rates positively affect voting, petitioning and protest alike. H5 seems to correctly predict the effect of the deficit on party engagement, but not on voting. In total, four of our ten hypotheses can be fully and one can be partially accepted for now, including our main hypotheses on the relationship between political trust and participation.

In addition, we do find evidence for a gender and education bias in the use of different modes of participation which is in line with previous research. For the chances to vote, petition and protest, education seemingly makes a big difference: the higher the level of education, the higher the chance to use the respective form. The influence of gender on voting is inconclusive. The reason behind this finding might be the fact that the survey question was formulated prospective rather than retrospective. Yet, women tend to engage less in a party and protest less often while petitioning more often than men. These results call into question the often claimed ability of innovative means of participation to be more inclusive than the traditional forms and to bring more people back into the political system.

Conclusion

Is there a relationship between political trust and political participation? And if so, are different means of participation influenced in the same way? These questions were posed by this article in the light of mass protests and even violent eruptions in several European countries in 2011. We thus relate to the ongoing public and scientific debate about the relationship between representatives and represented in today's Western democracies.

The discussions usually center on the notion of 'political disenchantment', a feeling that is allegedly growing all over the continent and combines the more diffuse sentiments of alienation, frustration or distance between voters and politicians and is said to ultimately affect the willingness to participate in politics.

Multilevel modeling is employed to simultaneously test the impact of individual and context variables on different modes of political participation with levels of political trust always serving as the main independent variable. We, first, find that context variables do affect individual behavior and, second, obtain new insights into the incentives for political participation: According to our results, institutionalized and non-institutionalized forms of participation are affected differently by our set of variables, and as hypothesized, also by different levels of political trust. Here, higher levels of political trust seem to favor more traditional forms of participation, while more innovative means of action are apparently furthered by lower levels of political trust.

These findings support the argument that decreasing levels of trust are not necessarily threatening the very foundations of democracy, but rather cause citizens to choose other means of voicing their opinions. According to Dalton (2008, 85), elections "are infrequent and blunt tools of political influence" no longer satisfying the needs of Inglehart's postmodern and 'elite-critical' citizen (Inglehart and Catterberg 2002, 314). Instead, people make use of other instruments that allow them to influence political decision-making on non-Election Days. Further research is therefore needed on the normative and practical implications and consequences of these changes as well as on whether the conclusions reached here hold when other modes of participation, other countries or longer time-periods are studied. The results also suggest that more sophisticated statistical methods like multilevel modeling can enrich our knowledge on political participation and that concentration on voting alone should be avoided to get the full picture.

Appendix

Table 5 displays the variables used in the analyses, their operationalization and their expected influence on political participation. If institutionalized and non-institutionalized forms of participation are expected to be influenced differently, this is indicated by +/– or –/+with the sign before the dash standing for institutionalized forms.

TABLE 5   *Variable overview and descriptive statistics*

Factor	Operationalization	Expected influence	Minimum/ Maximum	Mean/ Standard deviation
Voting	Item v263: vote intention in next election. Dummy.		0/1	0.84/0.37
Party engagement	Dummy built from items v14 and v32: belong to political party/ group, do unpaid work for party. 0 = none of the two; 1 = at least one of the two.		0/1	0.06/0.25
Petition	Recode of v187: 0 = never done, might do; 1 = have done		0/1	0.46/0.50
Protest	Dummy variable built from v188 (boycott), v189 (lawful demonstration), v190 (unofficial strike), v191 (occupy building). 0 = would never do, might do; 1 = have done at least one of the four		0/1	0.28/0.45
Individual level (Level 1)				
Political trust	Additive index built from items v211, v221 and v222: confidence in parliament, government, parties. Index ranges from 0 to 9.	+/−	0/9	3.45/2.04
Political interest	Item v186, rescaled 0 to 3.	+	0/3	1.56/0.92
Politics important	Item v5.	+	0/3	1.35/0.90
Self-placement left	Item v193, Left-right self-assessment. Left = 1, 0 = 5 or higher (middle or right)	+	0/1	0.29/0.45
Government good	Additive index of items v223 and v224: satisfaction with democracy, evaluation of government. Index ranges from 0 to 12.	+/−	0/12	5.30/2.67
Education	Item 336. 0 = primary or no school diploma, 1 = secondary education, 2 = tertiary education.	+	0/2	1.14/0.59

TABLE 5   *Variable overview and descriptive statistics* (cont.)

Factor	Operationalization	Expected influence	Minimum/ Maximum	Mean/ Standard deviation
Age	Item v303. Age in years at time of interview.	+/–	16/108	48.84/17.60
Gender	Item v302. Dummy, male = 0, female = 1	+/–	0/1	0.52/0.50
Nation level (Level 2)				
Electoral system	Electoral system. 0 = most majoritarian, 5 = most proportional. Armingeon et al. (2011)	–/+	0/5	2.91/0.92
Federalism	Federal system. 0 = no, 1 = yes. Armingeon et al. (2011)	+/–	0/1	0.19/0.39
Direct democracy	Additive index of direct democratic instruments. +1 for every instrument provided out of 4. Armingeon et al. (2011)	–	0/4	1.27/1.20
Unemployment change	Change of the unemployment rate between 2005 and 2007. World Bank.	–/+	–8.2/0.4	–1.7/1.74
Public deficit	Annual deficit (primary government balance) as a percentage of GDP. source OECD	–/+	–1.8/14.8	1.89/3.36

Note: All individual level variables are taken from the EVS, 4th wave. For the national level, we used information from the year 2007, the year prior to the 4th wave of the EVS, as we assume lagged effects.

References

Armingeon, Klaus, Romana Careja, David Weistanner, Sarah Engler, Panajotis Potolidis, Marlène Gerber, and Phillip Leimgruber. 2011. *Comparative Political Data Set III 1990–2009.* Institute of Political Science: University of Berne.

Baglioni, Simone. 2007. "The Effects of Direct Democracy and City Size on Political Participation. The Swiss Case." In *Participatory Democracy and Political Participation. Can Participatory Engeneering Bring Citizens Back In?*, edited by Thomas Zittel and Dieter Fuchs, 91–106. London: Rouledge.

Barnes, Samuel H., and Max Kaase. 1979. *Political Action. Mass Participation in Five Western Democracies*. Beverly Hills: Sage.

Brady, Henry E., Sidney Verba, and Kay Lehman Schlozman. 1995. "Beyond Ses: A Resource Model of Political Participation." *American Political Science Review* 89:271–94

Budge, Ian. 2006. "Direct and Representative Democracy: Are They Necessarily Opposed?" *Representation* 42:1–12.

Chanley, Virginia A., Thomas J. Rudolph, and Wendy Rahn, M. 2000. "The Origins and Consequences of Public Trust in Government: A Time Series Analysis." *Public Opinion Quarterly* 64:239–56.

Dalton, Russel J. 2008. "Citizenship Norms and the Expansion of Political Participation." *Political Studies* 56:76–98.

———. 2004. *Democratic Challenges, Democratic Choices. The Erosion of Political Support in Advanced Industrial Democracies*. Oxford: Oxford University Press.

Dalton, Russell J., David M. Farrell, and Ian McAllister. 2012. *Political Parties and Democratic Linkage. How Parties Organize Democracy*. Oxford: Oxford University Press.

Dalton, Russell, Alix Van Sickle, and Steven Weldon. 2009. "The Individual-Institutional Nexus of Protest Behaviour." *British Journal of Political Science* 40:51–73.

Delhey, Jan, and Kenneth Newton. 2005. "Predicting Cross-National Levels of Social Trust: Global Pattern or Nordic Exceptionalism?" *European Sociological Review* 21:311–27.

Downs, Anthony. 1957. *An Economic Theory of Democracy*. New York: Harper and Brothers.

Easton, David. 1965. *A Systems Analysis of Political Life*. New York: Wiley.

EVS. 2010. "European Values Study 2008, 4th Wave, Integrated Dataset." GESIS Data Archive Cologne, Germany:ZA4800 Data File Version 2.0.0 (2010-11-30) doi:10.4232/1.10188.

Fatke, Matthias, and Markus Freitag. 2012. "Direct Democracy: Protest Catalyst or Protest Alternative?" *Political Behavior* forthcoming:1–24.

Freitag, Markus, and Marc Bühlmann. 2009. "Crafting Trust. The Role of Political Institutions in a Comparative Perspective." *Comparative Political Studies* 42:1537–66.

Freitag, Markus, and Isabelle Stadelmann-Steffen. 2010. "Stumbling Block or Stepping Stone? The Influence of Direct Democracy on Individual Participation in Parliamentary Elections." *Electoral Studies* 29:472–83.

Freitag, Markus, and Richard Traunmüller. 2009. "Spheres of Trust: An Empirical Analysis of the Foundations of Particularized and Generalized Trust." *European Journal of Political Research* 48:782–803.

Geys, Benny. 2006. "Explaining Voter Turnout. A Review of Aggregate-Level Research." *Electoral Studies* 25:637–63.

Gray, Mark, and Miki Caul. 2000. "Declining Voter Turnout in Advanced Industrial Democracies, 1950 to 1977." *Comparative Political Studies* 33:1091–122.

Hetherington, Marc J. 1998. "The Political Relevance of Trust." *American Political Science Review* 92:791–808.

Hox, Joop J. 2010. *Multilevel Analysis. Techniques and Applications.* New York: Routledge.

Inglehart, Ronald. 1999. "Postmodernization Erodes Support for Authority, but Increases Support for Democracy." In *Critical Citizens. Global Support for Democratic Government*, edited by Pippa Norris, 236–56. Oxford: Oxford University Press.

Inglehart, Ronald, and Gabriela Catterberg. 2002. "Trends in Political Action: The Developmental Trend and the Post-Honeymoon Decline." *International Journal of Comparative Sociology* 43.

Keele, Luke. 2007. "Social Capital and the Dynamics of Trust in Government." *American Journal of Political Science* 51:241–54.

Klingemann, Hans-Dieter. 2009. "The Impact of Political Institutions. A Contribution of the" Comparative Study of Electoral Systems "(CSES) to Micro–macro Theories of Political Attitude Formation and Voting Behavior." In *Comparative The Study of Electoral Systems*, edited by Hans-Dieter Klingemann, 3–27. Oxford: Oxford University Press.

Kriesi, Hanspeter. 2008. "Political Mobilisation, Political Participation and the Power of the Vote." *West European Politics* 31:147–68.

Kumlin, Staffan, and Bo Rothstein. 2005. "Making and Breaking Social Capital. The Impact of Welfare-State Institutions." *Comparative Political Studies* 38:339–65.

Lenard, Patti Tamara. 2008. "Trust Your Compatriots, but Count Your Change: The Roles of Trust, Mistrust and Distrust in Democracy." *Political Studies* 56:312–32.

Levi, Margaret, and Laura Stoker. 2000. "Political Trust and Trustworthiness." *Annual Review of Political Science* 3:475–507.

Lijphart, Arend. 1999. *Patterns of Democracy. Government Forms and Performances in Thirty-Six Countries.* New Haven: Yale University Press.

Luke, Douglas A. 2004. *Multilevel Modeling.* Thousand Oaks: Sage Publications.

Mair, Peter, and Ingrid van Biezen. 2001. "Party Membership in Twenty European Democracies, 1980–2000." *Party Politics* 7:5–21.

Marien, Sofie, and Marc Hooghe. 2011. "Does Political Trust Matter? An Empirical Investigation into the Relation between Political Trust and Support for Law Compliance." *European Journal of Political Research* 50:267–91.

Marien, Sofie, Marc Hooghe, and Ellen Quintelier. 2010. "Inequalities in Non-Institutionalised Forms of Political Participation: A Multi-Level Analysis of 25 Countries." *Political Studies* 58:187–213.

Meyer, David S. 2004. "Protest and Political Opportunities." *Annual Review of Sociology* 30:125–45.

Miller, Arthur H. 1974. "Political Issues and Trust in Government: 1964–1970." *American Political Science Review* 68:951–72.

Mishler, William, and Richard Rose. 1999. "Five Years after the Fall: Trajectories of Support for Democracy in Post-Communist Europe." In *Critical Citizens. Global Support for Democratic Governance*, edited by Pippa Norris, 78–99. New York: Oxford University Press.

———. 1997. "Trust, Distrust and Skepticism: Popular Evaluations of Civil and Political Institutions in Post-Communist Societies." *Journal of Politics* 59:418–51.

Möckli, Silvano. 2007. "Direct Democracy and Political Participation from a Cross-National Perspective." In *Participatory Democracy and Political Participation. Can Participatory Engineering Bring Citizens Back In?*, edited by Thomas Zittel and Dieter Fuchs, 107–24. London: Routledge.

Nannestad, Peter. 2008. "What Have We Learned About Generalized Trust, If Anything?" *Annual Review of Political Science* 11:413–36.

Nevitte, Neil, André Blais, Elisabeth Gidengil, and Richard Nadeau. 2009. "Socioeconomic Status and Nonvoting: A Cross-National Comparative Analysis." In *Comparative The Study of Electoral Systems*, edited by Hans-Dieter Klingemann, 85–108. Oxford: Oxford University Press.

Newton, Kenneth. 2001. "Trust, Social Capital, Civil Society, and Democracy." *International Political Science Review* 22:201–14.

Nooteboom, Bart. 2007. "Social Capital, Institutions, and Trust." *Review of Social Economy* 65:29–53.

Norris, Pippa. 2011. *Democratic Deficit. Critical Citizen Revisited*. Cambridge: Cambridge University Press.

Norris, Pippa, Stefaan Walgrave, and Peter Van Aelst. 2005. "Who Demontsrates? Anti-State Rebels, Conventional Participants, or Everyone?" *Comparative Politics* 37:189–205.

Nyckowiak, Justyna 2009. "Political Activity. Is Trust in Democratic Institutions Really a Relevant Determinant?" *International Journal of Sociology* 39:49–61.

Nye, J.S. 1997. "In Government We Don't Trust." *Foreign Policy* 108:99–111.

Parry, Janine A., Daniel A. Smith, and Shayne Henry. 2012. "The Impact of Petition Signing on Voter Turnout." *Political Behavior* 34:117–36.

Paxton, Pamela. 2007. "Association Membership and Generalized Trust: A Multilevel Model across 31 Countries." *Social Forces* 86:47–76.

Perea Anduiza, Eva. 2002. "Individual Characteristics, Institutional Incentives and Electoral Abstention in Western Europe." *European Journal of Political Research* 41:643–73.

Rudolph, Thomas J., and Jillian Evans. 2005. "Political Trust, Ideology, and Public Support for Government Spending." *American Journal of Political Science* 49:660–71.

Scarrow, Susan. 2001. "Parties without Members?" In *Parties without Partisans*, edited by Russell J. Dalton and Martin Wattenberg. New York: Oxford University Press.

Scholz, John T., and Mark Lubell. 1998. "Trust and Taxpaying: Testing the Heuristic Approach to Collective Action." *American Journal of Political Science* 42:398–417.

Snijders, Tom, and Roel Bosker. 1999. *Multilevel Analysis. An Introduction to Basic and Advanced Multilevel Modeling*. London: Sage Publications.

Stoker, Gerry. 2006. "Explaining Political Disenchantment: Finding Pathways to Democratic Renewal." *Political Quarterly* 77:184–94.

Tolbert, Caroline J., John A. Grummel, and Daniel A. Smith. 2001. "The Effects of Ballot Initiatives on Voter Turnout in the American States." *American Politics Research* 29:625–48.

Tolbert, Caroline J., Ramona S. McNeal, and Daniel A. Smith. 2003. "Enhancing Civic Engagement. The Effect of Direct Democracy on Political Participation and Knowledge." *State Politics and Policy Quarterly* 3:23–41.

Tolbert, Caroline J., and Daniel A. Smith. 2006. "Representation and Direct Democracy in the United States." *Representation* 42:25–44.

Van Aelst, Peter, and Stefaan Walgrave. 2001. "Who Is That (Wo)Man in the Street? From the Normalisation of Protest to the Normalisation of the Protester." *European Journal of Political Research* 39:461–86.

van Biezen, Ingrid, Peter Mair, and Thomas Poguntke. 2012. "Going, Going, ...Gone? The Decline of Party Membership in Contemporary Europe." *European Journal of Political Research* 51:24–56.

van der Meer, Tom. 2010. "In What We Trust? A Multi-Level Study into Trust in Parliament as an Evaluation of State Characteristics." *International Review of Administrative Sciences* 76:517–36.

van Deth, Jan W. 1986. "A Note on Measuring Political Participation in Comparative Research." *Quality and Quantity* 20:261–71.

Vatter, Adrian. 2009. "Lijphart Expanded: Three Dimensions of Democracy in Advanced Oecd Countries?." *European Political Science Review* 1:125–54.

Vatter, Adrian, and Julian Bernauer. 2009. "The Missing Dimension of Democracy. Institutional Patterns in 25 Eu Member States between 1997 and 2006." *European Union Politics* 10:335–59.

Verba, Sidney, Kay Lehman Schlozman, and Henry Brady. 1995. *Voice and Equality: Civic Voluntarism in American Politics*. Cambridge: Harvard University Press.

Verba, Sidney, Kay Lehman Schlozman, Henry Brady, and Norman H. Nie. 1993a. "Citizen Activity. Who Participates? What Do They Say?" *American Political Science Review* 87:303–18.

——. 1993b. "Race, Ethnicity and Political Resources. Participation in the United States." *British Journal of Political Science* 23:453–97.

Whiteley, Paul F. 2011. "Is the Party Over? The Decline of Party Activism and Membership across the Democratic World." *Party Politics* 17:21–44.

CHAPTER 5

The Role of Electoral Systems for the Translation of Political Trust into Electoral Participation

Christoph Arndt

Introduction

Disenchantment, political cynicism and declining levels of turnout constitute almost ubiquitous phenomena in Western countries. The decline of political trust has been identified as both driving force for and consequence of these trends (Dalton 2004; Dogan 2005; Hay 2007; Norris 2011). Nevertheless, there is considerable variation between countries in the disenchantment of voters, political trust and electoral participation (e.g. Franklin 2004; Dogan 2005; Hay 2007; Karp and Banducci 2008; Marien 2011; Norris 2011). Whereas some countries see low levels of turnout in times of crumbling political trust, some others do not experience a huge drop in turnout, but see the rise of protest or anti-establishment parties, typically on the fringes of the party systems. Yet, we lack a clear and systematic understanding of how low levels of political trust do lead to low turnout in one electoral context, but not in another one. This constitutes a blind spot in the literature even though previous studies found electoral systems to be a crucial determinant for both political trust and turnout, but lacked a systematic account for how electoral systems affect the translation of trust into turnout.

Only few studies have so far looked at the role of electoral systems for the problem whether citizens' democratic attitudes do affect abstention at the ballots (Banducci, Donovan, and Karp 1999; Karp and Banducci 2008). This is striking as two branches of literature have identified electoral systems as major determinant for political attitudes and turnout. The first branch has argued that political trust and satisfaction with democracy is generally higher in polities that have highly open and proportional electoral systems (e.g. Weil 1989; Miller and Listhaug 1990; Lijphart 1999; Farrell and McAllister 2006; Marien 2011). This is because disaffected voters still have a chance to express their preferences by casting a ballot for new or protest parties and thus remain attached to the political system. The second branch has found a positive and direct effect of proportional systems on turnout since these provide a bunch of alternatives for the electorate compared to majoritarian systems which lead to few parties (Jackman 1987; Blais and Carty 1990; Blais and Dobrzynska 1998; Ladner and Milner, 1999). In other words, PR systems have been found to be more inclusive for disaffected voters and small parties.

This chapter claims that the electoral system is one important structural cause for the translation of political (dis)trust into turnout. In what follows, I will use the insights from the respective literatures to examine the role of electoral systems as structural determinant for the translation of political trust into electoral participation. My argument is that under open and highly proportional electoral systems does the absence of political trust among voters still produce higher levels of turnout as protest parties can canvass these voters with the respective appeals. In contrast, non-proportional majoritarian systems do produce lower levels of turnout if a number of citizens lack political trust as they have no chance to get their disaffection voiced. This chapter contributes to our understanding of these mechanisms since it provides an individual level-based explanation why electoral systems produce different levels of turnout in times of low political trust among Western electorates. In other words, not in all electoral contexts do disenchanted voters leave the democratic process completely, but turn to parliamentary protest. The remainder of this chapter is structured as follows. The next section reviews the relevant literatures and develops the theoretical arguments. The third section describes the data, measurements and methods used. Subsequently, the fourth section contains the results of the analysis. The fifth section summarizes and discusses some implications of the findings.

Political Trust, Electoral Systems and Turnout

Electoral Systems and Political Trust

Political trust has traditionally been a core subject in political science and the study of democratic elections (Hetherington 2005, Marien 2011 for reviews of the literature). In recent decades, scholars have increasingly directed their attention to the role of political trust in the study of electoral and political behaviour. A certain level of political trust has been seen as necessary condition for democratic polities and their well-functioning (e.g. Easton 1965; Citrin 1974; Hetherington 1998, 2005; Dalton 2004). This is essential in times of an increasing number of critical and more demanding citizens (Norris 1999). With regard to the chapter's purpose, several authors have argued that the electoral system is a strong determinant for the level of political trust among citizens (Miller and Listhaug 1990; Dalton 2004, 177 ff.; Vowles, Banducci, and Karp 2006; Marien 2011).

In a seminal article, Miller and Listhaug (1990) argue that differences in the party system explain variation of political trust across time and space. Differences in the party systems are understood as differences in the electoral systems (majoritarian versus proportional in their case) and other electoral rules such as thresholds. According to Miller and Listhaug (1990, 363), political trust is expected to be higher under proportional systems which are open to new parties thanks to a sufficiently low threshold. This is because citizens have a better chance to express dissatisfaction by voting for a protest party that has a fair chance to represent their discontent in the political arena.

Similarly, if segments of the electorate have the feeling that the existing parties fail to offer a solution for the problems they are concerned with, new parties may offer a response to those problems and promote policies these citizens favour (ibid, 368). Hence, under open and proportional systems, dissatisfaction does not lead to growing distrust towards the political system and its institutions as protest parties can act as the vehicle of expressing discontent within the political system (ibid, 366).

In contrast, a very rigid party system impeding the chances for new parties to enter the political arena will produce declining levels of political trust (in their example the majoritarian U.S. two party system). The same goes for thresholds or other formal and informal rules that hamper the entrance of new challengers, in their case Sweden. Here, disaffected voter have no viable option to get their disaffection represented in parliament and thus become less trusting over time as they have no voice within the system.

Their results demonstrate that, in contrast to Sweden and the USA, political trust recovered in Norway after a period of decline. In the latter case, new parties – in particular the Progress Party (*Fremskrittspartiet*) – brought the voices of the disaffected back into the political arena. This was not the case in the two other countries with more rigid party systems and the lack of new challengers. Progress Party supporters were the least trusting when the party started to contest elections in 1973, but the level of trust among its supporters caught up to the level found among the other parties' constituencies in the following elections. Thus, an open and proportional electoral system was able to keep political trust at a higher level, when political trust declined in other more restrictive contexts.

In line with these reasoning and findings, later scholars found that electoral systems do matter for a polity's level of political trust, or the related concepts of satisfaction with the democratic system and political efficacy (Lijphart 1999; Norris 1999; Dalton 2004; Farrell and McAllister 2006; Marien 2011). Several contributions have used the New Zealand case, where a referendum in 1993 changed the electoral system from first-past-the-post to mixed member proportionality. It has been argued that the electoral reform made the party system more responsive to the New Zealanders' demands and preferences. Under proportional representation, various measures of political trust, political efficacy and satisfaction with democracy revealed more positive attitudes over time (Banducci, Donovan, and Karp 1999; Vowles and Aimer 2004; Vowles, Banducci, and Karp 2006). Moreover, the electoral reform was at least temporarily able to offset the country's trend towards declining turnout.

Marien's recent analysis (2011) shows that highly proportional systems and systems with high accountability foster political trust among citizens. The more party alternatives citizens have to choose from the more they tend to trust, even though Marien argues that there is a ceiling effect if the party system is too fragmented (cf. also Weil 1989 for a similar proposition).[1]

Given the arguments of Miller and Listhaug (1990) and the results of more recent empirical studies, we can suspect that the electoral system does play a non-trivial role not only for the amount of political trust in a democratic polity, but also for the problem whether disenchantment and distrust leads into abstention and to which extent. After briefly reviewing the literature on electoral systems and turnout, I will develop a framework that conceptualizes the interplay between political trust, electoral systems and turnout.

Electoral Systems and Turnout

The study of the effect of electoral institutions on turnout has been a long history in political science. The literature has typically argued that proportional systems (PR) foster turnout, whereas majoritarian systems decrease it (e.g. Blais and Carty 1990; Sartori 1997, Lijphart 1999). The study of Blais and Carty (1990, 167) sums up the three main arguments in this respect. First, proportional system increase the voters' efficacy as the votes gained by a party also translate more likely into seats, even for small parties. Second, as PR typically applies multi-member constituencies, it is less likely that some districts remain non-competitive. Third, PR leads to a higher number of parties and thus a higher number of alternatives for the electorate. All three features of PR make citizens more inclined to vote as they feel more represented. The authors found a net effect of PR systems on turnout; that is turnout is 7 percentage points

---

1   There are, however, some studies which point to weak or non-existing relationship between electoral systems and political attitudes (e.g. Listhaug, Aardal, and Ellis 2009; Norris 2011). One should note that these studies do not use political trust as dependent variable as such, but rather different concepts like satisfaction with the democratic process, political efficacy or attitudes towards allegiant behaviour.

higher under proportional systems even after controlling for a variety of other possible determinants.

Other studies have found similar results pointing to a positive effect of proportional electoral systems on turnout in Western democracies (Jackman 1987; Blais and Dobrzynska 1998; Ladner and Milner, 1999). However, almost all of them use aggregate measures of turnout and we thus lack knowledge on how individual attitudes interact with features of the electoral system when it comes to electoral participation. Only the study of Karp and Banducci (2008) examines the effect of electoral systems on how political efficacy matters for the decision to participate. Using a multilevel design, they find that proportional systems enhance the voters' efficacy, which in turn fosters turnout. Under non-proportional systems, voters that may want to opt for a small party are aware of the limited chance to get their vote into parliament and thus have a higher degree of abstention (Blais and Carty 1991). This fits to the above-stated claim by Miller and Listhaug on the function of protest parties under PR.

The Role of Electoral Systems for Translating Trust into Electoral Participation[2]

Given the evidence found by Karp and Banducci and the arguments provided by Miller and Listhaug, we can apply a similar reasoning on the relationship between political trust, electoral systems and the citizens' allegiance to vote. As to the contingent effect of electoral systems for the translation of efficacy into political participation, we should expect a similar logic to be true for political trust respectively the lack thereof. In a nutshell, I argue that the electoral system mediates whether political trust (or the lack thereof) will translate into abstention. Under proportional representation, discontent with politics and the lack of political trust does not essentially lead to high levels of abstention. First, the respective segment of voters has still a chance to get their disaffection represented in the electoral arena. Second, the more permissive an electoral system is, the more likely have protest and minority parties a fair chance to contest elections and win parliamentary representation and thus keep disillusioned voters at the ballots (Miller and Listhaug 1990). In contrast,

---

2 The paper's focus will be on the direct effects of electoral systems on turnout since I argue that the electoral system comes first in the causal chain and voters are to a sufficient degree aware of how electoral systems work and whether their choice will translate into seats (Blais and Carty 1991; Dunleavy 2005). Thus, I will not use the indirect effects of electoral systems such as disproportionality or the effective number of parties as measures since these are partly caused by the voter's decisions and thus imply a certain degree of endogeneity.

under majoritarian or other non-proportional systems, disenchanted voters have no viable alternative than staying home as they feel to waste their votes otherwise. Here, political distrust will much more likely lead to abstention.

Nevertheless some qualifications for proportional systems need to be made. These concern the formal electoral threshold and district magnitudes. PR systems with no or low electoral thresholds allow protest parties or other new challengers to contest the electoral arena more easily, and thus to mobilize the discontent vote. Here, distrust into politics should not cause low levels of turnout since protest and populist parties have the lowest entry costs. PR systems with higher thresholds do produce higher burdens for these parties and make it more difficult for disaffected voters to express preferences for non-established parties. Similar effects are to be expected for PR systems where the district magnitudes are low and lead to a marginalization of small parties. The work of Willey (1998) has shown that low district magnitudes increase the entry costs for new parties. This is because each constituency applies a rather high natural threshold if the number of seats to be distributed is rather small irrespective of the formal threshold applied. In contrast larger district magnitudes do enhance the chances of success for new and smaller parties. With respect to the problem whether distrust affects the level of abstention, countries with sufficiently high district magnitudes should open the electoral market for those challengers that can soak up the votes of the disaffected.

Accordingly, I will not only use the legal threshold to distinguish between electoral systems, but also account for the district magnitudes as outlined in the next section. In countries classified as PR with high thresholds, I expect that low levels of trust will lead to higher levels of abstention compared to PR systems applying low thresholds. Lastly, majoritarian systems are expected to translate political distrust into higher degrees of abstention than PR does since these systems marginalize parties that may soak up the discontent.

Data, Methods and Measurement

Data

The second, third, and fourth wave of the European Social Survey (ESS 2004, 2006, 2008) have been used to analyze the relationship between electoral systems, political trust and electoral participation. The ESS covers currently more than 30 European countries and is ideally suited for the analysis of the effect of political trust on political behaviour.[3] I chose fourteen Western European countries that have a longer history of democratic rule and that have not changed the electoral system frequently such as Italy which is typically excluded in similar analyses (Karp and Banducci 2008; Marien 2011).[4] The ESS waves II–IV consist of items measuring trust in politicians, political parties, and the national parliaments. The respondents had been asked:

> Please tell me on a score of 0–10 how much you personally trust each of the institutions I read out. 0 means you do not trust an institution at all, and 10 means you have complete trust.

I used the variables on trust in politicians, political parties, and the national parliaments as they capture the trust in national political institutions quite well and constructed a political trust index by simple addition following the procedure in Marien (2011).[5] The index on political trust serves as my main independent variable at the individual level. It has been multiplied by minus 1 in the multilevel models to demonstrate the effects of lower levels of political trust on the probability of electoral participation. To measure electoral participation, the ESS contains a variable asking the respondents whether they casted a ballot at the last national election. This has been used to capture turnout as my dependent variable (yes/no) after eliminating those respondents which were not entitled to vote in the last election. Additionally, age, education and gender have been included as control variables since some authors presumed them to have an effect on political trust (Inglehart 1999; Marien 2011). The former is included as continuous variable and the latter two as dummies in the analysis. A further control is political interest to rule out that political trust and electoral participation is mainly mediated by political interest. This constitutes also a sort of robustness check as political interest could be expected to be a determinant of both trust and voting behaviour.

At the country level, the electoral system constitutes the main independent variable. Electoral systems were classified according to whether they are

---

3   The data can be accessed at http://www.europeansocialsurvey.org/. This web page provides detailed information and documentation of the data, the fieldwork, the sampling procedures and further methodological aspects.

4   Countries included are: Austria, Belgium, Denmark, Finland, France, Germany, Ireland, the Netherlands, Norway, Portugal, Spain, Sweden, Switzerland, and the United Kingdom.

5   Reliability tests reported a Cronbach's alpha of 0.89 and a principle component analysis yielded a one-factor solution. This shows that the three items can be used as one-dimensional index capturing political trust (Hooghe 2011).

majoritarian, PR with higher, or PR with lower thresholds. I used the information from the respective chapters in the edited volumes of Gallagher and Mitchell (2005) and Niedermayer, Stöss, and Haas (2006) that provide comprehensive compilations of electoral and party systems. Majoritarian systems are France and the United Kingdom since they have single-member constituencies with majority or plurality rule. These two countries have also no formula for proportional representation or compensatory seats to secure at least some proportionality.

Countries with PR that apply a threshold higher than 4 per cent were classified as PR with higher thresholds. The same was true for countries with lower or no thresholds, but low district magnitudes that constitute equivalents to high thresholds. The criterion was an average district magnitude of 10 and below as calculated by Gallagher and Mitchell (2005, Table C.6). Values of 10 and below go typically in hand with rather low effective nationwide district magnitudes. Here, many constituencies have natural thresholds of 10 per cent or even above. Under these circumstances, it is more difficult for small parties to gain representation despite that there are no or only low legal thresholds. This is for instance the case in Portugal, Spain and Switzerland which apply no legal threshold (Portugal, Switzerland) or a 3 per cent threshold (Spain), but produce considerably disproportional or even majoritarian outcomes as almost all constituencies have small district magnitudes limiting the number of competitive parties to two or three at the local level.[6]

Countries with thresholds of 4 per cent or lower have been classified as PR with low thresholds if the average district magnitude was above 10. Countries with such features of the electoral systems are the most open ones for new parties. Examples are Denmark, the Netherlands or Sweden which have all more than 7 parties represented in parliament. The analysis does also control for compulsory voting since this is the case in Belgium. Table A1 in the Appendix reports the classification of electoral systems according to these criteria.

Cross-level interactions between the electoral system dummies and the political trust index where constructed to analyze the conditional effect of electoral systems for the relationship between political trust and abstention. Hence, the respective interaction terms test the hypotheses on the electoral systems' role in translating the level of political trust into electoral participation and whether there are pure additive effects as advanced in the theoretical

---

6 According to the average district magnitude of 10.5, Portugal provides a borderline case for a classification according to district magnitudes. However, since it has been characterized as one of Europe's least proportional PR systems and the effective electoral threshold was calculated as above 5 per cent (see Freire 2006), it was classified as PR with high threshold.

section above or even multiplicative effects, respectively. In sum, the rationale of this empirical analysis is to regress the decision to vote on political trust for individuals, and to examine the respective moderator function of electoral systems by introducing cross-level interactions.

Analysis

Descriptive Analysis

A first step is to look briefly at the descriptive statistics for the levels of political trust and turnout across the three electoral systems. Table 1 yields the average level of political trust and turnout across the three electoral systems.

The results for political trust show that citizens in highly open proportional systems have a higher level of political trust compared to majoritarian or proportional systems with higher thresholds. On the 30-point index for political trust, the difference is larger than 3.5 points to the other two systems. Put differently, political trust among citizens in countries holding elections under proportional systems with low or no thresholds is 10 per cent higher compared to electoral systems with plurality rule or high thresholds. This confirms the arguments and findings of previous studies (Lijphart 1999; Norris 1999; Aarts and Thomassen 2008; Marien 2011). On the other hand, there is only a small, weakly significant difference between the majoritarian system and the proportional system applying higher thresholds.

The figures for average turnout across the three electoral systems confirm the findings from previous studies (Jackman 1987; Blais and Carty 1990; Blais and Dobrzynska 1998; Ladner and Miller 1999). There are highly significant differences between the three electoral systems. We find the highest turnout in proportional systems applying low or no thresholds, followed by proportional systems with higher ones. Turnout in majoritarian systems is at least 6.5 per cent lower than in proportional system corroborating the effect found by Blais

TABLE 1   *Political trust and turnout across electoral systems*

Electoral system	Majoritarian	PR-High threshold	PR-Low threshold
Mean political trust	11.16*	11.36*	14.93***
Average turnout	74.36% ***	80.92% ***	86.20% ***

Note: N = 79,079 for political trust; N = 72,247 for turnout; Sign.: * $p < 0.05$, ** $p < 0.01$, *** $p < 0.001$; significant result indicates that value is significantly different from other values in the same row.

and Carty (1990). Having found different levels of political trust and turnout across the three electoral systems, the question is now how the electoral system affects the conversion of political trust or distrust into electoral participation. The next section presents the results from the statistical model applied.

Multilevel Logistic Model of Political Trust, Electoral Systems and Turnout

A multilevel logistic regression analysis was used to test the translation of political distrust into abstention across the three electoral systems. Since the expectation is that there is not only variance between individuals, but also between countries with different electoral systems which form clusters the individuals are nested in, it is necessary to model the multilevel structure to avoid biased standard errors (Goldstein 2003; Gelman and Hill 2007; Rabe-Hesketh and Skrondal 2008). This was done by performing a logistic random-intercept model using the command *xtmelogit* in Stata (Rabe-Hesketh and Skrondal 2008, 248–251). This model is useful if the number of clusters is relatively small (in this case: 14 countries) and the cross-level interactions are of the main interest. In this respect, the cross-level interactions represent the slopes for the effect of distrust on electoral participation for each electoral system. Compulsory voting was included as a control variable since this is the case in Belgium. The results of this analysis are presented in Table 2.

First, the null model confirms that there is significant variation on the country level as the likelihood ratio test for the intraclass correlation rejects the null-hypothesis of rho = 0. The intraclass correlations in all models indicate that between 4 and 8 percent of all variance in turnout can be attributed to the country level. In other words, there is not only significant variation between individuals in electoral participation, but also between countries and hence electoral systems.

Model 1 includes the individual level variables, that is the index for political trust and the demographic control variables. The higher the value of the political trust index in Table 2 is the less trust has a respondent in politics. As expected, declining levels of political trust among individuals decrease the probability of turning out at Election Day since the sign is negative and the coefficient is highly significant. The other three demographic controls confirm the results of various other studies, namely that the high educated, males, and older citizens have a higher propensity to turn out since all three controls are highly significant and have a positive sign. Since this is the case in all models analyzed and the coefficients do not vary substantially, I will not further comment these coefficients in detail in what follows. On the country level, only the coefficient for the PR systems applying low thresholds can be distinguished

TABLE 2 *Effects of political trust and electoral systems on electoral participation, random effects logistic regression*

	Model 0	Model 1	Model 2	Model 3
Individual level variables				
Political trust (negative)		−0.058***	−0.052***	−0.033***
Gender (male = 1)		0.058**	0.056**	−0.085***
Education (intermediate)		0.534***	0.529***	0.359***
Education (high)		1.027***	1.019***	0.656***
Age		0.034***	0.034***	0.031***
Political interest				−0.665***
Country level variables				
PR-high threshold		0.175	0.195	0.233
PR-low threshold		0.656*	0.375	0.351
Cross-level interactions				
Trust*PR-high			0.002	0.002
Trust*PR-low			−0.023***	−0.023**
Constant	1.585***	−0.057	0.012	2.220***
Measures of fit and test statistics				
S.d of Random effect	0.536	0.373	0.366	0.398
loglikelihood	−33,579.902	−30,802.680	−30,782.467	−29,491.381
Intraclass corr. (Rho)	0.080***	0.040***	0.039***	0.046***
McKelvey & Zavoina R^2	0	19.25	19.67	25.46
N (countries)	72,247 (14)	71,664 (14)	71,664 (14)	71,587 (14)

Notes: Dependent variable is participation in last national election (0 = no, 1 = yes); Coefficients are non-standardized estimates from multilevel logistic regressions. Sign.: * $p < 0.05$, ** $p < 0.01$, *** $p < 0.001$. The models contain a control variable for compulsory voting in Belgium (not shown). PR: Proportional representation, s.d.: standard deviation.

significantly from majoritarian systems, but not the one for PR systems with higher thresholds. This means that there is a significant difference in turnout between highly proportional and majoritarian systems after controlling for political trust.

A next step is to add the cross-level interactions between the electoral system dummies and the political trust index. Model 2 allows testing the respective propositions on the role of the electoral system. The coefficient for political trust is now a constitutive term given the electoral system effect is zero, in my case the majoritarian system (cf. Brambor, Clark, and Golder 2006 for the interpretation of constitutive terms after interaction terms have been added). After controlling for other electoral systems than the majoritarian ones, we see that low political trust in the latter still leads to lower turnout. Surprisingly, the coefficient for the interaction PR–high threshold with political trust is not significant in statistical terms. This means also that there is no significant difference between majoritarian systems and proportional systems with high thresholds; this was not expected and will be further discussed below. However, in line with the expectation on highly open PR systems, we find a highly significant coefficient. This indicates a difference between majoritarian systems and this electoral system when it comes to the translation of low levels of political trust into turnout. Highly open PR systems translate political distrust to a lesser degree into abstention than PR systems with high thresholds and plurality rule. This effect is mainly additive given the respective coefficients in Model 2, but Model also reveals an interactive component as the slope changes slightly, but significantly for this electoral system.

Finally Model 3 controls whether political interest represents a mediator for political trust and turnout. Even though some coefficients lose some strength due to the inclusion of political interest, this does not change the results found in Model 2 substantially. The interaction between PR with low thresholds and trust is still significant and no other coefficient becomes insignificant. Gender changes sign as male respondents have a higher level of political interest, which is now controlled for by the model. Beyond that the model indicates that political interest does not explain the translation of political trust into turnout across electoral systems to a substantial degree. Hence, the findings are robust if controlled for political interest as an important determinant of both political trust and electoral behaviour.

To visualize the effects found in Model 2 and to ease their interpretation, I calculated predicted probabilities based on the model's coefficients, where the three controls were kept at their means and compulsory voting was said to be absent. Figure 1 graphs the respective predicted probabilities.[7] The predicted probabilities demonstrate that the electoral system contingents the translation of low levels of political trust into abstention of voters. Generally and not surprisingly, high levels of trust lead to very high rates of electoral participation as at least nine out of ten voters turn out if they have complete trust in politics in all three electoral systems.

In line with the propositions formulated in section 2, we can observe that the main difference in turnout is between highly open proportional systems

---

7   A similar pattern can be found if the predicted probabilities are calculated on the basis of
    Model 3; that is controlled for by political interest.

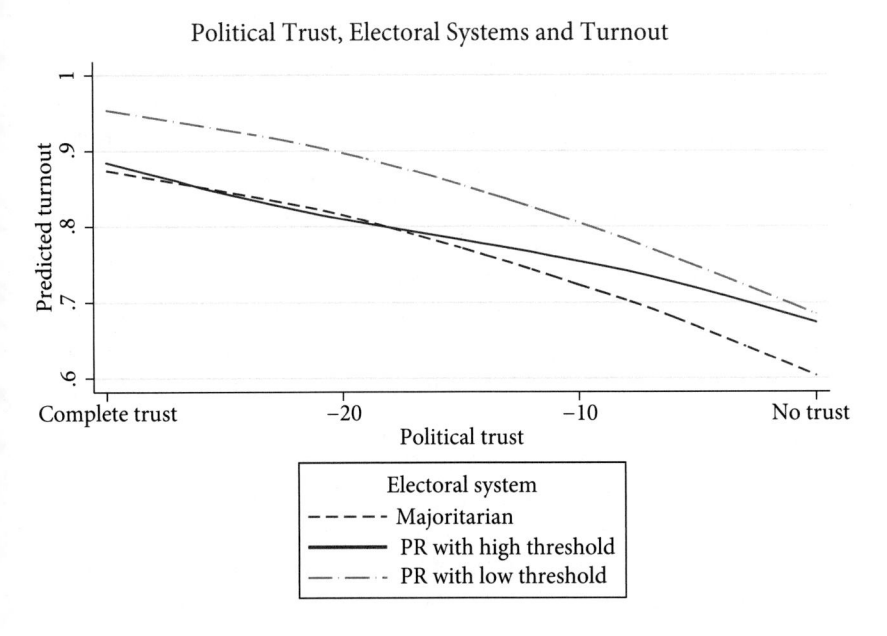

FIGURE 1   *Visualizing the coefficients from Model 3 in Table 1*

and the other two electoral systems distinguished above. Voters with lower levels of political trust do still have a three to four per cent higher propensity of turning out if the electoral system is open as no high threshold or a marginalization of minor parties hampers their participation. Majoritarian systems in contrast produce higher levels of abstention as political trust among the electorate declines. Together with the results from Table 1, Figure 1 confirms the expectation concerning PR systems with low thresholds. However, the line for PR systems with high thresholds does not confirm the expectations. Surprisingly, turnout declines even stronger with decreasing levels of trust than in majoritarian systems as the lines cross each other in the graph at some point. The fact that the lines cross each other may also explain the insignificant difference in the coefficients for PR with high thresholds and majoritarian system reported in Table 1. Another notable effect in this respect is that there is nonetheless a convergence of the two proportional systems among those voters with extremely low levels of political trust (right-hand side of Figure). This indicates that the effect of different electoral systems in translating low political trust into participation is at some point offset by the alienation of very disenchanted voters. Citizens do not use their voting rights if they have no political trust at all irrespective of whether the party system could provide them with an alternative.

These deviations were not expected, but refer to similar effects found by Marien (2011) with political trust as dependent variable. In her analysis, countries with intermediate levels of disproportionality have the lowest levels of political trust, whereas highly disproportional majoritarian system produce higher levels of political trust. Intermediate levels of disproportionality roughly equals PR systems with high thresholds as operationalized in this chapter, and my results may thus reflect the curvilinear effect in Marien's analysis to some extent. On the other hand, some of the differences may also be driven by outlier countries as a plotting the predicted probabilities for three countries representing typical cases for each electoral system (Great Britain, Germany, and Denmark) yield much more straightforward and intuitive patterns as shown in Figure 2.

Figure 2 demonstrates that the highly open Danish electoral system keeps dissatisfied voters to a stronger degree at the ballots than its German neighbour as the gap widens with increasing political distrust. This effect is even stronger in comparison with the British case, where turnout drops sharply as political distrust grows. Using three model countries for electoral system also

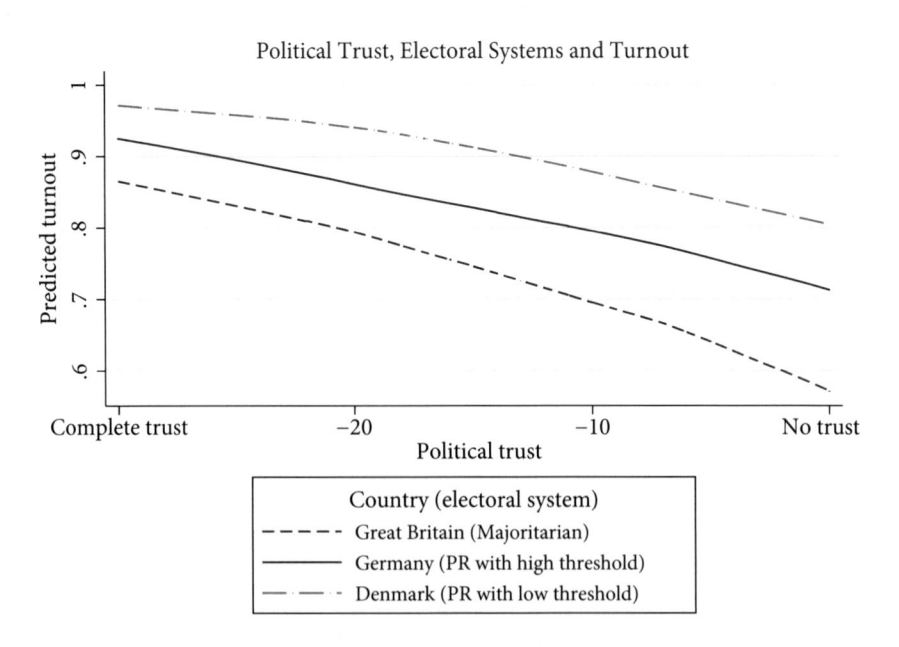

FIGURE 2 *Predicted probabilities for three typical countries, probabilities derived from Model 3, Table 1*

yields a clearer difference between PR systems with high thresholds and majoritarian countries since the gap in participation for Britain and Germany widens if political trust decreases.

In sum, the differences found between the electoral systems should reflect feedback effects found by Karp and Banducci (2008) and Marien (2011). Different electoral systems do produce different levels of turnout and political trust. Nonetheless, it is striking that proportional systems with higher thresholds do to some extent conform to majoritarian systems which have typically no chance of getting one's disaffection represented in parliament. This will be further addressed in the conclusion.

Conclusion

The ambition of this chapter was to enhance our understanding of how electoral systems translate political trust respectively the lack thereof into electoral participation. Based on the literature on political trust and its institutional determinants as well as the literature on electoral systems and turnout, I developed a framework conceptualizing the role of electoral systems in mediating the effect of political trust on turnout. I argued that highly open proportional systems understood as low thresholds and large district magnitudes will produce higher levels of turnout among disaffected voters. Such systems allow the existence and emergence of new and/or protest parties. These parties bring the disaffection back into the electoral arena and thus lead to higher turnout among voters with political distrust. In contrast majoritarian systems were expected to produce higher abstention among disenchanted voters because these systems rarely allow new competitors to enter the electoral arena and thus bereave these voters a viable alternative to express their dissatisfaction.

The empirical analysis supported the suspected difference between open proportional systems and majoritarian systems. In the former, lower levels of political trust still produce higher levels of turnout compared to majoritarian systems. Proportional systems applying high thresholds either through formal thresholds or low district magnitudes were expected to fall in between, but surprisingly showed more unclear patterns. The analysis yielded mostly additive effects of the electoral systems and the trust index, but there were also signs for a multiplicative effect in case of the PR-systems with low entry costs. Moreover, if we take three model countries for each electoral system, we observe clearer differences in the translation of distrust into abstention across the electoral systems distinguished.

As to this deviation from the expectations, some features of PR systems with high thresholds could partly explain the results. First, the thresholds may in some cases be too high to make the party system responsive to the political preferences and attitudes of the disenchanted which feel to waste their vote for a party that may not surpass the threshold at Election Day. Second, another effect of PR with high thresholds is the difficulty of 'throwing the rascals out', this means voters have the opportunity to vote for a complete shift of the parties in government (see Aarts and Thomassen 2008, 7; Norris 2011, 217ff). The virtue of the threshold often allows at least one governmental party to stay in office, whereas a vote for the largest opposition party can be useless.

This can be exemplified by Germany which since 1949 experienced only one complete change of government in 1998. In all other instances, only one coalition partner had been substituted after the elections. Another case is Ireland where a formally proportional system often allowed the Fianna Fáil to stay in office as the country's major party irrespective of its actual election result. These features of PR systems may cause cynical voters to stay home as they feel lower efficacy and are less trusting in politics in this type of electoral systems. Related to this was the finding that among voters with lower levels of trust, majoritarian systems produced somewhat higher turnout than PR with high thresholds. Especially under British-style first-past-the-post systems, the cynical and disaffected may simply turn to the largest opposition party to produce a complete change of government, even though new parties that may cater the disaffected voters remain marginalized. Future work should thus be directed to the problem to which extent and why some proportional systems converge to majoritarian system concerning political trust, efficacy and turnout. Another particular thing to examine, are potential outliers such as Switzerland that may have affected the analysis in this chapter, but also in similar analyses such as Marien's (2011).

In view of the findings, it is highly imaginable that distrusting citizens still harbour higher levels of political efficacy in countries with highly open proportional systems. Here, these voters have a fair chance to express dissatisfaction by voting for the respective parties as argued above and see their votes represented in parliament. Moreover, protest and wing parties having gained parliamentary representation are often able to influence the political agenda with those issues distrusting voters are concerned with (e.g. immigration, scepticism towards the political elite or recently the Euro crisis). In countries with majoritarian systems or those applying PR with high thresholds, distrusting voters should feel less efficacious since they lack a competitive party to express their dissatisfaction and the political system is thus fairly unresponsive to their preferences and dissatisfaction. Similarly, voting for parties failing to obtain parliamentary representation under such circumstances may reinforce the feeling that ones vote does not make a difference. Karp and Banducci's (2008) recent analysis on the interplay between political efficacy and turnout under different electoral systems point to this presumption although they did not account for political trust. There are higher levels of efficacy and turnout in countries applying 'pure' PR in their case compared to countries with mixed electoral systems (e.g. Germany) and plurality voting. Similarly, voters expressing a preference for small parties in the former feel more efficacious than in the latter groups of electoral systems (cf. also Banducci, Donovan, and Karp 1999 for the New Zealand case).

In this respect, the chapter's analysis also provided considerable support for the claims of feedback effects between political trust, electoral systems and citizen's attachment to political system as well as the suspected interplay with political efficacy (Miller and Listhaug 1990). The highest levels of trust have been found in highly open proportional systems and this type of electoral system produced in turn also the highest level of turnout among the less trusting. This confirms claims that new, populist, or protest parties can have a particular function when it comes to the problem under which conditions citizens reinvest trust in the political system. Since such parties typically try to mobilize disaffected or cynical voters, these voters remain more attached to the democratic system as they get their voice represented in the electoral arena. Consequently turnout remains higher as does the level of political trust in the long run. In contrast, if disenchanted voters have no realistic chance to get their voice into the electoral and parliamentary arena, the voter turnout declines and political trust can be expected to fall over time. Under these circumstances, non-conventional forms of political participation such as demonstrations or the mushrooming of political activism can be one distinct political consequence.

Acknowledgements

I am grateful to the two reviewers and the participants of the GESIS' authors' conference: "Declining Political Trust, Disenchantment with Politics, and Methods of Political Participation," January 26–27, 2012, Cologne, Germany for their helpful comments.

Appendix

TABLE A1   *Classification of electoral systems according to thresholds and average district magnitudes*

Country	Electoral system[a]	Formal threshold[b] (effective if no formal and relevant)	Average district magnitude[c]	Classified as
Austria	PR	4*	183	PR-low
Belgium#	PR	5*	10.7	PR-high
Denmark	PR	2*	175	PR-low
Finland	PR	–	14.2	PR-low
France	Single member majority	12.5 to qualify for second round	1	Majoritarian
Germany	MMP	5*	598	PR-high
Ireland	STV-PR	–	4	PR-high
Netherlands	PR	– (0.67)	150	PR-low
Norway	PR	4*	169	PR-low
Portugal	PR	– (>5)	10.5	PR-high
Spain	PR	3	6.7	PR-high
Sweden	PR	4*	349	PR-low
Switzerland	PR	–	7.7	PR-high
United Kingdom	Single member plurality	–	1	Majoritarian

Notes: PR: Proportional representation; MMP: Mixed member proportionality; STV: Single transferable vote. [a] Own classification based on Gallagher and Mitchell (2005: various chapters); [b] Own classification based on Gallagher and Mitchell (2005: various chapters), Niedermayer, Stöss, and Haas (2006: various chapters); [c] Gallagher and Mitchell (2005: Table C.6) and own calculations. # indicates compulsory voting; * indicates that it is possible to win constituency seats even though a party remains below the formal threshold nationwide.

References

Aarts, Kees, and Jacques Thomassen. 2008. "Satisfaction with Democracy: Do Institutions Matter?" *Electoral Studies* 27:5–18.

Banducci, Susan A., Todd Donovan, and Jeffrey A. Karp. 1999. "Proportional Representation and Attitudes about Politics: Results from New Zealand." *Electoral Studies* 18:533–555.

Blais, André, and Ronald K. Carty. 1990. "Does Proportional Representation Foster Turnout?" *European Journal of Political Research* 18:167–181.

Blais, André, and Ronald K. Carty. 1991. "The Psychological Impact of Electoral Laws: Measuring Duverger's Elusive Factor." *British Journal of Political Science* 21:79–93.

Blais, André, and Agnieszka Dobrzynska. 1998. "Turnout in Electoral Democracies." *European Journal of Political Research* 33:239–261.

Brambor, Thomas, William R. Clark, and Matt Golder. 2006. "Understanding Interaction Models: Improving Empirical Analyses." *Political Analysis* 14:63–82.

Citrin, Jack. 1974. "Comment: The Political Relevance of Trust in Government." *American Political Science Review* 68:973–988.

Dalton, Russell J. 2004. *Democratic Challenges, Democratic Choices: The Erosion of Political Support in Advanced Industrial Democracies*. New York: University Press.

Dogan, Mattei, edit. 2005. *Political Mistrust and the Discrediting of Politicians*. Leiden and Boston: Brill.

Dunleavy, Patrick. 2005. "Facing Up to Multi-Party Politics: How Partisan Dealignment and PR Voting Have Fundamentally Changed Britain's Party Systems." *Parliamentary Affairs* 58:503–532.

Easton, David. 1965. *A Systems Analysis of Political Life*. New York: John Wiley & Sons.

ESS: European Social Survey Round 2 Data. 2004. Data file edition 3.2. Norwegian Social Science Data Services, Norway – Data Archive and distributor of ESS data.

ESS: European Social Survey Round 3 Data. 2006. Data file edition 3.3. Norwegian Social Science Data Services, Norway – Data Archive and distributor of ESS data.

ESS: European Social Survey Round 4 Data. 2008. Data file edition 4.0. Norwegian Social Science Data Services, Norway – Data Archive and distributor of ESS data.

Farrell, David M., and Ian McAllister. 2006. "Voter satisfaction and electoral systems: Does preferential voting in candidate-centred systems make a difference?" *European Journal of Political Research* 45:723–749.

Franklin, Mark N. 2004. *Voter Turnout and the Dynamics of Electoral Competition in Established Democracies since 1945*. New York: Cambridge University Press.

Freire, André. 2006. "The Party System of Portugal." In *Die Parteiensysteme Westeuropas*, edited by Oskar Niedermayer, Richard Stöss, and Melanie Haas, 373–396. Wiesbaden: VS Verlag für Sozialwissenschaften.

Gallagher, Michael, and Paul Mitchell. 2005. *The Politics of Electoral Systems*. Oxford: Oxford University Press.

Gelman, Andrew, and Jennifer Hill. 2007. *Data Analysis Using Regression and Multilevel/Hierarchical Models*. Cambridge: Cambridge University Press.

Goldstein, Harvey. 2003. *Multilevel Statistical Models*. 3rd edition. London: Arnold.

Hay, Colin. 2007. *Why We Hate Politics*. Cambridge: Polity Press.

Hetherington, Marc J. 1998. "The Political Relevance of Political Trust." *American Political Science Review* 92:791–808.

Hetherington, Marc J. 2005. *Why Trust Matters. Declining Political Trust and the Demise of American Liberalism*. Princeton: Princeton University Press.

Hooghe, Marc. 2011. "Why There is Basically Only One Form of Political Trust." *British Journal of Politics and International Relations* 13:269–275.

Inglehart, Ronald. 1999. "Postmodernization Erodes Respect for Authority, But Increases Support for Democracy." In *Critical Citizens: Global Support for Democratic Governance*, edited by Pippa Norris, 236–256. Cambridge: Cambridge University Press.

Jackman, Robert W. 1987. "Political Institutions and Voter Turnout in the Industrial Democracies." *American Political Science Review* 81:405–424.

Karp, Jeffrey A., and Susan A. Banducci. 2008. "Political Efficacy and Participation in Twenty-Seven Democracies: How Electoral Systems Shape Political Behaviour." *British Journal of Political Science* 38:311–334.

Ladner, Andreas, and Henry Milner. 1999. "Do Voters Turn Out More Under Proportional than Majoritarian Systems? The Evidence from Swiss Communal Elections." *Electoral Studies* 18:235–250.

Lijphart, Arend. 1999. *Patterns of Democracy: Government Forms and Performance in Thirty-six Countries*. New Haven: Yale University Press, 1999.

Listhaug, Ola, Bernt Aardal, and Ingunn Opheim Ellis. 2009. "Institutional Variation and Political Support: An Analysis of CSES Data from 29 Countries." In *The Comparative Study of Electoral Systems*, edited by Hans-Dieter Klingemann, 311–332. Oxford: Oxford University Press.

Marien, Sofie. 2011. "The Effect of Electoral Outcomes on Political Trust: A Multi-level Analysis of 23 Countries." *Electoral Studies* 30:712–726.

Miller, Arthur H., and Ola Listhaug. 1990. "Political Parties and Confidence in Government: A Comparison of Norway, Sweden and the United States." *British Journal of Political Science* 29:357–386.

Niedermayer, Oskar, Richard Stöss, and Melanie Haas, edit. 2006. *Die Parteiensysteme Westeuropas*. Wiesbaden: VS Verlag für Sozialwissenschaften.

Norris, Pippa, edit. 1999. *Critical Citizens: Global Support for Democratic Governance*. Cambridge: Cambridge University Press.

Norris, Pippa. 2011. *Democratic Deficit. Critical Citizens Revisited*. New York: Cambridge University Press.

Rabe-Hesketh, Sophia, and Anders Skrondal. 2008. *Multilevel and Longitudinal Modeling Using Stata. Second Edition*. Texas: Stata Press.

Sartori, Giovanni. 1997. *Comparative Constitutional Engineering. An Inquiry into Structures, Incentives and Outcomes*. 2nd Edition. Houndmills: Macmillan.

Vowles, Jack, and Peter Aimer. 2004. "Political Leadership, Representation and Trust." In *Voters' Veto. The 2002 Election in New Zealand and the Consolidation of Minority Government*, edited by Jack Vowles, Peter Aimer, Susan A. Banducci, Jeffrey Karp, and Raymond Miller, 167–183. Auckland: Auckland University Press.

Vowles, Jack, Susan A. Banducci, and Jeffrey A. Karp. 2006. "Forecasting and Evaluating the Consequences of Electoral Change in New Zealand." *Acta Politica* 41:267–284.

Weil, Frederick D. 1989. "The Sources and Structure of Legitimation in Western Democracies: A Consolidated Model Tested With Time-Series Data in Six Countries Since World War II." *American Sociological Review* 54:682–706.

Willey, Joseph. 1998. "Institutional Arrangements and the Success of New Parties in Old Democracies." *Political Studies* 46:651–668.

CHAPTER 6

Social Risk, Political Detachment and Welfare State De-Commodification

Maria Oskarson

Social Risk and Political Detachment

Do Western democracies risk polarizing democratic citizenship? There are several indications that the economic development of advanced democracies in recent decades has led to increased differences between various social groups, not only in material living conditions but also in relation to politics. Some researchers have claimed that the world is witnessing the emergence of new rifts in post-modern nations as a consequence of globalization, as well as increasing differences in life chances and conditions between the 'winners' and 'losers' of globalization (Kitschelt and Rehm 2004; Kriesi et al. 2006) and that this development also risks marginalizing weaker groups from politics altogether (Bobbio 1987; Dahl 2006). This chapter presents support for this proposition by analyzing the correlations between a risk-exposed social and economic position and detachment from politics around Europe in 2008. Furthermore, the correlations are found to correlate positively with the degree of welfare generosity, de-commodification, equality and national wealth.

Research to date has presented various results regarding the marginalization hypothesis – that social marginalization leads also to political marginalization. The conclusions of previous research depend on how political involvement or integration is defined, or, rather, whether the research considers the central dimension to be political interest and/or political participation or political trust. Political interest is clearly related to areas such as education and income, as well as the general level of economic inequality, and is generally seen as a quite stable attitude to politics (Prior 2010; Solt 2008; van Deth and Elff 2004); low levels of political trust, on the other hand, are found among younger and more highly educated citizens and are to a higher degree dependent on actual outcomes from the political system (Dalton 2004; Norris 1999). The link between political marginalization and the social and economic marginalization hypothesis in Dalton's book *Democratic Challenges – Democratic Choices* is defined in the same way as it is in most recent studies: as the opposite of political trust (Dalton 2004). In line with other findings, Dalton concluded that there is no strong relation between 'lower status' (operationalized as 'low education') and low trust. Instead, he found the decrease in trust to be present among the well-educated younger generations, in line with Inglehart's argument that post-materialists are demanding and distrustful (Dalton 2004; Inglehart 1997).

An explanation for why it has not yet been possible to reach a firm understanding of how social and economic marginalization or vulnerability relates to political disengagement is that most studies have been restricted to political interest and participation or political trust. The central argument presented here is that, in order to encircle and understand the mechanisms leading to increasing social cleavages in relation to politics we have to combine insights regarding effects of inequality and social determinants from two research areas – political engagement and political trust. This chapter sheds new light on the marginalization hypothesis by specifying political detachment as two-dimensional, incorporating both political interest and political trust.

Political Detachment—the Concept

Inspired by Angus Campbell's classic article on 'The Passive Citizen' (Campbell 1962), political detachment is in this study treated as a qualitative concept capturing the coincidence of low political interest and low political trust, thereby indicating a feeling of distance or 'non-includedness' to the political sphere of society. Political detachment is believed to capture the subjective separation from the 'elite groups' or 'establishment' of politics and implies something more than 'just' low political engagement and also something more than low political trust. Citizens could report low political trust but still be interested in politics and be ready to participate; their low level of political trust could be the result of disapproval of government performance or disenchantment with policy output. Regarding political detachment as solely a lack of engagement, apathy or passivity is also too narrow, since apathy could be the result of trust in others to handle politics in which one still feels included. The consequences of social and economic inequalities for the relationship to politics risk being overseen if the analysis is restricted to just either dimension of citizens' relation to politics, and for this reason the dual aspect of political detachment is vital, and in line with the work on political alienation of Kabashima et al. (2000). They presented the dimensions of political trust and civic-mindedness as comprising political alienation, where civic-mindedness is "interpreted as a measure of active psychological engagement with politics" (Kabashima et al. 2000, 786).

In order to identify the possible mechanisms behind political detachment, it is vital to consider previous research on variations in political interest as well as political trust. Political interest is generally seen as a core component in the broader concept of political engagement. It refers to the psychological aspects of political citizenship, and also relates to the psychological feeling of being incorporated or even participating in the political sphere. Political engagement is usually linked to interest or motivation for actual participation (or the like), while political interest per se can be seen as a more general attitude, usually referring to "'the degree to which politics arouses a citizen's curiosity" (van Deth 1989, 278). It is well-proven that political interest co-varies with social characteristics such as education, age and gender (van Deth 1989; van Deth and Elff 2004; Verba and Nie 1972; Verba, Schlozman and Brady 1995). Political interest has also proven to be a very stable attitude, not sensitive to short-term factors (Prior 2009, 2010). The perspective presented here claims that involvement in the political sphere of society has one more dimension besides political interest: namely, trust and support. In order for citizens to feel like participants and supporters of the system, they must feel as though the political system or sphere can be trusted to treat them as participants, that is, with respect (Rothstein 1998). A general conclusion from earlier research on political trust was that one of the strongest explanations for political support was evaluation of policy and/or government performance, that is, trust in politicians and in political institutions (Miller and Listhaug 1999). Furthermore, there is a well-proven relationship between economic evaluations and political support (Dalton 2004; Listhaug 1995; Miller and Listhaug 1999). A continuing discrepancy between the citizens' expectations and the actual policies the government implements might lead to growing distrust (Borre 2000; Hay 2007; Miller 1974; Stoker 2006). This has led commentators to fear that the economic restructurings and consequential welfare retrenchments caused by the current economic crisis might result in a fall in trust and support for political institutions and actors. A lack of political support, however, does not necessarily indicate political passivity. It is sometimes claimed to imply a well-informed and 'sound' skepticism toward politics. Accordingly, this 'sound skepticism' would need to be separated from actual marginalization or detachment in order to be able to test the marginalization hypothesis. Since we also know that political interest varies with individual resources such as education and occupational status, the combination of low trust and low interest in politics is probably over-represented in weaker social groups, most vulnerable and risk-exposed when welfare policies are down-sized.

Political detachment as the combination of low political trust and low political interest captures the situation when disenchantment or dissatisfaction with political matters such as government performance or political outcomes occurs among people with weak political resources and low political interest. The consequences of political distrust or disenchantment among low interest groups are believed to be different from when more interested or 'critical' citizens get disenchanted. Politically detached citizens constitute what could be termed a risk group for democracy. Citizens who are politically detached do not seek information on political matters, and even if political information does reach them, they are not receptive to the information since they do not trust the political actors (Strömbäck and Shehata 2010). Whereas the resourceful citizens might 'voice' their grievances, the citizens with low interest might simply take the 'exit option' from politics. And without the 'voice', these groups risk being overlooked in the political debates and the decision processes, and thus become totally politically marginalized (APSA 2004; Bartels 2008).

The Marginalization Hypothesis

The 'marginalization' or 'modernization losers' hypothesis identifies low-educated, manual labor as the victims of modernization and globalization and as being at risk of unemployment and deteriorating standards of living. From the same perspective, the winners would be the well-educated middle class, especially in cultural or knowledge-intensive sectors. The argument is that globalization processes lead to increasing social differences whereby citizens with lower education, 'unqualified' jobs or a weak relationship with the labor market bear greater costs and receive less benefits from changing economic conditions (Bobbio 1987; Scholte 2005). Furthermore, this social and economic marginalization is expected to lead to political detachment in the sense of decreased political trust, engagement and involvement (Dalton 2004; Goul Andersen and Hoff 2001; Kabashima et al. 2000). The hypothesis states that, rather than being expressed politically, risk exposition (modernization losers) might actually lead to a detachment from politics altogether. It also states that the consequences of increased social and economic inequality have stronger political implications among more risk-exposed groups with low or few political resources, which could lead to political dissatisfaction and detachment. This could lead to the over-representation of political detachment in identifiable groups in society, which could have consequences for the representation of the interests of these groups and, therefore, for political decisions and policies. Taking the argument one step further, if the probability of political detachment can be linked to certain policy arrangements, this group's lack of political articulation could lead to policies that do not consider the group, which could bring about political detachment and even lead to the growth of the group. This leads to the overarching hypothesis for this analysis: social risk positions increase the risk of political detachment (H1).

The Rebound of Welfare Policies

The consequences of a social risk position, or acute economic problems due to such issues as unemployment, vary between different welfare contexts. Consequently, it is commonly believed that a social risk situation is more dev-astating in weak welfare states as compared to more generous welfare states where the citizens are more protected. This line of argumentation, which emanates from the central role of a welfare state, is what is often labelled 'de-commodification', that is, protecting individuals from the full consequences of market forces through various forms of social insurance schemes and social transfers (Esping-Andersen 1990; Esping-Andersen 1999). These social trans-fers allow the welfare policies to compensate to some extent for a weak market position, thereby reducing the risk of poverty. The degree to which these kinds of welfare policies reduce the risk of poverty varies between different coun-tries, due to 'welfare regimes'. For example, the Scandinavian countries are known for having a high degree of de-commodification and generosity, while other countries, such as Britain or the United States, apply a lower degree of de-commodification.

When it comes to the consequences of social risk position for political involvement and integration, a more de-commodifying and encompassing welfare system is sometimes supposed to detach weaker groups less than a more market-oriented welfare system (Goul Andersen and Hoff 2001). The argument is that a more de-commodifying system eases the consequences of a weak social position, making social marginalization less marginalizing. Furthermore, since policies recognize weaker groups, these groups are more likely to feel like political stakeholders. However, another aspect of the design of the welfare state is that welfare systems embody and create norms about what is fair and just, and they also form citizens' expectations and demands (Mau 2003, 2004; Rothstein 1998; Svallfors 2003, 2007). A social risk position could actually be more politically alienating in a welfare system that is expected to be highly de-commodifying and generous than in one where less exposure to risk could be seen as a politically relevant issue (Hay 2007; Oskarson 2007). When the welfare state is believed to protect and ease negative consequences of a risk-exposed social situation, the experience of being in a social risk situa-tion might to a higher degree be considered an unfulfilled responsibility of the welfare state, and thus a source of disenchantment with and detachment from politics (Stoker 2006). In a system with a more limited welfare state, there are no expectations that the state should take any further responsibilities for an individual's weak position. Instead, risk protection is seen as an individual or private responsibility, for which the state or government is not to blame. When expectations are lower, the risk of disenchantment due to unfulfilled promises decreases. For the analysis here, this would be reflected in a stronger effect of social risk position on political detachment in more de-commodifying and generous welfare systems (H2).

However, variations in how a social risk position is related to political detachment might be related to the general level of inequality rather than welfare state generosity. Richard Solt has found that increasing inequality depresses political engagement, especially among citizens with lower incomes. He concludes that inequality increases the relative power of richer citizens, leading to decreasing political focus on political issues regarding redistribution and thereby alienating poorer citizens (Solt 2008). In the same line we would expect the levels of detachment to be higher in more unequal societies. But with a higher general level of detachment, the effect of a social risk position would be weaker since citizens with a more secure social and economic situation are also alienated or detached from politics. There would in other words not be much difference if you are in a risk-exposed situation or not. Rather, we would expect the effect of a social risk position to be stronger where those exposed to risk are few and the general level of detachment from politics is low or moderate. The third hypothesis therefore states that the effect of social risk position on political detachment is stronger in more equal societies (H3).

The focus of this analysis is Europe in 2008. Even though Europe is considered to belong to the 'rich' part of the world, there are significant differences in national gross incomes around Europe. Not least are many countries in east and central Europe comparatively poor. This means that the proportion of the population in what is here labeled as a social risk-exposed situation is higher in poorer countries than in rich countries, thus being more of normality. To be in a weak position is therefore not as stigmatizing as the relative deprivation is lower. In richer countries, on the other hand, the stigmatization and relative deprivation of being poor or risk-exposed is stronger, which leads to the final hypothesis that the effect of social risk position on political detachment is positively related to the wealth of the country (GDP) (H4).

The following analysis explores the relationship between social risk positions and political detachment for 20 European countries in 2008, based on round 4 of the European Social Surveys. The chapter proceeds with a discussion of measurement and analytical models, followed by the empirical analysis, performed in several steps. In a first step the relationship between the social risk position and political detachment is measured for each of the 20 countries individually. How this relationship is related to welfare state contexts is evaluated by a series of bivariate graphs and random-intercept, random-coefficient multi-level models in which the effects of social risk on political detachment are nested in welfare contexts, measured by reduction of the poverty rate after social transfers, social transfers as a percentage of GDP as indicators for de-commodification, and by inequality in income distributions and GDP per capita.

Data and Measurement

This section analyzes the questions and hypothesis posed above in the context of Europe in 2008. The countries in Europe present a wide variety of economic and social structures, as well as welfare arrangements, which makes them suitable for an analysis such as this. The data used for the analysis come from round 4 of the European Social Survey from 2008/9.[1] The analysis here includes 20 countries for which all the needed variables are available, as presented in Table 1.[2]

Measurement of Political Detachment

The most central variable for this analysis is, of course, the variable for political detachment. As stated above, this variable incorporates two dimensions – interest and trust – which is why we must start with the matter of measurement. Political interest and, to an even greater extent, political trust are theoretical concepts that can be defined and measured in various ways. The analysis presented here is based on round 4 of the European Social Survey (2008), which means that the measurement is restricted to variables included in this study.

---

1   The European Social Survey (the ESS) is an academically-driven social survey designed to chart and explain the interaction between Europe's changing institutions and the attitudes, beliefs and behavioral patterns of its diverse populations. The survey covers up to 30 nations and employs the most rigorous methodologies. A repeat cross-sectional survey, it has been funded through the European Commission's Framework Programmes, the European Science Foundation and national funding bodies in each country. More information and data can be found at http://www.europeansocialsurvey.org/.

2   The analysis is performed with the weighting procedures presented on the ESS webpage. This means that analysis of the countries uses a separate design weight, corrected for national unrepresentative samples.

Political interest is measured with the single variable based on the traditional question of 'subjective political interest'. The variable is standardized and reversed in order to range from 0 (low interest) to 10 (high interest). An alternative would be to construct an index and thereby increase the validity and reduce measurement errors. The ESS studies include some potential candidates for such an index, namely, questions regarding how frequently respondents follow political news on television and in the newspapers. However, there are strong arguments against incorporating variables that measure any kind of activity, such as participation in political discussions or media usage, in an index on political interest. Firstly, these kinds of action could actually be seen as dependent on political interest. Secondly, the correlations between these variables and the traditional question on subjective political interest are quite modest. An alternative variable that could be included in an index is the importance of politics in the respondent's life. No such question is included in the ESS studies, however.

Political trust is actually measured with an index. The additive index is based on four items related to explicit trust (in the country's parliament, politicians, parties and the European Parliament). The European Parliament is included since the European Union is a relevant part of the political system in the countries under consideration here. The item values are reversed and standardized to range from 0 to 10, then added together and divided by four, giving an index ranging from 0 (extremely low political trust) to 10 (very high political trust).[3]

Political detachment is operationalized as a combination of the variable for political interest and the index for political trust. An additive index is constructed from the political interest index and the political trust index described above. In order to ease interpretations, both indexes are turned and then divided by two in order to construct a political detachment index where 0 indicates the least politically detached (i.e. attached) and 10 indicates the most politically detached.

Table 1 presents the mean values for the detachment index for political interest and political trust, as well as the bivariate correlations between the two, for the countries included. The table shows some variation in the levels of political detachment/integration. The lowest score on the detachment index (3.89) is found in Denmark, which is due to that country showing the highest average values on both political interest and political trust. More variation is found on the higher end of the detachment index, where the Czech Republic has the highest average value (6.85). This means that the Czechs are more politically detached than the Danes.

---

3 Cronbach's alpha = 0.89.

TABLE 1   *Political interest, political trust and political detachment index (means 0–10)*

	Detachment index	Political trust index	Political interest	Degree of satisfaction with the national government	Correlation trust and interest (r)	N
Belgium	5.4	4.58	4.58	3.92	0.25**	1703
Bulgaria	6.37	2.71	4.33	2.22	0.15**	1858
Czech Republic	6.85	3.33	2.90	3.71	0.15**	1906
Germany	4.96	4.16	5.81	4.23	0.11**	2514
Denmark	3.89	5.73	6.33	5.48	0.16**	1445
Estonia	5.52	4.11	4.70	3.53	0.16**	1368
Finland	4.87	5.35	4.85	5.94	0.21**	2099
France	5.29	4.23	5.10	3.89	0.19**	1988
United Kingdom	5.45	3.83	5.13	3.60	0.20**	2136
Greece	6.49	3.47	3.52	2.69	0.20**	1997
Hungary	6.51	2.85	4.00	1.88	0.15**	1338
Latvia	6.61	2.54	4.19	1.80	0.07**	1753
Netherlands	4.51	5.30	5.56	5.53	0.19**	1663
Norway	4.86	5.17	4.98	5.16	0.20**	1336
Poland	6.15	3.27	4.29	3.57	0.17**	1391
Portugal	6.54	3.50	3.14	3.27	0.27**	1911
Romania	5.81	4.09	4.16	3.49	0.30**	1883
Sweden	4.65	5.05	5.44	5.12	0.24**	1602
Slovenia	5.49	4.22	4.69	4.53	0.24**	1158
Slovakia	5.56	4.29	4.52	4.79	0.10**	1672
Total	5.6	4.07	4.60	3.89	0.24**	34727

Note: All indices vary between 0 and 10. For the political interest index and the political trust 10 indicates high interest and high trust. The index for political detachment is turned, and 10 indicates a high degree of detachment from politics. Satisfaction with government varies between 0 (very low satisfaction) and 10 (very high satisfaction).

The correlations between political interest and political trust illustrate that these are two separate aspects of individuals' attitudes towards politics, but it is also seen that the correlations vary somewhat between different countries (these variations are not explored further here). However, the levels of detachment are not the main focus here, but rather how it covaries with being in a social risk position.

Measurement of Social Risk Position and Welfare State Generosity

As an indication of 'globalization losers' this study will take its departure in the notion of 'social risk position'. What I try to capture here is different identifiable aspects of social position and situation pointed out as creating a vulnerability of decreasing life standards and life chances. In order to avoid more cultural aspects or relative deprivation, I here depart from a perspective of exposition to risk of poverty (Beck 2007; Esping-Andersen 1999; Whelan and Maitre 2008). A first risk category is to be in an unskilled manual labor class position, and a second is to have low education. These are the groups generally seen as easiest to replace on the labor market, and also most exposed to increasing competition due to the globalized economy (Kitschelt and Rehm 2004). Unskilled manual labor class is measured according to the European Socio-economic classification (ESEC) and identifies present, or in case of leave from the labor market, previous occupation (Harrison and Rose 2006). Low education is here measured as below upper secondary (or equivalent). A third risk exposition is to be outside of the labor market, and thus without market income. Unemployment, long-time sickness and disability are generally related to financial hardships and perhaps also social exclusion, and this is used as a third indicator. The various reasons for being outside the regular labor market are not separated, as the delineation between the three is to a certain degree due to various policies. The indicator is therefore constructed as belonging to any of these categories versus all others. The indicators of social risk position presented imply a risk of financial difficulties but say nothing about how respondents actually evaluate their present economic situation. The analysis therefore includes a question about how the respondent '...feels about the household incomes currently'. Two answers – 'finding it difficult' and 'finding it very difficult' – are combined to form 'difficult to cope on present income', which is used as the fourth indicator of social risk. Consequently, we have four independent variables indicating social risk and a weak market situation: occupied as routine manual worker, low education, a position outside the regular labor market – unemployed, disabled or in early retirement – and finally the subjective experience of finding it difficult to cope on the present household income. For the present analysis these four indicators are added into a social risk index ranging from 0 = no risk position to 4 = all four risks, that is a highly risk-exposed position. This index for social risk position is believed to capture the groups most exposed to risk of deteriorating situation. By not employing the sole categories of unemployed, outside the labor market or social exclusion of any other kind we avoid selection processes due to actual policies in varying situations in different welfare regimes. Rather than using this sharp delineation, the idea is to include broader groups, where the risks of economic hardships due to market income dependency are highest, regardless of the actual social policies and unemployment policies. The alternative of using dummy variables and multiple interactions is also rejected due to the statistical limitation for the proceeding analysis of the multi-level model as well as pedagogic clarity (Maas and Hox 2005).[4]

The distribution of social risks varies between the countries, due not least to differences in wealth. In the poorer countries, a larger proportion of the population belongs to what is here labeled risk categories due to lower average educational level and higher dependence on unskilled jobs. No further inquiries into this will be made here as the focus is on the relationship between risk positions and political detachment, but the variations in risk distribution between the countries is vital to bear in mind and will be considered in the interpretation of the results.

The way in which social risk is related to political detachment is expected to vary between different welfare contexts, mainly due to varying degrees of de-commodification and social protection schemes. De-commodification is generally measured with an index constructed by Esping-Andersen that is based on replacement rates and generosity in the social insurance systems (unemployment, sickness and pensions) (Esping-Andersen 1990; Scruggs and Allan 2006). However, the database produced by Lyle Scruggs and James Allen does not cover all European States and is not updated to 2008. In the absence of any precise data on de-commodification, the present analysis focuses on two more general aspects of welfare policies: the reduction of the poverty rate after social transfers, and social expenditure as a percentage of GDP, based on Eurostat's figures.[5] Social expenditure data do not represent an ideal indicator, since they do not really give information about how the welfare policies affect the actual situation of the individual. Therefore, the present analysis also uses the reduction of poverty as an additional indicator. The risk of poverty is the share of persons with an equalized disposable income below the risk-of-poverty

---

4   Crombach's alpha at 0.46 indicates scalability of the four indicators, however limited. The four indicators form one single factor capturing 38% of the variance. Each of the four indicators of social risk significantly correlate with each other, as well as with the social risk index, and also have significant effects on political detachment. All analyses presented in this chapter are also performed with the different risk factors as separate dummy variables. The respective strength between the risk variables differs somewhat between the countries, but the overall patterns are the same as when the risk index is used for the analysis here. Full documentation of this is available from the author.

5   See http://epp.eurostat.ec.europa.eu.

threshold, which is set at 60% of the national median equivalised disposable income. The reduction of poverty rate is simply the difference in the poverty ratebeforeandaftersocialtransfers(2010).Asdiscussedpreviously,twoothermacro-economic factors will also be used. Inequality is measured as the ratio of total income (equalized disposable income) received by the 20% of the population with the highest income (top quintile) to that received by the 20% of the population with the lowest income (lowest quintile). The wealth of the country of the respondent is measured with the gross domestic production (GDP) per inhabitant, presented in euros.[6]

Empirical Analysis

The analytical strategy includes three steps. The first step is to employ multiple regression analysis with social risk position and political detachment separately for the 20 countries included here in order to conclude whether there is a general pattern in the correlations and, accordingly, to test the first hypothesis. The second and third hypotheses are first tested by plotting the b-coefficients from the first step to the macro indicators of welfare state generosity, inequality and wealth. This enables us to identify the overall correlations and also the location of individual countries (Shalev 2007). In the final step, linear multi-level models are estimated in order to validate the pattern found in the previous steps. This also enables us to estimate the interaction effects between the individual level and country level. Employing a multi-level model when we have only 20 observations on the higher (country) level is somewhat doubtful from a statistical point of view (Maas and Hox 2005), but with this three-step strategy we do not solely rely on the estimates from the MLA, and it is thus believed to be appropriate for validating results found with other methods.

The Correlation between Social Risk and Political Detachment
The overarching hypothesis for this study is that a social risk position increases the risk of political detachment (H1) due to high vulnerability of globalization and increasing competition on the labor market. This marginalization hypothesis has so far received limited empirical support in research. The argument presented here as a reason for this limited support is that the measurement of political detachment has been limited to low political trust or low political engagement, and that, once we define political detachment as the combination of low political trust and low political interest, the hypothesis will find

---

6 http://epp.eurostat.ec.europa.eu.

support. This means that we expect clear correlations between the social risk index and political detachment, and that this is valid for all the countries included.

TABLE 2   *Social risk, government satisfaction and political attachment 2008, by country.* OLS *regression, unstandardized b-coefficients*

	Social risk index	Government satisfaction	Adjusted R²	N
Belgium	0.50***	-0.30*	0.19	1481
Bulgaria	0.30***	-0.34***	0.21	1661
Czech Republic	0.26***	-0.30***	0.21	1625
Germany	0.35***	-0.31***	0.24	2246
Denmark	0.45***	-0.07***	0.06	1332
Estonia	0.26***	-0.33***	0.25	1260
Finland	0.26***	-0.34***	0.18	1989
France	0.53***	-0.20***	0.15	1770
Great Britain	0.61***	-0.30***	0.26	1997
Greece	0.21***	-0.22***	0.13	1570
Hungary	0.28***	-0.26***	0.12	1157
Latvia	0.17***	-0.29***	0.16	1564
Netherlands	0.47***	-0.32***	0.25	1559
Norway	0.44***	-0.31***	0.25	1290
Poland	0.32***	-0.30***	0.22	1197
Portugal	0.48***	-0.29***	0.21	1529
Romania	0.16**	-0.40***	0.25	1208
Sweden	0.48***	-0.20***	0.13	1534
Slovenia	0.40***	-0.15***	0.13	926
Slovakia	0.31***	-0.25***	0.17	1444
All countries included	*0.41 ****	*-0.30 ****	*0.25*	*30.359*

Note: Data from ESS 2008. Regression models include controls for gender and age (not shown). Weighted by design weight in accordance with guidelines. Significance levels *** p < .001, ** p < .01, * p < .05. Constructions of the detachment index and the index for social risk position are presented in the text.

Given that satisfaction with government is an important factor behind political trust as one of the dimensions in political detachment, this factor is included in the model in the analysis in order to sort out short-term effects due to government performance and sympathy for governing parties.[7] This means that we separate political detachment from more directly output-oriented political disenchantment. Gender and age (three categories) are included in all the models in order to control for compositional effects. Table 2 below presents the relevant variables from the regression model, separately for all countries.[8]

As expected, Table 2 shows clear and statistically significant positive coefficients between social risk position and political detachment in all countries. This means that the higher the social risk, the higher the political detachment, or, vice versa, the lower the political integration and attachment. As expected, negative coefficients were also found between government satisfaction and political attachment, meaning that respondents content with the present government are more attached with politics, while disapproval of the present government is more related to political detachment. This means that there is a short-term factor behind political detachment, apart from the more long-term factors of social risk position. The conclusion is that the first hypothesis, that social risk positions increase the risk of political detachment (H1), is confirmed. However, Table 2 does reveal variations in the strength of the coefficients between the countries. The coefficients for social risk vary from 0.61 in the United Kingdom to 0.16 in Romania, even when controlled for government satisfaction. In other words, as expected, there seems to be something on the country level that varies and is related to the way in which social risk affects the individuals' relation to the political sphere, which leads to the next step of the analysis.

Effects of De-Commodification, Inequality and National Wealth
The general assumption presented above stated that the variations in the way social risk position is related to political detachment are related to welfare arrangements, inequality and wealth. The theoretical perspective applied put a focus on disenchantment and relative deprivation as explanations for why a social risk position might lead to detachment from politics altogether.

---

7   The formulation of the question is "Now thinking about the [*country*] government, how satisfied are you with the way it is doing its job?" Response alternatives range from 0 (extremely dissatisfied) to 10 (extremely satisfied).

8   Full documentation available from the author

The second hypothesis put a focus on de-commodification and generosity in the welfare systems. This hypothesis stated that a social risk position would be more connected to political detachment in more generous and de-commodifying welfare systems (H2). Being poor and risk-exposed in a generous and protecting welfare system could be seen as something of an anomaly, thereby alienating from politics to a higher degree than in a system where a person in a social risk position has lower expectations of the political sphere. In addition, in a more generous and encompassing welfare system, social risk exposure and poverty are probably seen as a political responsibility to a higher degree. In less encompassing welfare systems, these factors might be regarded more as personal or private responsibilities. The third hypothesis for the analysis is that the effect of social risk exposure would be higher in more equal societies where those who are exposed to risk are few and the general level of detachment from politics is low or moderate. The fourth hypothesis states that the positive correlation would be higher in richer countries where the stigmatization and relative deprivation of being poor or risk-exposed is believed to be stronger.

The first step in testing these opposing hypotheses is through simple bivariate scatterplots, in order to discern the general patterns (Figures 1 through 4). Reductions of poverty after social transfers and social expenditure are used as indicators for welfare generosity and the level of de-commodification, as discussed above. The b-values from Table 2 are taken as indicators of the association between social risk position and political detachment. Since political detachment is measured with an index ranging from 0 (attached) to 10 (detached), the positive b-values indicate that the higher the risk, the more politically detached the individual is. Accordingly, the patterns in Figures 1 and 2 should be interpreted as suggesting that the higher the reduction of poverty or social expenditure, the stronger the positive b-coefficient. This means that a social risk position has a stronger relation with political detachment in more de-commodifying welfare states.

Both aspects of welfare state generosity show positive relationships between the effects of social risk on political detachment. The higher the poverty reduction, the stronger are the b-coefficients between social risk position and political integration. The same pattern, only even stronger, is found for social expenditure. The scatterplots thus present support for the second hypothesis, that social risk position is more connected to political detachment in more generous and de-commodifying welfare systems.

The third hypothesis stated that the effect of social risk on political detachment would be stronger in more economically equal countries as well as in richer countries, due to effects of stigmatization and relative deprivation. The bivariate scatterplots are presented in Figures 3 and 4.

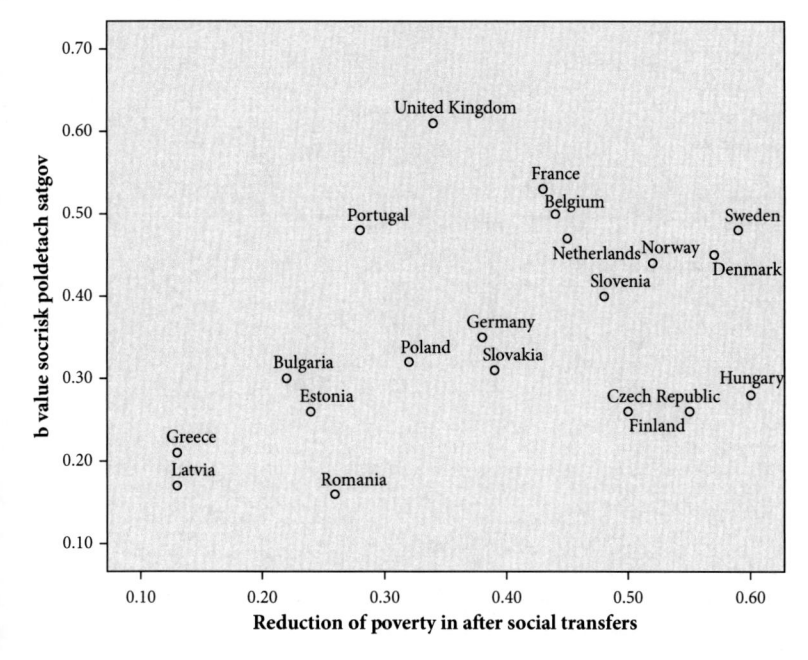

FIGURE 1   *Effect of social risk position on political detachment and reduction of risk of poverty in 2008*

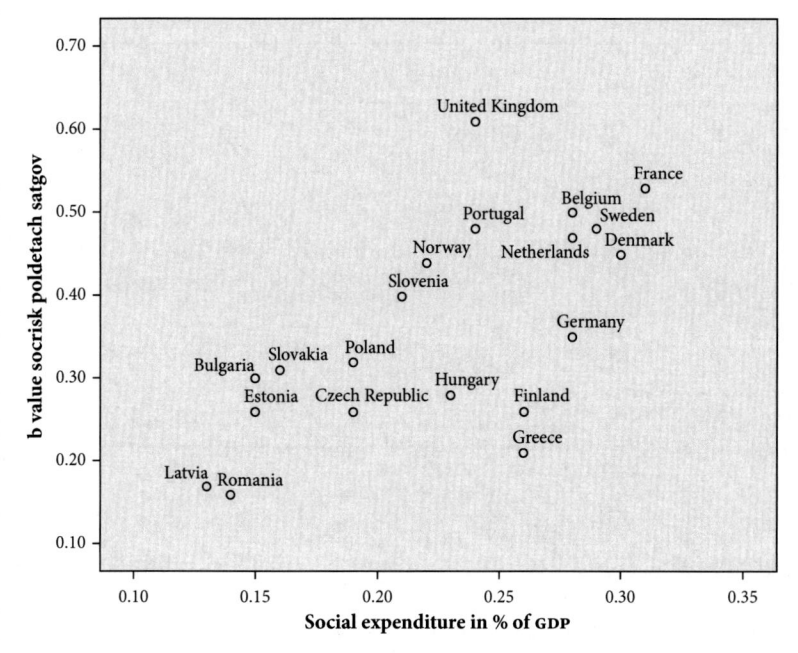

FIGURE 2   *Effect of social risk position on political detachment and social expenditure as a percentage of GDP in 2007*

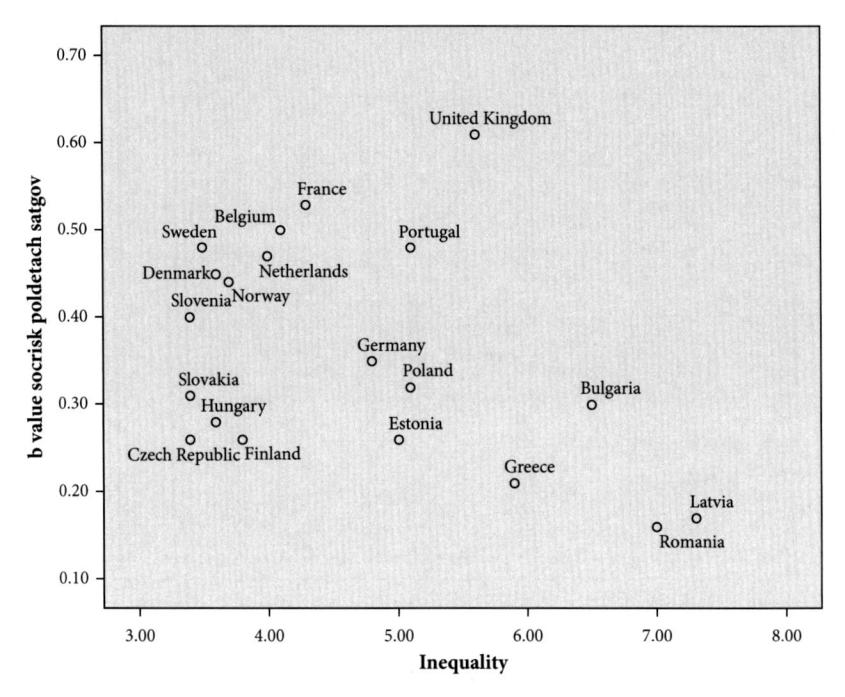

FIGURE 3   *Effect of social risk position on political detachment and income inequality*

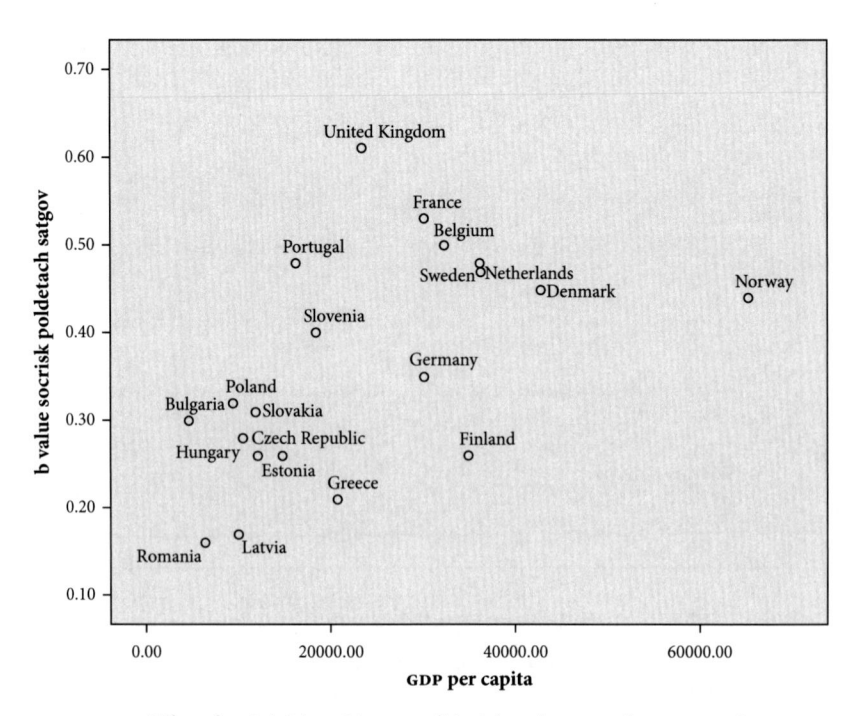

FIGURE 4   *Effect of social risk position on political detachment and GDP per capita*

In line with the hypothesis, the scatterplots do in fact indicate a stronger effect of risk position on political detachment in countries with a lower degree of income inequality and also a stronger effect in countries with higher GDP per capita. The results so far do in fact indicate that a social risk position is more devastating for political attachment in more generous, equal and wealthy welfare states. Even though the general level of political detachment is lower in these countries, it is more linked to a weak social and economic situation. And even though a lower proportion of the population is at risk, to actually be there is more related to political detachment. Table 3 below sorts out these patterns by presenting all relevant bivariate correlations.

The bivariate correlations confirm the patterns found. The strongest correlation with the effect of social risk on political detachment is with social expenditure in percent of GDP, but the correlation with wealth of the

TABLE 3   *Correlations between social risk position, political detachment, de-commodification, inequality and wealth. (Pearson's r)*

	Reduction of poverty after social transfers	Social expend-iture in % of GDP	Income inequality	GDP per capita	Mean level of detach-ment	Mean number of risks
ue socrisk* chment	0.41	0.66**	-0.41	0.54*	-0.50*	-0.39
ction of rty after l transfers	1	0.52*	-0.88**	0.54*	-0.50*	-0.51*
l nditure of GDP		1	-0.51*	0.66*	-0.58**	-0.48*
me uality			1	-0.50*	0.46*	0.56**
per capita				1	-0.75**	-0.73**
n level chment					1	0.78**

Comment: The bivariate correlations are based on the 20 countries included.
Significance levels *** p < .001, ** p < .01, * p < .05.

country is also clearly significant. Further, the different macro factors are clearly correlated, as expected. The correlations with income inequality are negative, since the low values on the scale indicate a high degree of income equality. The arguments based on relative deprivation and disenchantment receive support here, since we have negative correlations between the effect of social risks and the mean level of detachment in the country as well as with the average number of risks for the respondents of the country. This means that the political consequences of being in a social risk position is more severe where a social risk position is more of an anomaly than when it could be considered to be something shared with most other people in the country.

In order to fully discern how the effect of social risk position interrelates with political detachment in different welfare state contexts, the study also applied a linear random-intercepts, random-coefficients multi-level model to the data. This model enables interaction effects between aspects of social risk position and indicators of de-commodification in order to validate the pattern found in Figures 1 through 4. Table 4 presents the multi-level models. All data have been weighted with design weights that sum up to the total number of respondents that each country provides. Population weights are not used. The main reason for not using population weights is that such weights would distort the estimates of the standard errors and render the whole idea of using multi-level modeling meaningless. In multi-level modeling, standard errors should reflect sampling design and not population size (Asparouhov 2004). As countries have not been chosen randomly, all countries are assigned equal weights (1) in the regressions. There is also another, more substantial, reason why we only weight the models with the design weights, which is that our main interest is in exploring and explaining differences in effects between countries (see van Bavel 2010 for a similar argument in relation to ESS data).

The first model includes only the intercept and reports the grand mean, as well as the variation in political detachment between the countries, and shows that there is sufficient variance between the countries to proceed with the analysis. The second model puts the individual social risk position as a focal independent variable for political detachment, as well as the crucial control for satisfaction with government, as well as controls for gender and age.[9] Both effects are significant, and, for every additional risk on the risk index, the value on the political detachment index increases in 0.34 scale steps. This means that the average difference between a person with no risk position and a

---

9   These coefficients are not reported here but can be obtained from the author.

TABLE 4 Linear random-intercepts-random coefficients multi-level models of the effect of social risk on political detachment

FIXED PART:	Model 1	Model 2	Model 3a	Model 3b	Model 4a	Model 4b	Model 5a	Model 5b	Model 6a	Model 6b
Satisfaction with government		-0.27***	-0.28***	-0.28***	-0.27***	-0.27***	-0.27***	-0.27***	-0.27***	-0.27***
Social risk position		0.34***	0.35***	0.37***	0.36***	0.03	0.36***	056***	0.36***	0.25***
Intercept	4.43***	4.21***	4.22***	4.23***	2.57***	2.53***	5.13***	5.15***	3.67***	3.66***
Country level:										
Reduction of Poverty			0.01	0.02						
Social expenditure in % of GDP					-7.42**	-7.61**				
Inequality							0.19	0.19		
GDP per capita 10 000 euro									-0.25*	-0.25*
Cross-level interactions:										
Social risk position*inequality								-0.04		
Social risk position*GDP						1.48**				
Social risk position*reduction				-0.02						
Social risk position * GDP per capita									0.05**	0.05**

TABLE 4 *Linear random-intercepts-random coefficients multi-level models of the effect of social risk on political detachment* (cont.)

RANDOM PART:	Model 1	Model 2	Model 3a	Model 3b	Model 4a	Model 4b	Model 5a	Model 5b	Model 6a	Model 6b
Intercept (between countries)	0.59***	0.39**	0.50**	0.50**	0.30**	0.29**	0.43**	0.43**	0.34**	0.34**
Residual (within countries)	3.43***	2.80***	2.71***	2.71***	2.70***	2.70***	2.70***	2.70***	2.70***	2.70***
2Log Likelihood	164605.3	156714	122160	122164.9	118687	118675.8	118699.4	118701.6	118696	118695.1
Number of respondents	30359	30359	30359	30359	30359	30359	30359	30359	30359	30359
Number of countries	20	20	20	20	20	20	20	20	20	20

Note: Data ESS 2008. The mixed models include controls for gender and age (not shown) and are weighted by design weight in accordance with guidelines. Significance levels *** p < .001, ** p < .01, * p < .05. Number of observations for each country is reported in Table 2. All variables are described in the text.

person with the most risk-exposed position (four risks, as discussed above) is 1.36 scale steps (with all other factors being equal when all 20 countries are taken together). The addition of the individual factors results in a clear decrease in the variation between the countries, from 0.59 to 0.39. As discussed above, there is reason to believe that the way in which a social risk position affects political detachment partly depends on generosity in welfare policies, inequality and wealth.

Model 3a includes the reduction of poverty after social transfers, and model 3b also the cross-level interaction between social risk position and poverty after social transfers, none of which show significant effects. Model 4a takes social expenditure as a percentage of GDP into consideration, with the cross level interaction effect in model 4b. As in the bivariate analyses, social expenditure has a clearly significant negative effect. Since the dependent variable ranges from 0 (integrated) to 10 (detached), a negative coefficient here means that the higher the social expenditure, the less politically detached the population (having controlled for social risk position and satisfaction with government). In model 4b, the interaction between social risk position and social expenditure is included. The direct effect of social risk position basically vanishes in this model, while the positive coefficient for the interaction between social risk position and social expenditure (1.48) indicates that the positive association between social risk position and political detachment found in previous models is stronger when social expenditure as a percentage of GDP is higher than in countries that allocate a lower share of GDP to social expenditure. Models 5a and 5b test for effects of inequality, but neither the direct effect of income inequality nor the interaction between inequality and social risk position are significant. Finally, models 6a and 6b include GDP per capita on the country level and present significant effects of the expected sign, indicating that the level of disenchantment is lower where the GDP per capita is higher, but the effects of social risk position are at the same time stronger in richer countries.

All in all, the multi-level analysis confirms the pattern found in Figures 2 through 4 and Table 3 and support the hypotheses presented. The hypothesis that social risk position is more connected to political detachment in more generous and de-commodifying welfare systems (H2) receives clear support when social expenditure is used as a measurement and is somewhat more indecisive for risk of poverty after transfer. That the effect of social risk on political detachment would be stronger in countries with more equal income distributions (H3) did not show significant effects in the multi-level analysis. The fourth and last hypothesis, that the effect would be stronger in more wealthy countries (H4), did receive significant support.

Conclusion

Although the concept of political detachment is vague and contested, it remains hard to abandon. Not all individuals are integrated in the political world; not everyone votes or feels like a participant. While democratic citizenship might be equal in form and in theory, it is not equal in practice. Some people simply turn their back to politics; this 'back-turning' is quite often linked to a weak social and economic position. Furthermore, citizens detached from 'ordinary' politics are more open to populist arguments, since populist movements often describe themselves as 'outside' of ordinary politics, defending the 'ordinary citizen' against the political 'establishment' and thus articulating the kind of divides described here. This chapter has attempted to employ the concept of political detachment to capture the political marginalization discussed in relation to the globalization and development of post-modern democracies, and argues that political detachment could be defined and measured as the combination of the dimensions of political trust and political interest.

Treating political detachment in such a multi-dimensional manner, as opposed to solely with a lack of political trust, identifies the linkage with social risk position in the 20 European countries included in the analysis. The results show a clear relation between social risk position and political detachment. The analysis of what impact welfare policies, inequality and national wealth have on the relation between a social risk position and political detachment point at the notion that the effect of a weak or risk-exposed situation is connected to a higher grade of political detachment in more generous, equal and wealthy nations. This supports the notion that it is one thing to talk about average levels of political detachment, or average risk exposition in different countries, and another to look into how a social risk position is related to political detachment. Even though the average levels of political detachment and political risks are higher in more limited welfare states, unequal income distribution and lower national GDP, how social risk positions actually relate to political detachment shows the opposite pattern.

The results here show that being in a social risk position is more strongly related to political detachment in generous welfare states, under more equal income distribution and in wealthier nations. The general explanation for this maybe counter-intuitive pattern points to the importance of social norms, political expectations and relative deprivation. Being poor and risk-exposed in a context where most people have a high living standard and secure positions is believed to be stigmatizing and alienating to a higher degree than when this situation is shared with most of the people who are around you. Furthermore, generous and de-commodifying welfare states give rise to norms and expectations for individual protection and welfare; when these promises are unfulfilled, this is seen as a lack of political responsibility, and there is a risk of political detachment. In times of financial and economic crisis, the risk of unfulfilled expectations increases, as does the risk of social marginalization, which also leads to political marginalization. The higher the expectations of the political sphere in terms of protecting weaker groups, the higher the risk that unfulfilled expectations will lead to increased cleavages in relation to politics between those in more risk-exposed positions and those living in secure and prosperous circumstances. If the weakest groups detach from ordinary politics, their interests might not articulated or mobilized and their interests overlooked in policy making, which might further deepen the social cleavages and weaken the support for the political system, even in the most stable and thriving nations of Europe.

References

APSA. 2004. American Democracy in an Age of Rising Inequality. APSA Task Force Report. *Perspective on Politics* 2 (4): 651–666.

Asparouhov, Tihomir. 2004. 'Weighting for Unequal Probability of Selection in Multilevel Modeling." Mplus Web Notes: No. 8 Version 3, December 09, 2004. http://statmodel2.com/.

Bartels, Larry M. 2008. *Unequal Democracy. The Political Economy of the New Gilded Age.* Princeton: Princeton University Press.

Beck, Ulrich. 2007. "Beyond class and nation: Reframing Social Inequalities in a Globalizing World." *British Journal of Sociology* 58 (4): 679–705.

Bobbio, Norberto. 1987. *The Future of Democracy* Minneapolis: University of Minnesota Press.

Borre, Ole. 2000. "Critical Issues and Political Alienation in Denmark." *Scandinavian Political Studies* 23 (4): 285–309.

Campbell, Angus. 1962. "The Passive Citizen". *Acta Sociologica* 6 (1–2): 9–21.

Commission, European. 2010. *The Social Situation in the European Union 2009.* European Commission.

Dahl, Robert A. 2006. *On Political Equality.* New Haven & London: Yale University Press.

Dalton, Russell J. 2004. *Democratic Challenges, Democratic Choices. The Erosion of Political Support in Advanced Industrial Democracies.* Oxford: Oxford University Press.

Esping-Andersen, Gösta. 1999. *Social Foundations of Postindustrial Economies.* Oxford: Oxford University Press.

Esping-Andersen, Gøsta. 1990. *The Three Worlds of Welfare Capitalism*. Cambridge: Polity Press.

Goul Andersen, Jørgen and Jörgen Hoff. 2001. *Democracy and Citizenship in Scandinavia*. New York: Palgrave.

Harrisons, Eric and David Rose 2006. *The European Socio-economic Classification (ESeC) User Guide*. University of Essex Colchester, UK Institute for Social and Economic Research

Hay, Colin. 2007. *Why We Hate Politics*. Cambridge: Polity Press.

Inglehart, Ronald. 1997. *Modernization and Postmodernization. Cultural, Economic, and Political Change in 43 Societies*. Princeton: Princeton University Press.

Kabashima, Ikuo, Marshall, Jonathan, Uekami, Takayoschi Hyun, Dae-Song. 2000. "Causal Cynics or Disillusioned Democrats?" *Political Psychology* 21 (4).

Kitschelt, Herbert, and Philipp Rehm. 2004. "New social risk and political preferences." In *International conference of Europeanists organized by the Council for European Studies*. Chicago.

Kriesi, Hanspeter, Edgar Grande, Romain Lachat, Martin Dolezal, Simon Bornschier and Timotheos Frey. 2006. "Globalization and the transformation of the national political space: Six European countries compared." *European Journal of Political Research* (45): 921–956.

Listhaug, Ola. 1995. "Komparativ offentlig opinion i Europa." *Tidskrift för samfunnsforskning* 36 (4): 583–614.

Maas, Cora J.M., and Joop J. Hox. 2005. "Sufficient Sample Sizes for Multilevel Modeling." *Methodology* 1 (3): 86–92.

Mau, Steffen. 2003. *The Moral Economy of Welfare States. Britain and Germany compared*. London: Routledge.

Mau, Steffen. 2004. "Welfare Regimes and the Norms of Social Exchange." *Current Sociology* 52 (1): 53–74.

Miller, Arthur. 1974. "Political Issues and Trust in Government: 1964–1970." *American Political Science Review* 68 (3): 951–972.

Miller, Arthur, and Ola Listhaug. 1999. "Political Performance and Institutional Trust." In *Critical Citizens. Global Support for Democratic Governance*, ed. Pippa Norris. Oxford: Oxford University Press. 204–216.

Norris, Pippa, ed. 1999. *Critical Citizens. Global Support for Democratic Governance*. Oxford: Oxford University Press.

Oskarson, Maria. 2007. "Social Risk, Policy Dissatisfaction, and Political Alienation: A Comparison of Six European Countries." In *The Political Sociology of the Welfare State. Institutions, Social Cleavages and Orientations.*, ed. Stefan Svallfors. Stanford: Stanford University Press. 117–148.

Prior, Markus. 2009. "Why Are Some People More Interested in Politics than Others?." Woodrow Wilson School and Department of Politics.

Prior, Markus. 2010. "You've Either Got It or You Don't? The Stability of Political Interest over the Life Cycle." *The Journal of Politics* 72 (3): 747–766.

Rothstein, Bo. 1998. *Just Institutions Matter. The Moral and Political Logic of the Universal Welfare State*. Cambridge: Cambridge University Press.

Scholte, Jan Aart. 2005. *Globalization a Critical Introduction*. 2nd ed. Basingstoke: Palgrave MacMillan.

Scruggs, Lyle, and James Allan. 2006. "Welfare-state Decommodification in 18 OECD Countries: a Replication and Revision." *Journal of European Social Policy* 16 (1): 55–72.

Shalev, Michael. 2007. "Limits and Alternatives to Multiple Regression in Comparative Research." *Comparative Social Research* 24: 261–308.

Solt, Frederick. 2008. "Economic Inequality and Democratic Political Engagement." *American Journal of Political Science* 52 (1): 48–60.

Stoker, Gerry. 2006. "Explaining Political Disenchantment: Finding Pathways to Democratic Renewal." *The Political Quarterly* 77 (2): 184–194.

Stoker, Gerry. 2006. *Why Politics Matters. Making democracy Work*. New York: Palgrave Macmillan.

Strömbäck, Jesper, and Adam Shehata. 2010. "Media Malaise or a Virtuous Circle? Exploring the Causal Relationships Between News Media Exposure, Political News Attention and Political Interest." *European Journal of Political Research* 49: 575–597.

Svallfors, Stefan. 2003. "Welfare Regimes and Welfare Opinions: A Comparison of Eight western Countries." *Social Indicators Research* 64: 495–520.

Svallfors, Stefan. 2007. *The Political Sociology of the Welfare State. Institutions, Social Cleavages and Orientations*. Stanford: Stanford University Press.

van Bavel, J. 2010. "Choice of Study Discipline and the Postponement of Motherhood in Europe: The Impact of Expected Earnings, Gender Composition and Family Attitudes." *Demography* 47: 439–458.

van Deth, Jan. W., and Martin Elff. 2004. "Politicisation, Economic Development and Political Interest in Europe." *European Journal of Electoral Research* 43: 477–508.

van Deth, Jan.W. 1989. "Interest in Politics." In *Continuities in Political Action*, eds. Kent M Jennings and Jan.W. van Deth. Berlin: Walter de Gruyter & Co. 275–312.

Verba, Sidney, and Norman H. Nie. 1972. *Particiaption in America: Political Democracy and Social Equality*. New York: Harper & Row.

Verba, Sidney, Kay Lehman Schlozman, and Henry E. Brady. 1995. *Voice and Equality: civic Voluntarism in American Politics*. Cambridge, Mass.: Harvard University Press.

Whelan, Christopher T., and Bertrand Maitre. 2008. "Social Class Variation in Risk: a Comparative Analysis of the Dynamics of Economic Vulnerability." *British Journal of Sociology* 59 (4): 637–659.

CHAPTER 7

Contextual Income Inequality and Political Behavior

Michael P. McDonald

Income Inequality and Political Behavior

Politics is often defined as a competitive struggle by individuals and groups over scare resources: who gets what, when, and how (Lasswell 1936). In a democratic society, elections could serve as a means for individuals to translate their preferences over income redistribution into policy outcomes (Hill and Leighley 1992). Yet, if those of lower class are supportive of redistributing wealth, they do not translate well this desire into action. Scholars of American politics consistently find those of lower socio-economic status are less likely to participate in a gamut of civic activities, including voting (e.g., Lazarsfeld 1944; Wolfinger and Rosenstone 1980, Verba, Shlozman, and Brady 1985). The overwhelming evidence in support of a negative relationship between socio-economic status and voting further fits a stylized cross-national comparative correlation (Costa and Kahn 2003, 107) that the United States' high level of income inequality (United Nations 2006) contributes to its comparatively lower voter turnout (Hill 2006) by sculpting the electorate along the broad contours of income divisions within its society.

Differential participation rates of citizens by socio-economic status do not address directly how income inequality shapes political behavior. For inequality to affect individuals' behavior they must perceive its existence, how government functions to address it, arrive at judgments, and take – or fail to take – action. In the presence of income inequalities, those who believe the political system is working against them may become more distrustful and disengage from the political process (Costa and Kahn 2003; Uslaner and Brown 2005). Alternatively, dissatisfaction with the economic structure could stimulate participation as the disadvantaged petition the government about their economic grievances (Schattschneider 1960; Deutsch 1961). With the exception of a study of American municipalities (Oliver 1999), scholars generally find that income inequality is related to lower participation (Kawachi et al. 1997; Alesina and La Ferrara 2000; Tolbert and Hero 2001) or come to "surprising" (Uslaner and Brown 2005, 887) inconclusive findings.

Context matters. Oliver's (1999) seemingly contradictory finding with these other studies is a consequence of his choice to explore local level income inequality while other studies focus on state level income inequality. Both lines of research are supported here given their measurement of income inequality. Income inequality at the state level is *negatively* related to voting rates while at the county level it is simultaneously *positively* related. This insight helps resolve the scholarly debate, and presents new opportunities to understand how income inequality relates to civic participation and other political and social phenomenon such as trust, conflict and mobilization.

Linking Income Inequality to Voter Turnout

A long tradition of political thought argues that people perceive the world through the lens of inequality in their environment, "The nearer men are to a common level of uniformity, the less they are likely to believe blindly in any man or any class...[b]ut they are readier to trust the mass" (de Tocqueville 1969, 255). Three potential causal pathways linking income inequality to political participation are sketched in Figure 1. In a *trust model* income inequality affects an individual's trust towards other people, which in turn, affects voting propensities. The trust model also allows for a reverse, endogenous, relationship whereby participation builds trust through the act of participating. In a *policy conflict model* inequality breeds political conflict, which stimulates political participation. In a *mobilization model* elites act as political entrepreneurs within their communities through mobilization efforts. No single model may fully explain the link between income inequality and participation as all three models may act simultaneously.

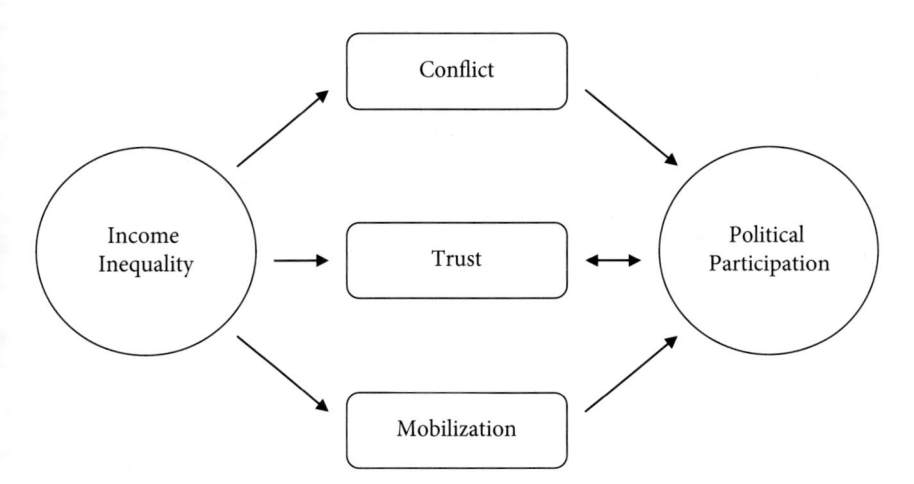

FIGURE 1   *Three causal models linking income inequality and political participation*

Trust. In a trust model, income inequality indirectly affects an individual citizen's voter participation as filtered through a two-step process whereby perceptions of inequality affect their levels of trust of others, which in turn shape their conception of citizen duty (Kawachi et al. 1997; Costa and Kahn 2003; Uslaner and Brown 2005).

The first stage of the trust model links income inequality to trust. Uslaner and Brown (2005) theorize that the presence of income inequality affects trust by two mechanisms. First, that when the poor observe inequality, they feel "powerless" and "opt out of civic engagement" (p. 896). Second, that "people at the top and the bottom will not see each other as facing a shared fate," (p. 896) which breeds distrust among both social classes. In a related formal model, Alesina and La Ferrara (2000) assume people do not see each other as sharing the same fate and therefore prefer to interact and join associations with others of their own 'type', which in economically heterogeneous communities degrades the building of social capital that manifests in lower voter turnout. The trust theory, combined with Putnam's (2000) arguments concerning social capital, therefore predicts communities with high inequality become mired in a brutal cycle of distrust and disengagement that can negatively affect the functioning of government, such as the quality of health care (Kawachi et al. 1997).

The theoretical underpinning of the second stage comes from a well-established literature that finds a positive correlation between trust and civic engagement, both broadly defined (e.g., Almond and Verba 1963; Brehm and Rahn 1997; Stolle 1998; Putnam 2000). Uslaner and Brown (2005, 872–873) aptly point out that the causal arrow may point backwards, since it may reasonably be true that people become more trusting when they become politically engaged.

Logically, in the trust model, if trust and participation are positively related and people become more distrustful when inequality rises, income inequality will be negatively related to voter participation. While Uslaner and Brown (2005) do not find strong support for their hypothesized relationships, other studies that find negative relationships between income inequality and participation couch their findings in these terms (Alesina and La Ferrara 2000; Tolbert and Hero 2001; Costa and Kahn 2003; Galbraith and Hale 2006).[1] While the trust causal path could work at any geographic level, a key assumption is that individuals observe others' income. One might therefore expect income inequality to effect trust and voter participation more at local levels where

---

1   Costa and Kahn's (2003) findings may be a result of omitting a measure of an individual's income in their model. Individual income variation is therefore absorbed into the coefficient on income inequality.

people have more contact with one another than at larger and more geographically remote levels, such as states.

Policy Conflict. A prescient critique of the trust model comes from Schattschneider (1960), who argues the political process is a primary vehicle for the disadvantaged to redress economic grievances, what I call a policy conflict model. Dominant economic interests prefer to keep economic conflict out of the public sphere, since "they are able to dictate the outcome as long as the conflict remains private" (Schattschneider 1960, 39). The disadvantaged, on the other hand, seek to "modify private power relations by enlarging the scope of conflict" (Schattschneider 1960, 39) to, in Schattschneider's analogy, call in the school teacher to disrupt the power balance between defenseless smaller boys and a predatory bully. Those economically disadvantaged persons thus have an incentive to engage politically to rectify perceived inequalities. Injecting economic inequality into the public arena heightens political conflict, which spurs participation among all citizens who engage in the ensuing meaningful policy debates. Oliver finds this conflict argument is "most consistent" (Oliver 1999, 198) with his findings that participation among the poor is low in poor or affluent communities, and higher in economically heterogeneous communities.

Two stages are implicitly assumed in the conflict model. In a first stage, citizens perceive inequality and adopt preferences over government policies to rectify it. In a second stage, citizens take action by voting. Which is the proper unit of analysis, the state or the county, in terms of government policies towards income inequality within the United States? In other words, should state or local income inequality spur participation? Hill and Leighley's (1992) state-level analysis of the electorate's class bias and welfare policy is predicated on the notion that "...states vary widely with respect to their turnout levels, class bias of the electorates, and redistributive policies" (1992, 353). This is not to say that local policies may also vary in terms of how resources are distributed among their residents, such as the location of schools and health facilities or the distribution of policing and emergency services. However, localities act within constraints imposed on them from above and are better described as agents acting within a delegation of power from state governments rather than as primary policy formulators. Thus, citizens may reasonably have different attitudes and opinions towards their state and local income inequality policies, with greater conflict emerging at the state level.

Mobilization. In a mobilization model, participation increases among the lower classes in the presence of income inequality when those with resources lend a hand to those without. Olson (1965) theorized those with resources are better able to overcome their collective action problem than those without, in

this case, the wealthy are better equipped than the poor to collectively organize into political organizations that will educate and mobilize citizens about
their political choices and the benefits of voting. Related, Huckfeldt (1984)
argues that those living in affluent communities reinforce higher participation
levels among the poor when "informal transmission of group-based norms
turns into a societal obligation" (1984, 105). In a mobilization model, formal or
informal transmission of participation bleeds down to lower classes when
inequality is present.[2] When the wealthy are intermingled with the poor, the
wealthy act as political entrepreneurs to help the poor overcome their collective action problem or act as exemplars of good citizens. The mobilization
theory, like the trust theory, relies upon direct or indirect personal contact. As
such, it may be reasonably expected that income inequality plays a more
important role at the local level.

Summary. The link between income inequality and voter participation is theoretically complex. In a trust model, inequality breeds distrust to negatively
affect participation. A conflict model predicts inequality spurs policy debates,
which increases participation. A distinction among these two models is individuals' reactions to inequality: in the former case people disengage and in the
latter they take action. In a mobilization model, wealthier individuals act as
political entrepreneurs or exemplars to mobilize the poor. Of course, it is
always possible that there is no linkage and that observed correlations are
products of "unmodeled individual characteristics" (Oliver 1999, 193; see also
Hauser 1970). State and local policy formation dynamics may differ, which suggest that state-level and county-level inequality may have different causal linkages to voter participation. State and local level income inequality may
reasonably both belong in a model of voter participation since both may have
effects independent of one another. Recognizing this insight may further help
explain why scholars have come to conflicting conclusions about income
inequality's effect on voter turnout as no existing study simultaneously controls for both state and local inequality.

Income Inequality in the United States

In a capitalist society some people will inevitably have more money than others. An inequality measure commonly used by policymakers and scholars to
quantify income inequality is the Gini coefficient, which ranges on a $[0, 1]$
interval and generally describes inequality of any given mathematical

---

2   For a similar argument regarding participation stimulus among lower socio-economic per-
    sons who are members of a labor union, see Radcliff and Davis (2000).

distribution (Gini 1912). Higher values of the Gini coefficient are related to higher levels of inequality. For example, if one person holds all of a state's wealth, then the Gini income inequality coefficient within the state equals one. Within the state's counties, however, income inequality only equals one in the county of residence of the wealthy individual; elsewhere it equals zero since everyone shares the same degree of absolute poverty. The Gini inequality coefficient thus has idiosyncratic characteristics such that the component parts may be seemingly unrelated to the aggregate unit (Lambert and Aronson 1993).[3] Gini income inequality coefficients constructed from the 2000 census are plotted among U.S. counties[4] in Figure 2 and among U.S. states in Figure 3.[5] Higher levels of inequality are shaded more darkly, which for both figures are identified by seven equal-interval categories of Gini coefficients ranging from the lightest-shaded [0.30, 0.35] interval to darkest-shaded [0.60, 0.65] interval.

The county level map reveals inequality is concentrated within regions, such as in Southern counties often referred to as the "Black Belt" for their African-American communities, the mining communities in that Appalachian Mountains of West Virginia and Eastern Kentucky, and a swath of inequality extending along the Mexican border through Texas. Although hard to perceive from the map, some of the highest inequality levels are concentrated within densely populated urban areas. Comparing the county level to the state level, state inequality is higher among states that encompass the regions of inequality identified in the county map. Yet, county-level inequality is apparently washed out of the state-level data, as a comparison of the two maps reveals more county-level variation than state variation. County-level Gini coefficients range between [0.32, 0.61] with a mean of 0.43 and a standard deviation of 0.04. State-level Gini coefficients have a tighter range between [0.40, 0.55] with a higher mean of 0.45 and a lower standard deviation of 0.03. The correlation between the county-level and state-level coefficients is 0.48, indicating there is

---

3 The Gini coefficient is ratio of the area of the Lorenz curve under a 45 degree angle (representing perfect equality) to the area outside the Lorenz curve (Gini 1912).

4 The Census Bureau classifies independent cities in Illinois, Maryland, Missouri, and Virginia as counties. Louisiana parishes are similarly classified. Townships, primarily located in northeastern states, are not classified as counties.

5 These data were generously provided by staff at the Income Surveys Branch of the U.S. Census Bureau. The state level Gini coefficients are not an average of county measures, they are both computed directly and independently from the canonical and confidential individual census data. It is possible to construct a higher level measure from lower level components, although there are certain assumptions and averaging is not appropriate given the distributional character of the Gini coefficient (for a method to calculate a Gini coefficient for aggregate data, see Brown 1994).

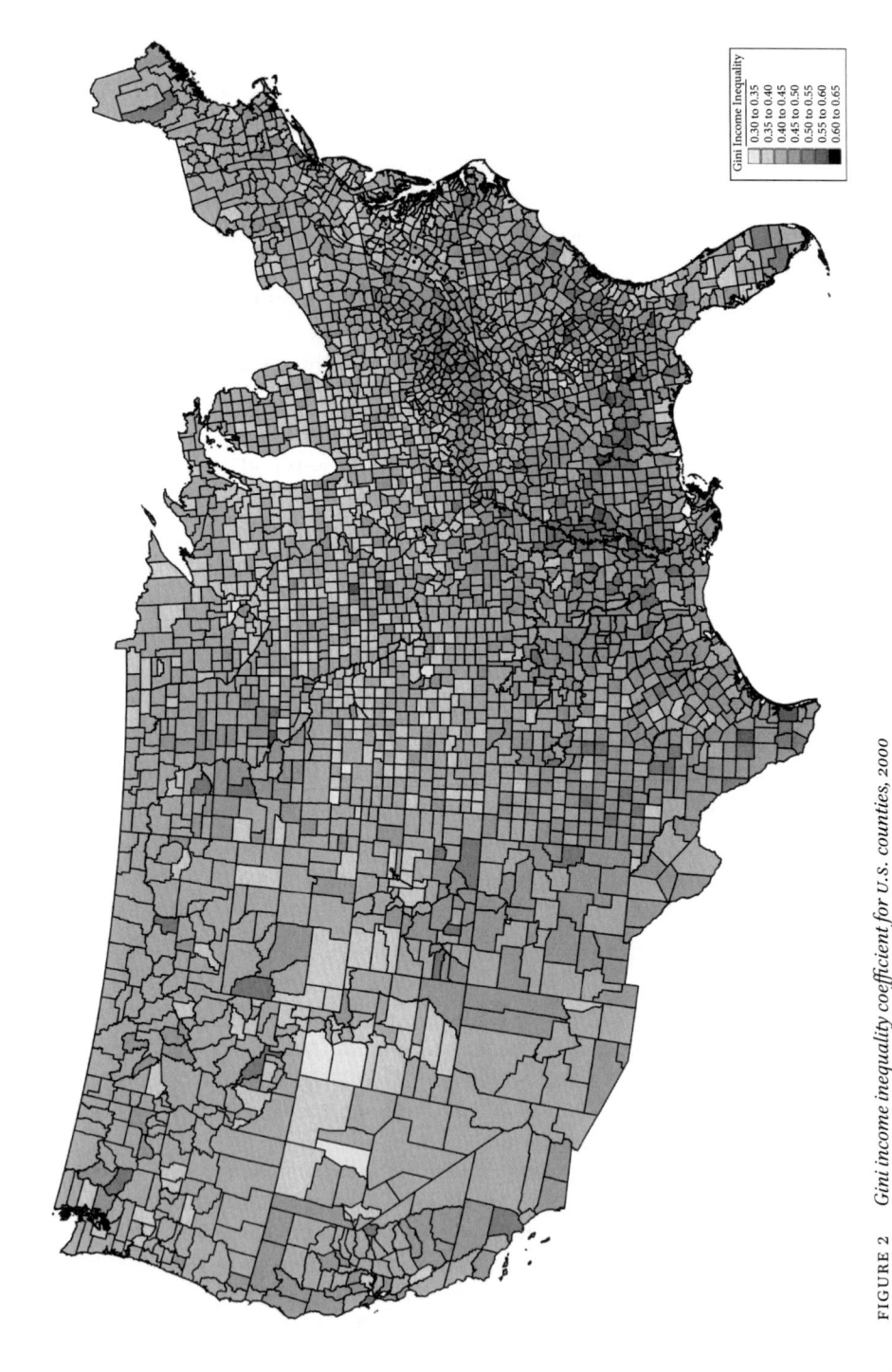

FIGURE 2   *Gini income inequality coefficient for U.S. counties, 2000*

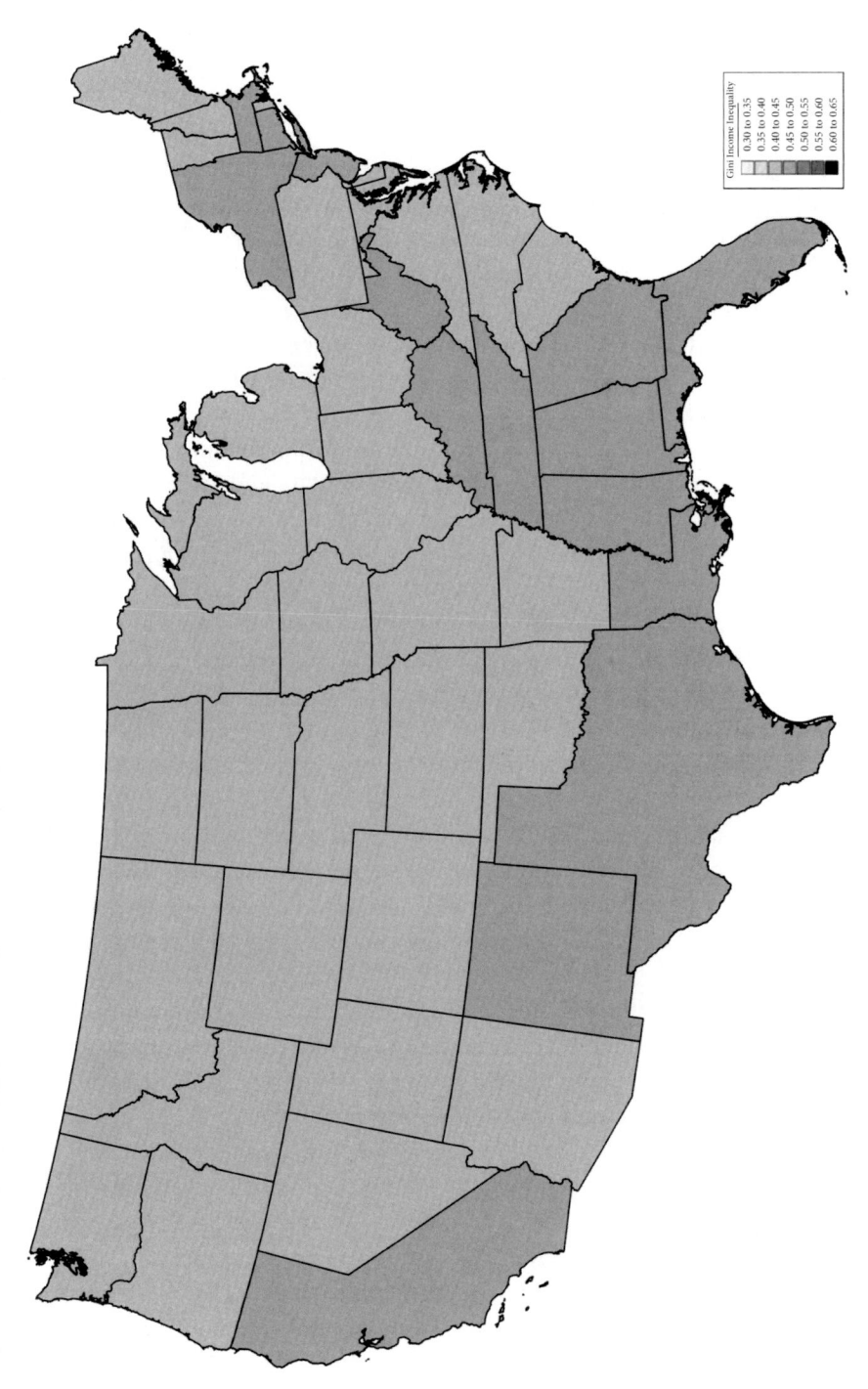

FIGURE 3   *Gini income inequality coefficient for U.S. states, 2000*

a statistically strong correlation, but that much unexplained variance remains between the two measures.

Income Inequality and Voter Turnout

To investigate the effects of state and county income inequality on voting behavior, I examine the Current Population Survey (CPS) and the American National Election Study (ANES). The CPS is a large-scale survey conducted by the U.S. Census Bureau used to calculate government statistics, such as the unemployment rate. In a November of an election year, the CPS includes a limited number of voting questions. The advantage of the CPS is that its large sample size of tens of thousands of respondents permits robust analysis at a fine aggregation level. The ANES is the premier scholarly U.S. election survey and respondents are asked attitudinal and behavioral questions that can be used to further investigate the trust, conflict, and mobilization models. However, the ANES is a smaller survey than the CPS and its cluster sample design results in a limited number of respondents within particular states and counties. This sampling feature of the ANES reduces variation and may result in seemingly-odd correlations, particularly on state-level or county-level independent variables. If the ANES and CPS analyses show similar patterns where they possess common independent variables, this provides confidence for modeling behavior possible only with the ANES.

These are multi-level data in that individuals are grouped into counties which are hierarchically organized into states. Failing to model the multi-level nature of these data may lead to under-estimates of coefficients' standard errors and an increased likelihood of committing a Type I error (Moulton 1990). A statistical method to address this issue is known as Hierarchical Linear Modeling (HML), and non-linear variants (Byrk and Raudenbush 1992). Primo, Jacobsmeier and Milyo (2007) analyze the 2000 CPS and find that HLM fails to converge for a two-level model where individuals are clustered solely by states. They attribute the failure to the relatively small number of clusters, fifty. These statistical computation problems are more severe for the ANES, which surveys respondents in about three-fifths of the states. The ANES cluster sizes are further unbalanced, ranging from one respondent (the modal number) to over fifty at the county level and from one to over a hundred at the state level. A multi-level model is therefore computationally impractical for these data. Another recommended solution to estimate standard errors is to compute robust clustered standard errors (Moulton 1990). However, the properties of robust clustered standard errors are poorly understood for small numbers of clusters with unbalanced cluster sizes (Cameron, Gelbach, and Miller 2008). In the analyses that follow I report simple standard errors, with the understanding that these errors are likely under-estimates of the true values.

The dependent variable is whether or not a citizen of voting-age voted and scores CPS and ANES respondents who did not know or refused to answer as not having voted.[6] In addition to state and county level Gini coefficients, a number of independent control variables commonly used in CPS analyses of turnout rates (e.g., Wolfinger and Rosenstone 1980; Leighley and Nagler 1992) are included in the analysis.[7] The independent variables are restricted in this first analysis to those available on the CPS, since the purpose of this exercise is to analyze comparable independent variables found on two independent surveys.

TABLE 1   2004 presidential election vote, CPS & ANES logit models

Variables	Current Population Survey			American National Election Study		
	Model 1	Model 2	Model 3	Model 1	Model 2	Model 3
Inequality						
State Gini Index	−0.776 **		−3.005 **	−3.031		−8.666 #
	(0.377)		(0.779)	(4.273)		(4.705)
County Gini Index		3.262 **	4.113 **		5.738 *	8.178 **
		(0.378)	(0.437)		(2.727)	(3.056)
Control						
Presidential	−0.525 **	−0.498 **	−0.258 **	−0.487	−0.218	−0.055
Victory Margin	(0.071)	(0.111)	(0.128)	(1.072)	(1.056)	(1.096)
Election Day	0.283 **	0.669 **	0.599 **	0.111	0.266	−0.088
Registration	(0.028)	(0.069)	(0.071)	(0.399)	(0.357)	(0.407)
Income	0.223 **	0.193 **	0.194 **	0.252 *	0.253 *	0.256 *
	(0.009)	(0.015)	(0.015)	(0.104)	(0.105)	(0.105)
Education	0.856 **	0.790 **	0.790 **	0.658 **	0.630 **	0.620 **
	(0.011)	(0.019)	(0.019)	(0.131)	(0.133)	(0.133)

6 The specification of "non-voter" is consistent with the Census Bureau definitions (see also, Leighley and Nagler 1992).

7 The control variables include state-level structural variables of the statewide presidential victory margin and the presence of Election Day registration; and individuals' demographic characteristics of education, age, sex, marital status, race (the omitted race/ethnicity category is Hispanic or Other race), home tenure, and home ownership. There are slight and unavoidable differences in variable definitions between the two surveys, which are detailed in the Appendix.

TABLE 1   *2004 presidential election vote, CPS & ANES logit models* (cont.)

Variables	Current Population Survey			American National Election Study		
	Model 1	Model 2	Model 3	Model 1	Model 2	Model 3
Age	0.024 **	0.028 **	0.028 **	0.046	0.051	0.053 #
	(0.003)	(0.004)	(0.004)	(0.031)	(0.032)	(0.032)
Age2	−0.000 **	−0.000 **	−0.000 **	−0.000	−0.000	−0.000
	(0.000)	(0.000)	(0.000)	(0.000)	(0.000)	(0.000)
Sex	−0.200 **	−0.204 **	−0.204 **	−0.359 #	−0.382 #	−0.374 #
	(0.017)	(0.028)	(0.028)	(0.196)	(0.196)	(0.197)
Married	0.384 **	0.375 **	0.374 **	−0.168	−0.149 *	−0.144
	(0.018)	(0.031)	(0.031)	(0.219)	(0.219)	(0.22)
Non-Hispanic White	0.480 **	0.631 **	0.629 **	0.428	0.520	0.451
	(0.025)	(0.036)	(0.036)	(0.552)	(0.551)	(0.555)
Non-Hispanic Black	0.906 **	0.823 **	0.821 **	0.505	0.441	0.417
	(0.036)	(0.051)	(0.051)	(0.581)	(0.582)	(0.585)
Recent Mover	−0.361 **	−0.363 **	−0.367 **	0.361	0.316	0.322
	(0.019)	(0.031)	(0.031)	(0.248)	(0.248)	(0.249)
Home Owner	0.324 **	0.314 **	0.314 **	0.543 *	0.566 *	0.545 *
	(0.021)	(0.034)	(0.034)	(0.26)	(0.261)	(0.263)
Constant	−1.891 **	−3.605 **	−2.641 **	−1.057	−5.157 **	−2.249
	(0.182)	(0.201)	(0.321)	(2.195)	(1.582)	(2.235)
Observations	87,483	60,988	60,988	812	812	810

Pseudo R²

Notes: Standard errors in parentheses, #$p < 0.10$, *$p < 0.05$, **$p < 0.01$, two-tailed tests.

Statistical analyses of both surveys are presented in Table 1 for three logit models estimating individual voting propensities in the 2004 presidential election. In Model 1, the state-level Gini income inequality coefficient is run alone (along with the control variables). In Model 2 the county-level Gini income inequality coefficient is run alone. In Model 3, the state and county level measures appear simultaneously. Standard errors are provided in parentheses below the coefficients, and for the control variables are generally statistically significant in the predicted directions from previous research (e.g., Wolfinger and Rosenstone 1980; Leighley and Nagler 1992).

Of interest are the income inequality variables. In Model 1, the estimated coefficient for the state-level Gini income inequality measure is negative and statistical significant ($p < 0.01$) for the CPS and is also negative but statistically insignificant for the ANES model. The difference between the two surveys may be a consequence of the smaller sample and other survey methodology issues present on the ANES. These statistically strong CPS and the weaker ANES results are consistent with previous research linking income inequality to lower turn-out (Alesina and La Ferrara 2000; Tolbert and Hero 2001; Costa and Kahn 2003; Galbraith and Hale 2006). In Model 2, the estimated coefficient for the county-level Gini coefficient is positive and strongly statistical significant for the CPS ($p < 0.01$) and for the ANES ($p < 0.05$), a finding that is consistent with Oliver's (1999) conclusion that local income inequality is related to higher turnout.

When the state and county level indicators are simultaneously tested in Model 3, the two inequality variables are estimated in a direction consistent with the respective previous research, depending on how scholars operational-ize their measure of income inequality. For the CPS, state income inequality is negatively related to turnout and county income inequality is simultaneously positively related (both at $p < 0.01$). For the ANES, state income inequality is negatively related ($p < 0.10$) and county income inequality is positively related ($p < 0.01$).[8] The implications are clear: the substantive disagreement in the scholarly literature over whether income inequality results in lower turnout, as mediated through trust, or is spurred by conflict is more apparent than real. It is a consequence of scholars' measurement choices.

Trust, Conflict, Mobilization and Voting

I turn next to models of trust, conflict, and mobilization using pooled ANES presidential election data from 1988–2004. The results of statistical models are presented in Table 2. All models have a binary dependent variable and logit

---

8   State and county income inequality variables are not entirely independent from one another, given that both measure inequality within their respective geographic units and that coun-ties are nested within states. Recall that the correlation between the two variables is 0.48. While the two variables are correlated, there is ample variation between the two variables to alleviate concerns that multi-collinearity alone is causing the coefficients to be estimated in more strongly opposite directions when the two variables are entered together in Model 3. Still, note that the coefficients of interest in Model 3 are three to four times as large as those in Model 1 and Model 2. Given that the two variables are related, the variables should not be viewed in isolation, as a change in county-level income inequality may affect a change in state-level income inequality. Unfortunately, due to the idiosyncratic measurement of Gini coefficients, it is impossible to describe how a change in county level income inequality is related to a change in state income equality.

TABLE 2 *Trust, conflict & mobilization models, ANES pooled logit models*

	Trust		Conflict		Mobilization	
Inequality Variables						
State Gini Index	−3.887 ** (1.622)	−0.043	2.967 * (1.153)	0.035	−13.421 ** (2.445)	−0.138
County Gini Index	−2.140 ** (0.943)	−0.041	1.118 # (0.638)	0.024	3.786 * (1.533)	0.193
Family Income x State Gini Index					−0.597 (2.007)	−0.157
Family Income x County Gini Index					−2.327 # (1.299)	−0.603
Control Variables						
Presidential Victory Margin					−1.867 ** (0.553)	−0.085
Family Income	0.145 ** (0.034)	0.083	−0.035 (0.024)	−0.022	0.161 ** (0.054)	0.845
Education	0.517 ** (0.039)	0.231	0.022 (0.027)	0.011	0.223 ** (0.064)	0.095
Age	0.049 ** (0.011)	0.412	0.020 ** (0.008)	0.185	0.045 * (0.018)	0.372
Age^2	0.000 ** (0.000)	−0.330	0.000 ** (0.000)	−0.202	0.000 (0.000)	−0.203
Sex	0.134 * (0.063)	0.033	0.096 * (0.043)	0.026	−0.254 * (0.102)	−0.060
Married	−0.031 (0.071)	−0.008	0.034 (0.048)	0.009	0.055 (0.111)	0.012
Non-Hispanic White	0.374 ** (0.104)	0.079	−0.125 # (0.067)	−0.029	0.352 # (0.191)	0.071
Non-Hispanic Black	−0.725 ** (0.145)	−0.118	0.357 ** (0.084)	0.063	0.011 (0.243)	−0.003
Recent Mover	0.014 (0.074)	0.003	0.099 * (0.05)	0.027	−0.294 ** (0.107)	−0.070
Home Owner	0.171 * (0.081)	0.040	−0.164 ** (0.054)	−0.042	0.665 ** (0.13)	0.147
Democrat	0.416 ** (0.108)	0.103	0.001 (0.072)	0.000	0.232 (0.173)	0.053

	Trust		Conflict		Mobilization	
Republican	0.252 *	0.061	0.242 **	0.064	0.090	0.020
	(0.111)		(0.074)		(0.177)	
Political Interest	0.262 **	0.061	0.205 **	0.053	0.501 **	0.116
	(0.07)		(0.047)		(0.112)	
Job Worries	−0.266 **	−0.054				
	(0.078)					
Observations	5.036		10,784		2,077	
Pseudo R²	0.11		0.02		0.14	

Notes: Unstandardized coefficients on the left. Standardized coefficients on the right. Standard errors in parentheses, # $p < 0.10$,* $p < 0.05$, ** $p < 0.01$, two-tailed tests. Year-fixed effects not reported.

models are used for the estimation. Additional attitudinal variables available on the ANES are added to these statistical models. These variables include the partisanship of the respondent, their level of political interest, and if they are worried about losing their job (for the trust model only). Additional year fixed-effects variables are included. State-level controls related to turnout present in the previous models are excluded. The trust model is limited to the years where both personal trust and job worries are present in the ANES questionnaire: 1992, 1996, 1998, and 2004.[9] A measure of job worries – which is used as an instrumental variable to test for endogeneity in subsequent trust models – is dropped in the policy conflict to increase the number of inclusive years from 1988 to 2004.[10] The contact model is run for 2000 and 2004 only, as these are the years that presidential campaigns began investing heavily in voter mobilization efforts.[11]

---

9   A personal trust question was asked in 1992, 1996, 1998, 2000, 2002, and 2004. A question about job worries was asked in 1988, 1990, 1992, 1994, 1996, 1998, and 2004. Excluding the job worries question adds 2000 and 2002 to the analysis, but this alternative model does not differ substantively from the one reported here with respect to contextual income inequality.

10   Conflict and mobilization models tested with job worries were included demonstrated that the variable is far from statistical significance, so there is little concern of omitted variable bias as a consequence of dropping this variable from the model.

11   In the presidential elections of 1988, 1992, and 1996, only 24% of ANES respondents reported contact. The frequency of contact increased to 38% in 2000 and 45% in 2004. For this reason, I examine 2000 and 2004 only.

Trust. Scholars who posit trust negatively affects participation emphasize a personal nature of trust. When people observe income inequality through the interactions with persons of different income levels, they do not perceive that they share a common fate, which lead to increased levels of distrust. The nature of trust posited to be affected by income inequality is therefore of a personal nature, not of trust of government institutions, elected officials, or non-governmental institutions such as the political parties or the media. It may affect both persons of higher and lower socio-economic status, as the poor become distrustful of the rich, and the rich become distrustful of the poor. Trust is thus commonly operationalized in terms of ANES respondents' answers to a simple question on personal trust, which asks if most people can be trusted or not (Uslaner and Brown 2005).

The results for the trust model are presented in the first column of Table 2. The control variables are generally strongly statistically significant in the expected direction. People of higher education and family income are more trusting of other people. So, too, are older people, though there is a negative diminishing trust among the elderly. Whites are more trusting than the omitted category of Hispanics or other race, while African-Americans are less trusting. Partisans and those who express interest in politics are more trusting. And those who are worried about their job situation are less trusting. These results are consistent with previous research and lend validity to the statistical modeling.

Of interest are the coefficients for income inequality. Here, both state and county level income inequality variables are statistically significant in the negative direction, consistent with the theory that income inequality breeds distrust. Interestingly, the results at the state and county levels are in the same direction and of same magnitude. When income inequality is low at both state and county levels, personal trust is at its highest, all other things equal. When it is high at both state and county levels, personal trust is at its lowest. These results imply that increased income inequality at either level breeds distrust.

Policy Conflict. Political conflict is a difficult concept to measure. It may manifest itself in electoral competition, but even in areas of one-party dominance there may be fierce localized intra-party competition. An assumption of the conflict model may thus lend itself to measurement. The model supposes that when persons perceive income inequality that those of lower status engage in politics to rectify it and those who oppose government intervention will work to maintain the status quo. Peoples' perceptions of the role of government in the economy may thus serve as an indicator of the presence of economic conflict, pitting those in favor of government regulation against those who believe in free market solutions. When income inequality is present, people become more aware of economic inequities and their opinion about government economic policies may become polarized.

The measurement is not of individuals' preferences over government policy, rather that they hold strong opinions. I fold a seven point scale of the level of government services, which ranges from support for decreasing government services to increasing government services. Respondents who scored in the middle range [3, 5] and those expressing no opinion are scored as not expressing a strong opinion on government services. Those on the remaining extremes are scored as expressing a strong opinion.[12]

The results of the estimation of the conflict model are presented in the second column of Table 2. The socio-economic variables of income and education are uncorrelated with redistributive policy polarization, but this is reasonable in that persons of lower and higher status could express different, but not necessarily stronger, opinions. The remaining relationships can be better understood in a similar light. People who are politically interested are more likely to express a strong opinion, as are older persons and African-Americans. Republicans are more likely to express an opinion, while Democrats are not, relative to the omitted category, independents, who are more ideologically moderate and are more willing to express opinions that range across the spectrum. Recent movers are more likely and home owners are less likely to express a strong opinion, which is perhaps a counter-intuitive finding that is present in simple cross-tabulations that show differences among these groups ($p < 0.01$).[13]

As predicted by the conflict model, where income inequality is higher, respondents are more likely to respond with stronger opinions on economic policy. These results are statistically significant for at the state level, but teeter on the edge of significance at the county level for a two-tailed test. These results are therefore consistent with theoretical framework posited by Schattschneider (1960) and the empirical results observed by Oliver (1999). However, with respect to Oliver, he observed only a relationship between income inequality and participation that he theorized was consistent with a conflict theory, while the results in Table 2 provide direct evidence that

---

12   In the 2000 ANES, only in-person interviews included this question.

13   Recent movers are more likely to support a role for government, which explains their propensity to express a stronger opinion. Overall, more homeowners lean towards favoring free markets, which might be expected of this group that holds wealth in their home equity, but more choose the moderate option of '3' on the seven point scale, which thus scores them as not holding a strong opinion. Perhaps home owners feel ambivalent because they are dependent on services supplied by local governments, such as police and fire protection.

contextual income inequality heightens economic policy conflict, both at state and county levels. As predicted, the correlation is stronger at the state level, where the meaningful policies tend to be made, than at the local level.

Mobilization. The results of the mobilization model for 2000 and 2004 presidential elections are presented in the third column of Table 2. The control variables perform as expected, respondents reported being contacted more frequently in states with a narrow presidential margin of victory. Those reporting higher levels of contact are those easier to find, such as people who own homes and those who have not moved recently (Highton 2000; McDonald 2008). Women are more likely to report contact, too, which may be a consequence of more often being at home in their child caregiver role. Higher frequency of contact reported among older, higher educated and married persons may be indicative of their higher levels of social capital (Putnam 2000). Those reporting being interested in politics are more likely to report being contacted, which raises endogeneity concerns since the contact may stimulate interest, although it is also likely that the politically interested have previously voted, and are thus targets for mobilization efforts.

The mobilization model predicts that those of lower income have heightened participation levels when intermingled with higher income individuals, with whom they come in direct or indirect contact with. These connections should reasonably occur primarily at the local level. As expected, county level income inequality is positively related to contact and an interaction of county income inequality and family income is negatively related to contact. The relationship is graphically presented in Figure 4, where the predicted probability of a respondent reporting contact is plotted for the lowest and highest family income categories across the meaningful range [0.32, 0.61] of county-level income inequality. Figure 4 confirms that the reported levels of contact between the rich and poor are in areas where income inequality is lowest, and least where income inequality is greatest. In areas of high income inequality, predicted levels of contact are nearly the same between the poorest and wealthiest family income categories.

While these county level findings conform to expectations, state level income inequality continues to exhibit a negative relationship. It may be that state political party organizations are weaker when income inequality is distributed widely across a state, making it difficult for the persons living in wealthy areas of a state to reach out to lend organizational support to less affluent areas.

Voting Reassessed. The full vote model diagrammed in Figure 1 can be evaluated from the information derived from these statistical models. The evidence

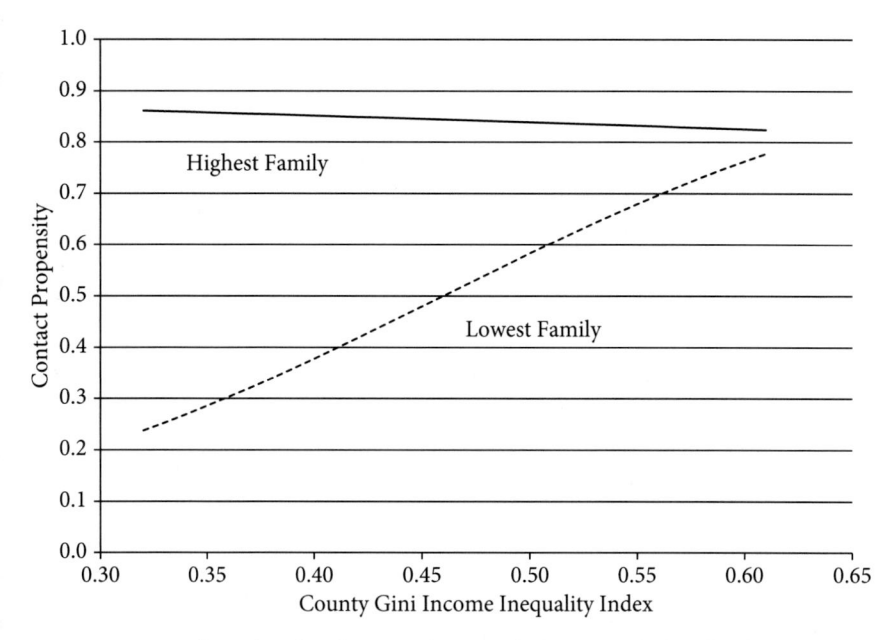

FIGURE 4   *Transformed predicted contact propensity for lowest and highest family income categories across meaningful ranges of county-level income inequality.*
Note: The graph is centered on a fifty percent probability of contact for respondents with the lowest family income for a county level income inequality of 0.46, which is the median of the income inequality range.

presented in Table 3 supports that income inequality at the county and state level affects personal trust, conflict, and mobilization. All variables may be simultaneously entered into a statistical model predicting voter participation so that their individual effects may be parsed out from one another, and to see if when controlling for these causal pathways, the direct effect of income inequality dissipates.

First, a potential endogenous relationship between trust and participation, where the act of voting reinforces personal trust, must be addressed. A common solution to testing and controlling for endogenous relationships is through an instrumental variables approach: a variable correlated with personal trust is used to predict trust in a first stage model and the resulting predictive values are entered into a second stage model predicting voting propensities. While instruments can be difficult to identify, fortunately, an instrument is ready at hand: the degree that an individual is worried about losing their job, which is correlated with personal trust but uncorrelated with economic policy conflict, self-reported contact by a political organization, and voting propensities. The difficulty in this case is that the two-stage approach is best suited to models where the dependent and endogenous variables are continuous, whereas here the variables are dichotomous. Uslaner and Brown (2005) circumvent this issue by aggregating their data to produce state-level percentages, an approach that will not work here due to small state cluster sizes. I approximate by using ordinary least squares estimation for the two stages. The resulting Durbin-Wu-Houseman endogeneity test is far from statistical significance ($p < 0.96$), which confirms Uslaner and Brown's (2005, 887) finding that, "there is little evidence that political action...leads to more trusting citizens."

Lacking evidence of endogeneity, the voter turnout model can be reassessed including the additional variables available on the ANES. Estimated models for the 1992, 1996, 2000, and 2004 presidential elections are presented in Table 3 (1988 is dropped because the trust measure was not asked). Variables identifying a respondent's self-reported partisanship and level of political interest are included as control variables in addition to those appearing in voting propensity model in Table 1. These control variables correlate in patterns that conform to theoretical expectations, but are not shown for space considerations. Two models are presented for each election, one with state and county level income inequality only and one that includes the three measures for personal trust, policy conflict, and mobilization.

The estimation results reveal that personal trust and self-reported contact by a political organization consistently correlate with voting propensities while strong opinions of economic policy do not. In all but the 2004 election, higher levels of personal trust are positively related ($p < 0.05$ or greater) to increased voting propensities. In all four elections, contact by a political organization is positively related to increased voting ($p < 0.01$). In none of the presidential elections is strong preference on government economic policy statistically significant.

The contextual income inequality measures are related to voting propensities only in 1992 and 2004. In 1992, state level income inequality is negatively related to voting propensities in both models ($p < 0.05$) and the county level inequality is positively related just outside ($p < 0.10$). In 1996 and 2000, the coefficients are in the predicted direction for all but the coefficient on county level income inequality for the 2000 full model, but in no case do the coefficients rise close to a level of statistical significance. In 2004, county level income inequality is positively related in increased voting propensities ($p < 0.05$) in both models, whereas state level income inequality is negatively related ($p < 0.10$) only when the causal pathways of trust, conflict, and mobilization are not present.

TABLE 3 *Contextual Income Inequality and Presidential Voter Turnout, 1992–2004*

| | | 1992 | | | | 1996 | | | |
		Reduced		Full		Reduced		Full	
Inequality Variables	*State Gini Index*	−9.784*	−0.077	−9.361 *	−0.072	−3.882	−0.034	−3.107	−0.027
		(4.024)		(4.112)		(−5.078)		(5.210)	
	County Gini Index	2.909	0.048	3.037	0.048	0.916	0.015	1.722	0.028
		(2.002)		(2.052)		(−2.362)		(2.415)	
Causal Variables	*Trust*			0.432 **	0.091			0.376 *	0.080
				(0.142)				(0.170)	
	Conflict			0.057	0.011			0.124	0.024
				(0.146)				(0.171)	
	Contact			0.880 **	0.068			0.830 **	0.163
				(0.208)				(0.203)	
Observations		1,852		1,829		1,376		1,365	
Pseudo R^2		0.23		0.24		0.22		0.23	

| | | 2000 | | | | 2004 | | | |
		Reduced		Full		Reduced		Full	
Inequality Variables	*State Gini Index*	2.816	0.028	4.752		0.050	−8.167 #	−0.098	−6.349	−0.074
		(4.344)		(5.379)			(−4.946)		(5.085)	
	County Gini Index	0.070	0.001	−0.907		−0.014	7.912 *	0.135	7.126 *	0.119
		(2.346)		(3.204)			(−3.286)		(3.280)	
Causal Variables	*Trust*			0.623 **		0.131			0.132	0.029
				(0.217)					(0.230)	
	Conflict			−0.110		−0.022			−0.009	−0.002
				(0.215)					(0.224)	
	Contact			1.002 **		0.200			0.814 **	0.182
				(0.256)					(0.237)	
Observations		1,270		713			810		806	
Pseudo R^2		0.23		0.26			0.20		0.22	

Notes: Unstandardized coefficients on the left. Standardized coefficients on the right. Standard errors in parentheses, $\#p < 0.10$, $^*p < 0.05$, $^{**}p < 0.01$, two-tailed tests. Control variables and year-fixed effects suppressed for space considerations.

There is a slight indication that income inequality indirectly affects turnout though trust and mobilization. When the trust, conflict, and mobilization variables are entered into the equations, the statistical significance of the income inequality coefficients is slightly lower. However, the drop in statistical significance is slight, suggesting that there is either a direct effect of income inequality on voting propensities or there is some yet-to-be-explained indirect causal path. Since the measure of policy conflict fares poorly in these models, as an dependent and independent variable, further exploration of the policy conflict model may provide better insights into the relationship between income inequality and political participation.

Another feature of the models is that they perform best in 1992 and 2004. Some caution is warranted in inferring much from this and all patterns since the cluster sample design of the ANES limits variation among states and counties. However, these elections are distinguished from 1996 and 2000 in that economic troubles were of greater salience. In 1992, the country was just emerging from a recession, and in 2004, the country was just emerging from a low economic growth following the terrorist attacks of 9–11. These results therefore suggest that contextual income inequality is more salient under times of economic stress. When difficult economic times exist, citizens become more aware of income inequality and predicate their voting behavior accordingly. When times are good and the proverbial economic pie is getting larger, all citizens enjoy greater economic benefits and are less likely to orient their voting in terms of income inequality. Still, if this were the case, one might expect conflict over redistributive policies to have some relationship in these years, but it does not.

Discussion

How do people behave when they observe income inequality around them? Two theoretical lines have developed that researchers have sought evidence in support of. A trust model predicts a negative relationship between income inequality and voter turnout, whereby economic inequality breeds distrust which in turn breeds lower turnout (Kawachi et al. 1997; Alesina and La Ferrara 2000; Tolbert and Hero 2001; Uslaner and Brown 2005). A policy conflict model predicts that inequality heightens political conflict, which spurs greater levels of participation (Oliver 1999). To these, I add a third, a mobilization model whereby those with resources lend a helping hand to those without. The results here suggest strongly that these studies of how income inequality affects civic engagement are talking past one another because none simultaneously control for income inequality at different levels of aggregation. Income inequality has a different effect on political behavior and voter engagement depending on the operationalization of the concept. When income inequality is measured at the state level, a *negative* relationship between income inequality and voter turnout is revealed, supporting the trust model. When measured at the county level, a *positive* relationship is revealed, supporting the conflict model. Both operate simultaneously.

This insight provokes further investigation. I find evidence that income inequality at both county and state levels is negatively related to personal trust and positively related to policy conflict. These results conform with theoretical expectations. I also find a positive effect of local income inequality on mobilization among lower income persons, as predicted by the mobilization theory. Unexpected is a sizable negative relationship between income inequality and mobilization at the state level. A plausible explanation is that geographically dispersed income inequality impedes strong political party organizations in wealthy areas from facilitating the creation of stronger political organizations to aid low income persons in economically depressed corners of a state.

When these dependent variables are introduced as independent variables in a turnout model, income inequality effects persist with a negative relationship among states and a simultaneous positive relationship among counties, particularly in years where economic issues were preeminent. The persistence of a direct effect of income inequality on participation when these other theories are controlled for presents an unresolved puzzle. Perhaps the variables testing for the three models of trust, conflict, and mobilization are not performing well. In particular, the policy conflict variable is correlated to income inequality, but it is not related to voter participation, suggesting that it may not adequately serve as a measure for conflict as conceptualized by Schattschneider (1960) and others. Or perhaps there exists an untested theory linking income inequality to turnout.

The findings here are weighted by normative implications. Milbrath (1965, 152), echoing Karl Marx, argues democratic elites prefer passivity among the masses as agitation upsets existing peaceful elite power structures. Indeed, some American Founding Fathers such as Adams and Madison argued in favor of limiting voting suffrage to prevent tyranny by the economically disadvantaged majority (Keyssar 2001). Later democratic elite theorists such as Lipset (1960, 121) further echo these Founding Fathers by arguing, "widespread anti-democratic tendencies of the lower classes" could undo democracy itself if the masses become engaged. Democratic elites thus prefer acquiesce to the social order among the poor by what Walker (1966, 287) calls a "noble lie" of framing disengagement as a personal choice (see also Morris-Jones 1954; Lipset, 1960; Milbrath 1965). I do not mean to imply that scholars who link inequality to political disengagement seek to perpetuate the elitist frame, as they may arrive at their research agenda from sincere concerns of how income inequality affects American society. Yet, the prevailing conventional wisdom is that income inequality lowers participation. Revisiting the arguments of those who critique democratic elite theory, such as Schattschneider (1960), along the lines proposed by Oliver (1999) may bear fruitful insights into the surprisingly complex role income inequality plays in American politics.

This study has applications for the social sciences, generally. Gini income inequality coefficients are used in a large number of contexts, for example, predicting levels of violence (e.g., Messner, Baumer, Rosenfeld 2004), quality of health care (e.g., Kawachi, et al. 1997; Ronzio 2003), and migration patterns among jurisdictions (Epple and Romer 1991) to name just a few examples among literally hundreds of articles that explore income inequality effects in economics, health sciences, environmental sciences, education, administration of justice, sociology, and political science. The results here suggest that researchers should take care in interpreting causal theories when they uncover a relationship between income inequality and the dependent variable of their research agenda. A relationship may only be valid at the level of aggregation level the researcher is looking at, which may lead researchers to inappropriately reject one theory in favor of another. Indeed, this admonishment applies to any contextual variable, including racial and social diversity indexes. Campbell's (2006, 108) caution in his analysis of religious threat should be well-heeded, "...aggregated measures require the assumption that the state [or any level of measurement] is the relevant geographic unit."

Appendix: Variable Definitions

Common Variables

State and County Level Gini Income Inequality Coefficients. Computed from the 1990 and 2000 census by the U.S. Census Bureau. Values are interpolated and extrapolated between 1990 and 2000 to measure income inequality for a particular election year. To prepare these data for analysis, they are appended to CPS and ANES records. While many CPS respondents are corresponded directly with a county, many CPS records do not have a county identifier.[14] 71% of CPS respondents are matched with a county Gini coefficient. Fortunately, matched respondents are comparable to those without a match.[15] Identifying the home county of ANES respondents is more straightforward and is accomplished by use of a county identifier present on that survey.[16]

Presidential Margin of Victory. Statewide margin of victory calculated as a percentage of total vote among all presidential candidates.

Election Day Registration. States with Election Day Registration are Idaho, Maine, Minnesota, New Hampshire, North Dakota (no registration), Rhode Island (presidential electors only), Wisconsin, and Wyoming.

Current Population Survey Variables

Family Income. 0 = household income < $20,000, 1 = household income < $40,000, 2 = household income < $100,000, 3 = household income > $99,999.

Education. 0 = persons with less than a high school diploma, 1 = persons with a high school diploma, 2 = persons with some college or an undergraduate degree, 3 = persons with at least some post-graduate education.

Age. Respondent's age top coded at 90. This variable is multiplied by itself to form its square.

Sex. 0 = woman, 1 = man.

Married. 0 = not married, 1 = married.

Non-Hispanic White. 1 = Non-Hispanic White, 0 = All others.

Non-Hispanic Black. 1 = Non-Hispanic Black, 0 = All others.

Recent Mover. 0 = resided at current address for 4 or more years, 1 = resided at current address for less than 4 years.

Home Owner. 0 = renter, 1 = owner.

---

14   For respondents without a county identifier, respondents were matched to counties based on their Combined Statistical Area (CSA) designation. CSAs can be a city or group of cites and many CSAs corresponded directly to single counties. Where a CSA obviously included two or more counties, I averaged the Gini coefficient across counties. Figure 2 shows that there is a high degree of spatial correlation for Gini scores, so the averaging approach, while imprecise, likely introduces small errors.

15   For example, the turnout rate among those that did and did not match was different by 0.01 percentage points. The income distribution among those with a matching county was slightly wealthier, with 31.3% reporting an income less than $20,000 compared to 35.5% among those without a matching county.

16   ANES county identifiers are publicly available prior to 2000. County identifiers from 2000 onward were obtained through an approved confidential data request.

American National Election Study Variables

Family Income. (VCF0114) 1 = household income 0–16 percentile, 2 = 17–33 percentile, 3 = 34–67 percentile, 4 = 68–95 percentile 5 = 96–100 percentile.

Education. (VCF0110) 0 = persons a grade school or less, 1 = high school or less, 2 = some college, 3 = persons with a college degree or more post-graduate education.

Age. (VCF0101) Respondent's age top coded at 99. This variable is multiplied by itself to form its square.

Sex. (VCF0104) 0 = woman, 1 = man.

Married. (VCF0147) 0 = not married, 1 = married.

Non-Hispanic White. (VCF0106 & VCF0108) 1 = Non-Hispanic White, 0 = All others.

Non-Hispanic Black. (VCF0106 & VCF0108) 1 = Non-Hispanic Black, 0 = All others.

Recent Mover. (VCF9002) 0 = resided at current address for more than 4 years, 1 = qresided at current address for 4 years or less.

Home Owner. (VCF0146) 0 = renter, 1 = owner.

Democrat. (VCF0303A) 0 = Republican, Independent, or Do not know, 1 = Democrat.

Political Interest. (VCF0313) 0 = Follow politics hardly at all, only now and then, and do not know, 1 = Some of the time or most of the time.

Job Worries. (VCF0155) 0 = Not much at all worried about losing job, not in the labor force, and do not know, 1 = worried a lot or somewhat.

Personal Trust. (VCF0619) 0 = Can't be too careful, 1 = Most people can be trusted.

Economic Policy Conflict. (VCF0839) 0 = 3–5 self-placement on a 7 point scale or respondents who did not know, 1 = self-placement at 1, 2, 6, or 7.

Contact. (VCF9030) 0 = No reported contact, 1 = contact by either party or another organization.

References

Alesina, Alberto and Eliana La Ferrara. 2000. "Participation in Heterogeneous Communities." *Quarterly Journal of Economics* 115(3): 847–904.

Almond, Gabriel, and Sydney Verba. 1963. *The Civic Culture.* Princeton, NJ: Princeton University Press.

Brehm, John and Wendy Rahn. 1997. "Individual-Level Evidence for the Causes and Consequences of Social Capital." *American Journal of Political Science* 41(3): 999–1023.

Brown, Malcolm. 1994. "Using Gini-Style Indices to Evaluate the Spatial Patterns of Health Practitioners: Theoretical Considerations and an Application Based on Alberta Data." *Social Science Medicine* 38: 1243–1256.

Bryk, Steven W. and Anthony S. Raudenbush. 1992. *Hierarchical Linear Models: Applications and Data Analysis Methods.* Thousand Oaks, CA: Sage Press.

Cameron, A. Colin, Jonah B. Gelbach, and Douglas L. Miller. 2008. "Bootstrap-Based Improvements for Inference with Clustered Errors." *The Review of Economics and Statistics* 90(3): 414–427.

Campbell, David E. 2006. "Religious 'Threat' in Contemporary Presidential Elections." *Journal of Politics* 68(1): 104–115.

Costa, Dora L. and Matthew E. Kahn. 2003. "Civic Engagement and Community Heterogeneity: An Economist's Perspective." *Perspectives on Politics* 1(1): 103–111.

Deutsch, Karl W. 1961. "Social Mobilization and Political Development." *The American Political Science Review* 55(3): 493–514.

Epple, Dennis and Thomas Romer. 1991. "Mobility and Redistribution." *The Journal of Political Economy* 99(4): 828–858.

Galbraith, James K. and Travis Hale. 2006. "State Income Inequality and Presidential Election Turnout and Outcomes." The University of Texas Inequality Project Working Paper 33.

Gini, Corrado. 1912. "Variabilità e mutabilità" Reprinted in *Memorie di metodologica statistica*, E. Pizetti and T. Salvemini, eds. Rome, Italy: Libreria Eredi Virgilio Veschi.

Hauser, Robert M. 1970. "Context and Consex: A Cautionary Tale." *The American Journal of Sociology* 75(4): 645–664.

Highton, Benjamin. 2000. "Residential Mobility, Community Mobility, and Electoral Participation." *Political Behavior* 22(2): 109–120.

Hill, David. 2006. *American Voter Turnout*. Boulder, CO: Westview Press.

Hill, Kim Quaile and Jan E. Leighley. 1992. "The Policy Consequences of Class Bias in State Electorates." *American Journal of Political Science* 36(2): 351–365.

Huckfeldt, Robert. 1984. "Political Loyalties and Social Class Ties: The Mechanisms of Contextual Influence." *American Journal of Political Science* 28(2): 399–417.

Kawachi, Ichiro, Bruce P Kennedy, Kimberly Lochner, Deborah Prothrow-Stith. 1997. "Social Capital, Income Inequality, and Mortality." *American Journal of Public Health* 87(9): 1491–1499.

Keyssar, Alexander. 2001. *The Right to Vote: The Contested History of Democracy in the United States*. New York, NY: Basic Books.

Lambert Peter J. and J. Richard Aronson. 1993. "Inequality Decomposition Analysis and the Gini Coefficient Revisited." *The Economic Journal* 103(420): 1221–1227.

Lasswell, Harold D. 1936. Politics: *Who Gets What, When, and How*. New York, NY: Whittlesey House.

Lazarsfeld, Paul. 1944. *The People's Choice*. New York, NY: Columbia University Press.

Leighley, Jan E. and Jonathan Nagler. 1992. "Socioeconomic Class Bias in Turnout, 1964–1988: The Voters Remain the Same." *The American Political Science Review* 86(3): 725–736.

Lipset, Seymour Martin. 1960. *Political Man*. New York, NY: Doubleday Company, Inc.

Messner, Steven F., Eric P. Baumer, and Richard Rosenfeld. 2004. "Dimensions of Social Capital and Rates of Criminal Homicide." *American Sociological Review* 69(6): 882–903.

Michael P. McDonald. 2008. "Portable Voter Registration." *Political Behavior* 30(4): 491–501.

Milbrath, Lester W. 1965. *Political Participation*. Chicago, IL: Rand McNally.

Morris-Jones, W.H. (1954) "In Defense of Apathy: Some Doubts on the Duty to Vote." *Political Studies* 2(2): 25–37.

Moulton, Brent R. 1990. "An Illustration of a Pitfall in Estimating the Effects of Aggregate Variables on Micro Units." *Review of Economics and Statistics* 72(2): 334–338.

Oliver, J. Eric. 1999. "The Effects of Metropolitan Economic Segregation on Local Civic Participation." *American Journal of Political Science* 43(1): 186–212.

Olson, Mancur. 1965. *The Logic of Collective Action: Public Goods and the Theory of Groups*. Cambridge, MA: Harvard University Press.

Primo, David M., Matthew L. Jacobsmeier and Jeffrey Milyo. 2007. "Estimating the Impact of State Policies and Institutions with Mixed-Level Data." *State Politics and Policy Quarterly* 7(4): 446–459.

Putnam, Robert D. 2000. *Bowling Alone: The Collapse and Revival of American Community*. New York, NY: Simon and Schuster.

Radcliff, Benjamin and Patricia Davis. 2000. "Labor Organization and Electoral Participation in Industrial Countries." *American Journal of Political Science* 44(1): 132–141.

Riker, William H. and Peter C. Ordeshook. 1968. "A Theory of the Calculus of Voting." *The American Political Science Review* 62(1): 25–42.

Ronzio, Cynthia R. 2003. "Urban Premature Mortality in the U.S. between 1980 and 1990: Changing Roles of Income Inequality and Social Spending." *Journal of Public Health Policy* 24(3/4): 386–400.

Schattschneider, E.E. 1960. *The Semi-Sovereign People: A Realist's View of Democracy in America*. New York: Holt, Rinehart and Winston.

Stolle, D. 1998. "Bowling Together, Bowling Alone: The Development of Generalized Trust in Voluntary Associations." *Political Psychology* 19: 497–526.

De Tocqueville, Alexis. 1969. Democracy in America, ed. and trans. J.P. Mayer. New York: Anchor Books.

Tolbert, Caroline and Rodney Hero. 2001. "Dealing with Diversity: Racial/Ethnic Context and Social Policy Change." *Political Research Quarterly* 54(3): 571–604.

United Nations. 2006. "Human Development Report, 2006." New York, NY: United Nations Development Programme. Table 15: "Inequality in Income or Expenditure."

Uslaner, Eric M. and Mitchell Brown. 2005. "Inequality, Trust, and Civic Engagement." *American Politics Research* 33(6): 868–894.

Verba, Sydney, Kay L. Schlozman, and Henry Brady. 1995. *Voice and Equality: Civic Voluntarism in American Politics*. Cambridge, MA: Harvard University Press.

Walker, Jack L. 1966. "A Critique of the Elitist Theory of Democracy." *The American Political Science Review* 60(2): 285–295.

Wolfinger, Raymond E. and Stephen Rosenstone. 1980. *Who Votes?* New Haven, CT: Yale.

CHAPTER 8

Thinking Outside the Democratic Box

Political Values, Performance and Political Support in Authoritarian Regimes: A Comparative Analysis

Wiebke Breustedt and Toralf Stark

Introduction

The downfall of the USSR was a decisive moment for all of its member countries. As such, the countries of Central and Eastern Europe, the Caucasus Region and Central Asia started out from a more or less comparable political situation into a new political future. Since then, democracy has been established in most Central and Eastern European countries. In Central Asia, however, the countries have not democratized successfully (Grotz and Müller-Rommel 2011, 11).

In light of this development, political culture research has experienced a revival as an explanatory approach (Fuchs 2007, 161). Its main argument is that the congruence between political culture (in terms of the citizens' values and attitudes) and the political institutions of a given country are essential for the effective functioning and persistence of any political regime (Almond and Verba 1963, 20–21; Diamond 1993, 422–426; Easton 1965, 157; Rose, Mishler and Haerpfer 1998, 91; Verba 1965, 513). So far, public opinion studies have mainly focused on democracies (Anderson et al. 2005; Dalton 2004; Inoguchi and Blondel 2008; Kaase and Newton 1995; Klingemann and Fuchs 1995; Norris 1999; Nye, Zelikow and King 1997; Pharr and Putnam 2000). However, political culture is a relevant societal basis for the maintenance and successful implementation of power not only in democratic systems but also in authoritarian regimes (Inglehart and Welzel 2005, 158, 187–188; Rose, Mishler and Haerpfer 1998, 8).

Among the many theoretical models of political support developed in the tradition of political culture research (Almond and Verba 1963; Dalton 2004; Easton 1965; Fuchs 1989, 2002, 2007; Lipset 1959; Norris 1999; Welzel and Inglehart 1999; Westle 1989) Fuchs' (1999, 2002, 2007) model is particularly suitable for the study of political support in authoritarian regimes.[1] It is better applicable than the other models as Fuchs clarifies the systemic consequences

---

[1] Other innovations include those by Inglehart and Welzel (2005), who focus more on modernization as a cause of change in political culture as well as the interaction between social and political values. For a comprehensive summary see Pickel and Pickel (2006).

of different types of political support with respect to regime persistence. In addition, it is innovative in so far as he clearly outlines the hierarchy of dimensions of the political system. However, for the sake of simplicity, Fuchs exclusively applies his model of political support to democratic political systems. Nevertheless, he states that "the assumption that a regime that wants to remain persistent in the long run, requires a political culture that is in congruency with the institutional structure, can be generally applied to all regime types" (Fuchs 2007, 163–164).

In line with previous research results indicating the importance of political support in authoritarian regimes (Inglehart and Welzel 2005, 186–191), we study in how far Fuchs' model can be applied to authoritarian systems. Fuchs states that support of democratic values and the democratic political regime are the most important aspects of political support in order to ensure the persistence of democratic political regimes. We argue that in authoritarian regimes the most important aspect of political support is trust in national government in order to maintain the authoritarian regime. Thus, it is crucial to study what determines trust in national government. According to the logic of political systems theory, the types of conditions that generate citizens' support of the political regime and authorities are the same independent of the regime type (Easton 1975). We therefore study empirically the conditions of high political trust in national government in Central Asia. Our analysis serves to answer the question: Is the fact that people trust their national government in Central Asia conditioned by their assessment of socio-economic and political performance and political values?[2]

The analysis focuses on Central Asian authoritarian regimes for several reasons. First, in general, there is little comparative research on the conditions of high political trust in authoritarian regimes. Most of the analyses are case studies and focus on East and Southeast Asia (Chu and Huang 2007; Dalton and Shin 2003; Inoguchi and Blondel 2008; Inoguchi 2008). While there are some case studies on Central Asian countries (Inoguchi 2008), so far, there have only been a few comparative, theory-testing studies (Dadabaev 2005; Dononbaev and Naskeeva 2004; Haerpfer 2008; Inoguchi 2008). However, the arguments upon which the conceptual political support framework is based have thus far not been adjusted to authoritarian regimes.

Second, the common political heritage of the Central Asian countries as former Soviet republics and their common status as authoritarian regimes provide sufficient homogeneity of the cases considered to ensure that they are

---

2 We would like to thank Claudius Wagemann and Carsten Schneider for helpful comments and remarks in the course of the ECPR SSMT 2011.

comparable with regard to the conditions of political trust. Third, due to the fact that the political systems of these countries can be characterized as authoritarian regimes to a different extent and since the political systems differ with regard to their socio-economic characteristics, the cases are diverse enough to supply maximum heterogeneity between the cases (Berg-Schlosser and de Meur 2009, 20–21).

In order to specify the conditional patterns of high trust in national government in Central Asia, we use individual-level data from the Asia Barometer Survey 2005. As social desirability is even more of an issue in authoritarian regimes than in democracies, we heed the advice to perform contextualized analyses by taking into account the characteristics of the countries' respective authoritarian political regime type (Inoguchi 2008, 17).

In order to derive the conditions of the outcome of high political trust in national government, we apply fuzzy set Qualitative Comparative Analysis (fsQCA). So far, QCA has rarely been applied to individual-level data due to its hitherto more case-oriented applications. However, the levels of application of QCA have been broadened to include the individual level (for a summary of applications see Rihoux et al. 2009, 173–174). Here, the unit of analysis, i.e. the individual himself, is not primarily of interest. Rather, the analysis of conditions of high trust in national government is intended to derive *types* of individuals as reflected in different conjunctions of conditions that lead to high trust in national government (Schneider and Wagemann 2010, 401).

FsQCA has several advantages for our analysis: First, unlike crisp set QCA (csQCA), it permits a differentiation between individuals both in terms of differences in kind – do they trust their government or not – as well as in terms of degree – to what extent do they trust their government.[3] Second, unlike standard statistical analyses it incorporates separate tests for necessary and sufficient conditions of the outcome (Wagemann and Schneider 2010, 380).[4] Third, it allows the researcher to study complex interaction effects. Previous studies of political support usually applied multiple regression analysis, which follows the principle of additivity (Catterberg and Moreno 2005; Dalton 2004; Inglehart

---

3 In csQCA, cases only differ in kind: they are either members (1) or non-members (0) of the set of high trusters in national government. FsQCA membership scores account for gradations in set membership.

4 Generally, "a *condition* is necessary if, whenever the *outcome* is present, the condition is also present, but there can be cases that are members of the condition but not the outcome" (Schneider and Wagemann 2012, 329–330; original emphasis). A condition is sufficient "if, whenever the conditions is present, the *outcome* is also present, but there can be cases that are members of the outcome but not the condition" (Schneider and Wagemann 2012, 333; original emphasis).

and Welzel 2005; Mishler and Rose 2001; Pharr and Putnam 2000; Wong, Wan and Hsiao 2011). As research has shown, citizens' political trust primarily results from their assessment of the socio-economic and political performance of the political system as well as their political values.[5] However, the literature suggests that these factors do not affect political trust in an isolated manner. Rather, they influence political trust *in conjunction*. Consequently, multiple regression analyses that determine the net effect of the single best predictor do not adequately take into account the causal complexity reflected in the research findings (Ragin 1987, 83; Ragin 2008, 176–182). In QCA, third, fourth and fifth order interaction terms are common, unlike in multiple regression analysis (Wagemann and Schneider 2010, 384).[6] Finally, QCA takes equifinality into account, i.e. "different constellations of factors may lead to the same result" (Berg-Schlosser et al. 2009, 8). This is important to bear in mind since the combinations or conjunctions of the conditions that affect political trust may differ both within and between the countries studied.

In sum, the article contributes theoretically by elaborating the model of political support developed by Fuchs as we apply it to authoritarian regimes. In addition, the article enhances the knowledge of the conditions of high political trust in national government in Central Asia from a comparative perspective, which is very seldom found in analyses of Central Asian countries thus far. Furthermore, the article contributes methodologically by applying fsQCA to test the newly developed theoretical arguments and by using individual-level survey data to study the conditions of high political trust in national government.

Theoretical Background

A Model of Political Support for Authoritarian Regimes
For our analysis, we refer to the model by Fuchs (1999, 2002, 2007), which is a recent and innovative elaboration of the political support model based on

---

5   For a recent summary of the different approaches to explaining political trust see Kotzian (2011, 26–28) and Wong, Wan and Hsiao (2011: 264–267).

6   Specifically, QCA enables the analysis of so-called INUS conditions. An INUS condition is a single condition that derives its name from the initial letters of the italicized words in the following definition: It is "an *insufficient* but *necessary* part of a condition which is itself *unnecessary* but *sufficient* for the result" (Mackie 1965, 245; original emphasis). In other words, it is a "single *condition* that is insufficient for producing the *outcome* on its own but which is a *necessary* part of a *conjunction* that, in turn, is unnecessary but *sufficient* for producing the outcome" (Schneider and Wagemann 2012, 328; original emphasis).

Easton. Political support is defined as "an attitude by which a person orients himself to an object either favorably or unfavorably, positively or negatively" (Easton 1975, 436). Fuchs first discerns between three hierarchically ranked dimensions of the political system each of which comprises different political objects, namely political values, the institutions of a regime and the political authorities. He then goes on to specify the corresponding types of political support for democratic political systems, namely commitment to democratic values, support of the democratic regime of the country and support of the political authorities, respectively. In line with Easton he further states that trust is an essential dimension of political support (Fuchs 2007, 164–166; see also Easton 1975, 447).

Conceiving political support as a system of attitudes, he, like other research-ers before him (Almond 1980; Easton 1975; Pappi 1986), assumes that the differ-ent dimensions of political support interact and are affected by citizens' assessment of political and socio-economic performance. However, he is the first to systematize and to justify theoretically the relationship between the different dimensions of political support (Fuchs 1999, 124; Fuchs 2002, 37–38; Fuchs 2007, 165).[7]

Furthermore, Fuchs derives the systemic consequences that arise from the different types of political support (Fuchs 2002, 37). He does so by relating the dimensions of political support to the dimensions of the political system. Based on Parsons (1971) and Luhmann (1970, 1984), he argues that political values can be attributed to the cultural dimension, support of the regime reflects the structural dimension and support of the authorities represents the procedural dimension of the political system (Fuchs 2002, 35–36).[8] He then states the respective consequences of the different dimensions of political support: per-sistence of a democratic system of the country, persistence of the type of demo-cratic system of the country, re-election or de-election of political authorities.

---

7 In "Critical Citizens" and "Democratic Deficit – Critical Citizens Revisited" Norris (1999, 2011) also presents a hierarchical model of political support. Unlike her, Fuchs clearly distinguishes between general democratic values and the democratic values inherent in the institutional structure of the current political regime (Fuchs 1999, 124–125; Fuchs 2002, 37; Fuchs 2007, 165, see also Dalton 2004, 6–7). In addition, he does not include 'identification with the political community' in the concept of political support (see Fuchs 2007, 169–172 for a detailed explanation).

8 He thus elaborates Easton's concept of political support. Easton differentiates the dimen-sions of political support by attributing them to individual objects of the political system, i.e. the political community, the regime as a whole and the political authorities. Fuchs takes on a more general approach by associating the types of political support to different kinds of dimensions of the overall political system.

Generally, there is no reason to believe why Fuchs' model of political support should not be equally applicable to democracies and autocracies. The dimensions of the political system and the respective dimensions of political support can be applied to both democratic and authoritarian regimes in line with the logic of political systems theory (Easton 1965, 8). His argument concerning the origins of political support is based on a universal assumption about human nature, namely that it derives from people's socialization experiences as well as their assessments of political and socio-economic performance. Therefore, he assumes that support develops in the same manner in all humans, independent of the type of political system they live in. Consequently, the fact that the different dimensions of political support and performance evaluations interact applies to authoritarian and democratic regimes.

However, the *consequences* of the different kinds of political support for the political system *differ*. Fuchs considers support of democratic rule, i.e. the commitment to democratic values, to be the most important dimension of political support for the persistence of democracies in general and states that support of the current political regime is indispensable for the persistence of the type of democratic regime in the respective country (Fuchs 2002, 31; Fuchs 2007, 166–167). We argue that in authoritarian regimes, high political trust in national government is crucial for the persistence of authoritarian regimes.

Since the national government is mainly perceived in terms of the political elites that represent the government, political trust in national government is located at the level of political authorities (Fuchs 1999, 124; Fuchs 2007, 165–166). Due to the non- or bare existence of a system of checks and balances, the locus of institutional power rests with the authorities. Since the authorities are not elected or the elections are mere charades, over time, the central political institutions are mainly framed by the political leader(s). Therefore, a clear separation between the authorities themselves and the institutions is no longer possible. Consequently, the extent to which the objects of political support of the political system can be distinguished is not as clear-cut as in democracies.[9] Instead, the values as well as the institutions of the regime are associated with the political authorities. In authoritarian countries, the authorities in national government and the ruling parties themselves personify the values of authoritarian rule.[10]

---

9   The question whether the objects of political support can be clearly distinguished in democracies has also been subject of a long debate (Miller and Citrin debate: Miller 1974a, 1974b; Citrin 1974; Citrin and Luks 2001).

10   Unlike in democracies where the constitutions specify the democratic values inherent in the political institutions of the political regime.

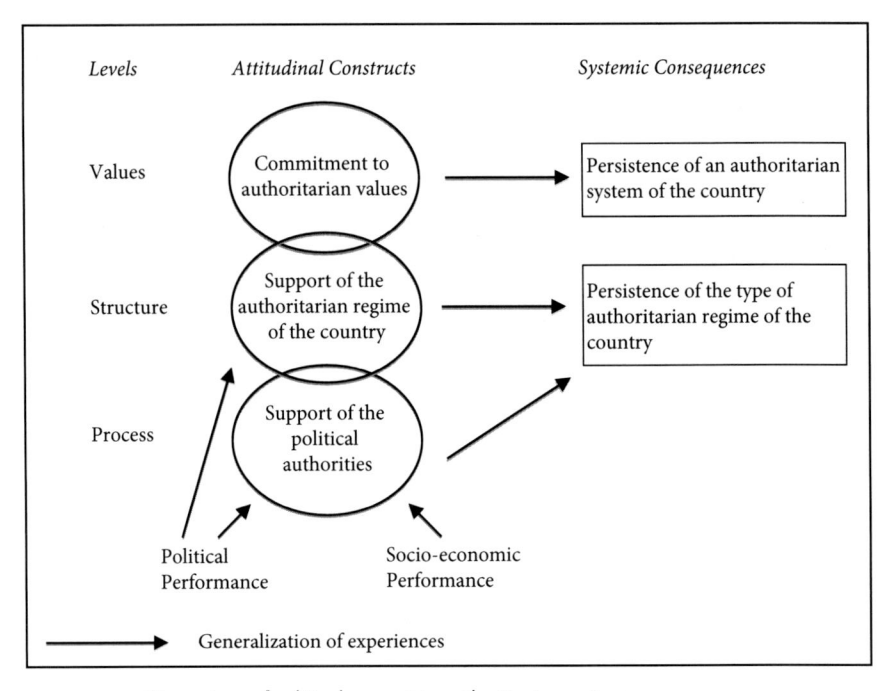

This has implications both for the most important aspect of political support for regime persistence as well as the interaction of the dimensions of political support. In general, based on this line of argument, it is high trust in national government that matters most for the persistence of the authoritarian regime in a given country (see figure 1). In authoritarian countries, it is therefore essential to study the conditions of high political trust in national government.

According to the original model by Fuchs, political trust in political authorities, i.e. the incumbents in political offices, results from the extent to which people are satisfied with their political and socio-economic performance (Easton 1975, 438–439; see also Fuchs 1999, 124). In addition, generalized trust in institutions provides political authorities with an advance in trust. According to our model, citizens also base their trust in the authorities on political values. Political trust in national government in authoritarian regimes can thus be considered to be affected by people's trust in the institutions of the regime, their political values as well as their evaluations of the political and socio-economic performance.

Since "[...] different kinds of authoritarianism differ from each other as much as they differ from democracy" (Geddes 1999, 121), we also have to consider the different manifestations of authoritarianism in Central Asia when choosing the conditions of high levels of trust in national government. In order to do so, initially, it is important to set autocracies apart from democracies as autocracies function according to regime-specific mechanisms and principles in their own right (Sartori 1997, 185). We do so in reference to a number of authors who distinguish between political regimes based on this dichotomous differentiation (Geddes 1999, 122–130; Linz 2000, 49–53; Sartori 1997, 185–186). Empirically, we draw on Freedom House and Polity IV, the two most commonly used empirical indices measuring the political performance of political regimes (Coppedge et al. 2011, 248).[11]

In terms of their political performance, the Central Asian countries highly differ, but none of them pass the democratic threshold (see figure 2).[12] With respect to the type of executive recruitment, constraints on executive authority and political competition, the countries have either remained autocratic (Uzbekistan), have fluctuated between autocracy and anocracy (Kazakhstan, Tajikistan) or have remained in an anocratic state between autocracy and democracy (Kyrgyzstan) (Marshall, Jaggers and Gurr 2011).[13]

Concerning the implementation of political rights and civil liberties, Freedom House has persistently rated some of the countries as not free (Uzbekistan), but has also assigned improving scores of freedom over time, while still categorizing the countries as not free (Kazakhstan, Tajikistan). Kyrgyzstan has been classified as either partly free or as not free.[14] This brief summary indicates that this region contains political regimes that have implemented the authoritarian rules in terms of electoral institutions, as well as political rights and civil liberties to different degrees (Freedom House 2012).

However, the differences between political regimes are not just a matter of quantitative degrees of authoritarianism but also a question of qualitative differences between authoritarian regimes. Possible qualitative differences should therefore also be considered when determining the conditions of high trust in national government.

---

11   Polity IV and Freedom House refer to two dimensions: "contestation" and "inclusiveness" based on Dahl's concept of polyarchy (Dahl 1971, 4–5).

12   Considering the fluctuations in Kyrgyzstan's assessment of political performance over the past years, it remains to be seen whether the country will manage to maintain its positive development.

13   Polity IV differentiates three regime types. Countries ranked between 10 and 6 are called democracy, countries ranked between 5 and –5 are referred to as anocracies and those ranging from –6 to –10 are entitled 'autocracy'.

14   Freedom House divides their scale into three dimensions: 1–2.5 = free; 3–5 = partly free; 5.5-7 not free.

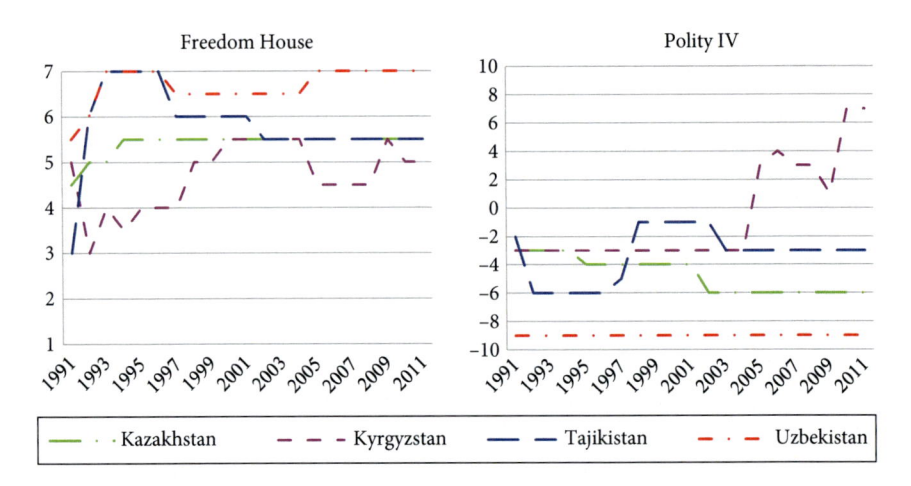

FIGURE 2   *Constitutional and actual rights of freedom and participation*
            SOURCE: FREEDOM HOUSE (2012)/ POLITY IV (2011)

In order to classify the types of authoritarian political regimes in Central
Asia in a qualitative manner, we use the approach by Hadenius and Teorell
(2006) which is based on Barbara Geddes' seminal proposal (1999). Hadenius
and Teorell elaborate Geddes' concept in two respects. First, they classify
authoritarian regimes based on three modes of political power maintenance:
(a) hereditary succession; (b) actual or threatened use of military force and (c)
popular election. The resulting regime types are monarchy, military regimes
and electoral regimes. These basic types can be divided into several subtypes.
Electoral regimes are differentiated into no-party regimes, one-party regimes
and limited multiparty regimes (Hadenius and Teorell 2006, 6–7). Following
Hadenius and Teorell, all Central Asian regimes are classified as limited multiparty regimes (Hadenius and Teorell 2006, 27). These arguments underline
that – in limited multiparty regimes as in Central Asia[15] – trust in parliament
should contribute to trust in national government, as parliament is the main
institutional display of the power of national parties.

Second, unlike Geddes, Hadenius and Teorell do not consider personalism
to be a regime type in its own right but state that it is a characteristic which is
more or less present in all authoritarian regimes (Hadenius and Teorell 2006,
4). Since personalism is characteristic of all authoritarian regimes, support of
strong political leadership (by a party or person) as a political value must be
considered as a condition of trust in national government when studying these
regimes. The importance of support of strong political leadership for citizens'

15   as well as in one-party regimes

trust in national government in authoritarian regimes is substantiated by Welzel and Inglehart (2009). They argue that citizens' intrinsic preference for authoritarianism is essential in order for them to support authoritarian rule in the long run (Welzel and Inglehart 2009, 134–135). According to them, citizens prefer authoritarianism intrinsically when they reject emancipative values, i.e. when they "give priority to authority and strong leadership over freedom and expression" (Welzel and Inglehart 2009, 131). They also show empirically that the congruence between citizens' values and political structures has systemic consequences (Inglehart and Welzel 2005, 186–191).

Assumptions

Fuchs' model implies that positive assessment of performance is a necessary condition of political trust in national government as political trust in national government mainly develops based on short-term evaluations of the political authorities (Easton 1975, 448), i.e. whenever people trust national government they also positively evaluate the socio-economic and/or political performance.

In addition, based on the arguments outlined in the previous section, support of strong leadership, positive assessment of socio-economic and political performance as well as political trust in parliament are sufficient for high trust in national government, i.e. whenever people support strong leadership and/ or positively evaluate the performance, they also trust national government. These conditions can be sufficient either by themselves or as INUS conditions.[16]

According to Fuchs' model, there should be sufficient conjunctions that exclusively include the positive assessment of socio-economic and political performance ('performance-driven' trusters). These conjunctions are likely to be complemented by trust in other institutions such as parliament. In contrast, according to our application of Fuchs' model to authoritarian regimes, we expect conjunctions of conditions that include performance, trust in parliament and support of strong leadership, as citizens in authoritarian regimes do not distinguish as clearly between the different dimensions of the political regime as in democracies. Support of strong leadership is expected to be part of a sufficient conjunction of conditions among the individuals in all countries due to the fact that the analysis is based on survey data from individuals who have all been socialized in Central Asian authoritarian regimes. Similarly, authoritarian values could also be sufficient by themselves ('value-driven' trusters).

---

16   see footnote 6.

Method and Data

We will now turn to the empirical determination of the necessary and sufficient conditions of high political trust in national government in authoritarian regimes in Central Asia. The study of the conditions of political trust is
not merely a question of whether and why people trust or not. It involves
both the question of qualitative states – do people trust or do they not
trust – as well as the question of degree – to what *extent* do people trust or
distrust. The most appropriate way to account for these differences in kind
(qualitative differences) and degree (quantitative differences) both in terms
of conceptualization as well as measurement when studying the conditions
of high political trust in national government is to apply fuzzy set Qualitative
Comparative Analysis (fsQCA) (Ragin 2008, 30; Schneider and Wagemann
2007, 184).

The individuals' responses to the survey questions in the Asia Barometer
2005 provide the raw data for the study of the conditions of high political trust
in national government in the countries of analysis. The Asia Barometer is a
regional public opinion survey project which has been conducted on an annual
basis in East, Southeast, South and Central Asia since 2003 (Inoguchi and Fujii
2008, 187). In 2005, the survey focused on South and Central Asian countries.
The survey items cover a range of issues pertaining to the quality of life, including political attitudes, political values and assessment of socio-economic and
political performance (Inoguchi and Fujii 2008, 164–197).

The selection of conditions is based on our model of political support.
Therefore, items pertaining to authoritarian values, political trust in parliament as well as the assessment of socio-economic and political performance
are included in the analysis (see Appendix A). With respect to the definition of
the outcome, we deviate from Fuchs' model. According to the argument outlined earlier, the choice of high political trust in national government as the
outcome is based on the assumption that high political trust in national government is comparatively more important for the persistence of authoritarian
regimes in a given country than authoritarian political values or high trust in
the political system and its institutions as such.

In order to perform a fsQCA to determine the necessity and sufficiency of
the conditions, first, those respondents of the Asia Barometer 2005 were
chosen which replied to the items pertaining to political performance, socio-
economic performance, political values and political trust.[17] The survey data

---

17   Kazakhstan N = 508; Kyrgyzstan N = 442; Tajikistan N = 414; Uzbekistan N = 353. A com-
      parison of the distributions of our sample with the distributions in the original sample

was then calibrated in order to perform a fsQCA to study the individual-level conditions of high political trust in national government. Each individual was therefore assigned set membership scores in the sets described by the characteristics of the conditions[18] and the outcome (see Appendix A).

According to the set-theoretic logic of fsQCA, the set membership scores range from 0 (full non-membership in the set, i.e. fully non-trusting) to 1 (full membership, i.e. fully trusting). The qualitative difference between the cases is determined by the 0.5 score, which represents the point of maximum ambiguity where cases are neither in nor out of a set (Ragin 2008, 30). This is why cases should not have a set membership of 0.5 because they cannot be clearly specified as members or non-members of a set. This in turn affects the ability to determine the specific truth table rows where they fit best (Schneider and Wagemann 2012, 28). The quantitative differences in the degree of set membership between the cases that are similar in kind are indicated by assigning different fuzzy set membership scores to the respective cases either above or below the point of maximum ambiguity (Ragin 2009, 89–90; Schneider and Wagemann 2007, 184–185).

In order to reflect the qualitative character, each fuzzy set score was assigned a linguistic qualifier (Schneider and Wagemann 2007, 184). Since the Asia Barometer Survey uses fully verbalized scales, the linguistic qualifiers of the fuzzy set values are actually inherent in the labels of the response categories. According to research in survey methodology, the response categories of survey items affect the respondents' cognitive process in choosing a response category when replying to the survey questions (see for example Mazaheri and Theuns 2009). These facts provide substantive reasons to assign a set membership score to each of the response categories. The endpoints of the scales were used as qualitative anchors to designate full membership and full non-membership, the crossover point was based on the meaning inherent in the labels of the response categories.[19] All 3-point scales were calibrated as follows:

(not shown here) regarding the socio-demographic characteristics (sex, age and education) according to which the representative sample was drawn showed that the distributions are similar.

18   Overall, there are 18 items that pertain to political performance, socio-economic performance, political values and political trust. Among these, there are several items in the Asia Barometer that are similar in terms of content. In these cases (f.ex. satisfaction with public safety and satisfaction with the way government is dealing with crime), only those items were chosen for the analysis that explicitly referred to government performance.

19   Due to the large number of respondents per country, the raw data are not presented here. However, the data set is available on the Asia Barometer website. While the raw data can

TABLE 1   *Calibration of three-point scales*

Fuzzy set membership scores	Survey item response categories	Linguistic qualifiers
1	1	Very good
0.55	2	Fairly good
0	3	Very bad

SOURCE: OWN CALIBRATION BASED ON ASIA BAROMETER 2005

The point of maximum ambiguity was set between response category 2 and 3, as indicated by the labels. Response category 3 was coded as 0.55 because the linguistic qualifier reflects a positive tendency and the assignment of a set membership of 0.5 should be avoided as mentioned above. The 4-point scales were calibrated according to the calibration rules in Table 2

TABLE 2   *Calibration of four-point scales*

Fuzzy set membership scores	Survey item response categories	Linguistic qualifiers
1	1	Trust a lot/very well/very satisfied
0.66	2	Trust to a degree/fairly well/ somewhat satisfied
0.33	3	Don't really trust/not so well/ somewhat dissatisfied
0	4	Don't trust at all/not well at all/very dissatisfied

SOURCE: OWN CALIBRATION BASED ON ASIA BAROMETER 2005

In the case of 4-point scales, the point of maximum ambiguity was set between response category 2 and 3 as the labels clearly indicate a qualitative difference. The 5-point scales were calibrated according to the calibration rules in Table 3. The point of maximum ambiguity was set between response categories 3

---

be calibrated according to the calibration rules outlined above, the fsQCA data set is also available upon request to facilitate the reanalysis of the data.

TABLE 3   *Calibration of five-point scales*

Fuzzy set membership scores	Survey item response categories	Linguistic qualifiers
1	1	Very satisfied/strongly agree
0.75	2	Somewhat satisfied/agree
0.55	3	Neither satisfied nor dissatisfied/ neither disagree nor agree[20]
0.25	4	Somewhat dissatisfied/disagree
0	5	Very dissatisfied/strongly disagree

SOURCE: OWN CALIBRATION BASED ON ASIA BAROMETER 2005

and 4. A detailed overview of the calibration of each of the conditions is listed in Appendix A.

Analysis of the Conditions of High Political Trust in National Government in Central Asian Authoritarian Regimes

First, we determined the necessary conditions of high political trust in national government (TG) as well as their consistency and coverage per country. Consistency indicates "the degree to which the empirical information at hand is in line with the statement of necessity, i.e., how far the outcome can be considered a subset of the condition" (Schneider and Wagemann 2012, 143). When studying necessary conditions, coverage indicates the relevance of a necessary condition (Schneider and Wagemann 2012, 325), Second, we derived the sufficient conditions of high political trust in national government (TG) in a separate analysis for each of the countries. We also report the fit measures of consistency and coverage for sufficient conditions. Again, "consistency provides a numerical expression for the degree to which the empirical information deviates from a perfect subset relation" (Schneider and Wagemann 2012, 129). When studying sufficient conditions, coverage reflects to which degree the solution term explains the outcome (Schneider and Wagemann 2012, 325).

---

20   The linguistic qualifier suggests a neutral middle category. However, due to the reasons elaborated with respect to table 1, cases should not be assigned a set membership of 0.50. We therefore assumed a positive response tendency in calibrating survey item responses '3' as 0.55.

Analysis of Necessity

When analyzing the necessity of the conditions, we sought to determine whether there are any conditions of which the outcome of high political trust in national government (TG) is a subset, i.e. whenever high political trust in national government (TG) is present, the condition is also present (Wagemann and Schneider 2010, 383). In order to determine whether the conditions listed in Appendix A are necessary for high political trust in national government (TG), we assessed their consistency. We considered only those conditions whose consistency was above 0.9, 1 being the highest possible consistency value (Schneider and Wagemann 2012, 143).

As expected, we found several political and socio-economic performance conditions that can be considered necessary based on their consistency value.[21] In *Kazakhstan, Kyrgyzstan* and *Uzbekistan*, high satisfaction with the current scope of the right to vote (SV) could be considered necessary. Counter-intuitively, in *Kyrgyzstan, Tajikistan* and *Uzbekistan*, the *absence* of the conviction that the government is dealing well with unemployment ($\sim$SU)[22] could be considered necessary, and in *Kazakhstan, Kyrgyzstan* and *Uzbekistan,* the same applies to the belief that there is widespread corruption among those who govern (C).[23]

However, "conditions that pass the consistency test as a necessary condition should not be deemed to be relevant necessary conditions unless they also obtain a high value in the relevance measure" (Schneider and Wagemann 2012, 147). The coverage of a necessary condition indicates the extent to which the set TG is smaller in relation to each conditional set. If the condition is irrelevant, its coverage will be low (Schneider and Wagemann 2012, 147, 237). This is the case for all conditions listed above. Therefore, we must conclude that there are no *relevant* necessary conditions. Nevertheless, the omnipresence of high satisfaction with the current scope of the right to vote (SV), the *absence* of the conviction that the government is dealing well with unemployment ($\sim$SU) and the belief that there is widespread corruption among those who govern (C) in the Central Asian countries indicated by the distribution of the values (not shown here) is in itself an important finding in terms of survey research as well as the quality of the political systems. We will elaborate this further when discussing the findings in the conclusion.

Analysis of Sufficiency

When analyzing the sufficiency of the conditions, we sought to determine which conditions are subsets of the outcome for high political trust in national

---

21   See Appendix B for the consistency and coverage values of each necessary condition with regard to the outcome 'high political trust in national government' (TG) for each country.

22   The '$\sim$' indicates the logical negation (Schneider and Wagemann 2012, 47).

23   The consistency level of 'widespread corruption' (C) is also very high in Tajikistan (0.88).

government (TG), i.e. whenever the condition is present, high political trust in national government (TG) is present (Schneider and Wagemann 2007, 32). QCA is characterized by causal complexity which is expressed by the fact that, a lot of the time, conjunctions of conditions instead of single conditions contribute to the outcome. This is indicated by "*" which stands for the logical AND. When considering the conjunctions of conditions, it is also possible that the outcome can result from both the presence and the absence of a certain condition, depending on which conditions it is combined with, i.e. $A^*B +\sim A^*C \rightarrow Y$ are permissible. In addition, QCA solution terms are characterized by equifinality, i.e. several conjunctions of conditions can be related to the same outcome (Berg-Schlosser et al. 2009, 8; Wagemann and Schneider 2010, 384; Schneider and Wagemann 2012, 54). This is indicated by '+' which stands for the logical OR. However, the OR is not exclusive but rather inclusive, i.e. an individual displays a high level of political trust if conjunction A^*B OR$\sim A^*C \rightarrow Y$ is present or both. Thus, the fsQCA solution term yields patterns of attitudes described by different solution paths. The arrow indicates that the expressions on the left side of the arrow are subsets of the outcome to the right side of the arrow. This subset relation implies sufficiency of the conditions for the outcome.

Based on our theoretical model, we included high trust in parliament (TP), the conviction that having a powerful leader (L) is good, and conditions characterizing socio-economic and political performance. With regard to the items measuring political and socio-economic performance, QCA's case-orientedness supports the idea of functionally equivalent conditions (Schneider and Wagemann 2010, 403). We chose those functionally equivalent items listed in Appendix A that yielded the best consistency and coverage values per country. The following conditions are included in the fsQCA in Kazakhstan, Kyrgyzstan, Tajikistan and Uzbekistan:

TABLE 4   *Conditions included in the analysis of sufficiency*

Dimensions of conditions	Political Support		Political performance (functional equivalents)	Socio-economic performance (functional equivalents)
Countries	Values	Structure		
Kazakhstan	L	TP	SI	SE, SL
Kyrgyzstan	L	TP	SI, SV	SH
Tajikistan	L	TP	SI	SE, SH
Uzbekistan	L	TP	SI	SU, SH, SC

SOURCE: SEE APPENDIX A

These conditions can be combined into 2^k conjunctions of conditions. Each logically possible conjunction represents one truth table row. The truth table rows are essential for the derivation of the solution formula that describes the sufficient conditions and conjunctions of conditions of high trust in national government presented below. For each country, we assigned each individual to the truth table row that described it best based on the fuzzy set scores, i.e. the ideal typical conjunction of conditions where the individual had a set membership of higher than 0.5. We then determined the outcome value for each truth table row (Schneider and Wagemann 2012, 179–186). In order to decide which rows are considered sufficient for the outcome and are therefore included in the logical minimization process, we used raw consistency as well as the proportional reduction in error (PRE). Whereas the raw consistency indicates the degree to which the conjunctions of conditions are a subset of the outcome, the PRE provides a numerical indication of truth table rows' simultaneous subset relations of the conjunctions of conditions in the outcome and the non-occurrence of the outcome (Schneider and Wagemann 2012, 242). We decided to include those rows with a raw consistency level of at least 0.90 *and* a PRE (proportional reduction in error) score of 0.79 or higher.[24] The analysis of sufficiency was performed using the QuineMcClusky truth table algorithm incorporated in the fsQCA program. With respect to the analysis of the individuals from Uzbekistan and Kyrgyzstan, several truth table rows (Uzbekistan: 22 rows; Kyrgyzstan: 3 rows) did not have cases with a set membership of more than 0.5. They are therefore logical remainders. However, we did not make any assumptions about them (Schneider and Wagemann 2012, 162). The truth table minimization yielded the following conservative solution terms:[25]

Kazakhstan: TP + L*SI*SL + L*SE*SL + SI*SE*SL ⟶ TG
Kyrgyzstan: L*TP*SH*SV + SI*TP*SH*SV ⟶ TG

---

24   The truth tables are included in Appendix C. The consistency threshold was set at 0.9 to ensure high consistency while allowing for some minor inconsistencies due to measurement error in the surveys. The 0.79 PRE threshold was chosen due to the fact that in all of the countries, all of the truth table rows with a consistency value of at least 0.9 exhibited a gap in the PRE score below 0.79.

25   The parsimonious solution for Uzbekistan is: TP*SU + SI*SH*SC*TP*~L. The parsimonious solution for Kyrgyzstan is: L*TP*SH*SV+~L*TP*SH*SI+TP*SH*SI*SV (solution includes all prime implicants). We chose not to present and interpret the parsimonious or intermediate solution as we did not want to make any assumptions about the logical remainders which would have to be justified. By presenting the conservative solution, we exclusively relied on our empirical data.

Tajikistan: TP + L*SE + SE*SH + SE*SI + L*SI*~SH +~L*SI*SH ⟶ TG

Uzbekistan: SC*SU*SI*TP + SC*SU*L*TP + SC*SH*SI*~L*TP + SI*SH*SU* ~L*TP ⟶ TG

The solution terms cover all sufficient truth table rows, i.e. all conjunctions of conditions that are sufficient for the outcome of high political trust in national government (TG). Since there are hardly ever any perfect subset relations in the social sciences, "it is important to assess the *degree* to which the empirical evidence is consistent with the set theoretic relation in question" (Ragin 2009, 108; original emphasis). Thus, before interpreting the solution terms, it is important to consider the consistency, the raw and unique coverage of the individual solution paths as well as the solution coverage and consistency. These parameters of fit are summarized in tables 5-8 below.

TABLE 5 *Kazakhstan*

Parameters of fit	Sufficient Conditions of TG				
	TP	+ L*SI*SL	+	L*SE*SL	+ SI*SE*SL
Raw coverage	0.813082	0.331405		0.382253	0.590487
Unique coverage	0.220254	0.005361		0.021054	0.030054
Consistency	0.922853	0.939832		0.933212	0.954417
Solution coverage			0.891546		
Solution consistency			0.901002		

SOURCE: OWN CALCULATIONS BASED ON ASIA BAROMETER 2005

TABLE 6 *Kyrgyzstan*

Parameters of fit	Sufficient Conditions of TG		
	L*TP*SH*SV	+	SI*TP*SH*SV
Raw coverage	0.401046		0.502772
Unique coverage	0.058800		0.160526
Consistency	0.936026		0.925965
Solution coverage		0.561572	
Solution consistency		0.925156	

SOURCE: OWN CALCULATIONS BASED ON ASIA BAROMETER 2005

TABLE 7   *Tajikistan*

Parameters of fit	Sufficient Conditions of TG					
	TP +	L*SE +	SE* SH +	SE*SI +	L*SI*~SH +	~L*SI*SH
Raw coverage	0.768204	0.353803	0.478605	0.446794	0.242735	0.315009
Unique coverage	0.223106	0.006323	0.010746	0.005974	0.011289	0.014509
Consistency	0.867634	0.948222	0.962025	0.969281	0.948893	0.962542
Solution coverage			0.866975			
Solution consistency			0.861727			

SOURCE: OWN CALCULATIONS BASED ON ASIA BAROMETER 2005

TABLE 8   *Uzbekistan*

Parameters of fit	Sufficient Conditions of TG			
	SC*SU* SI*TP +	SC*SU* L*TP +	SC*SH* SI*~L*TP +	SI*SH*SU* ~L* TP
Raw coverage	0.259300	0.105340	0.326887	0.220257
Unique coverage	0.023082	0.019583	0.112584	0.005955
Consistency	0.977099	0.981132	0.961018	0.975265
Solution coverage		0.397421		
Solution consistency		0.961818		

SOURCE: OWN CALCULATIONS BASED ON ASIA BAROMETER 2005

The consistency scores for sufficiency of the overall solutions in all four countries indicate that the statement that the solutions are sufficient for high political trust in national government (TG) is in line with the empirical survey data. Therefore, usually, individuals' membership score in the solution term is lower or equal to their membership score in high political trust in national government (TG). This means that there are very few instances where individuals have a membership score in the overall solution term that is larger than their set membership in high political trust in national government (TG).

The solution coverage for sufficiency shows how much of the outcome is explained by the solution paths. It is very high in Kazakhstan and Tajikistan and comparatively lower in Kyrgyzstan and Uzbekistan. While there is no lower threshold for coverage, a high coverage score for sufficiency indicates the empirical importance of the solution term (Schneider and Wagemann 2012, 137–138). Therefore, overall, the solution terms in Kazakhstan and Tajikistan are highly important whereas their importance in Kyrgyzstan and Uzbekistan is lower.

The consistency scores for sufficiency of the individual solution paths show that the conjunctions of conditions are empirically sufficient for high political trust in national government (TG). In terms of analytical content, this means that in Tajikistan, for example, the individuals in the survey usually trust parliament to the same (or lesser) extent as they trust national government (TG).

The raw coverage score of the individual solution paths "indicates how much of the membership in the outcome is covered by the membership in a single path" (Schneider and Wagemann 2012, 139). Overall, as reflected in the raw coverage scores, in Kazakhstan and Tajikistan, high political trust in parliament (TP) has the highest empirical importance, in Kyrgyzstan, it is SI*TP*SH*SV and in Uzbekistan, it is SC* SH* SI*~L*TP.

Due to the inclusiveness of the logical or, individuals can have a set membership of more than 0.5 in more than one solution path, i.e. we cannot state from the raw coverage scores in how far certain conditions have a 'higher effect' on individuals.[26]

At the same time, in fsQCA it is also possible to determine 'types' of trusters, i.e. those who are 'value-driven' and those who are 'performance-driven'. In order to do so, we need to consider the unique coverage score. The unique coverage score indicates the unique contribution of each solution path to the outcome (Schneider and Wagemann 2012, 137, 139).[27] Only those individuals which have a membership of greater than 0.5 in a single path are uniquely covered. According to the results, there are exclusively performance-based sufficient conjunctions of conditions. These uniquely cover the 'performance-driven trusters': SI*SE*SL in Kazakhstan and SE*SI as well as SE*SH in Tajikistan. However, there are no 'value-driven trusters' in any of the countries.

Conclusions Regarding the Assumptions

As outlined above, according to Fuchs' model, a positive assessment of performance is a necessary condition of high political trust in national government. In the analysis of necessity, we found that satisfaction with the current scope of the right to vote (SV) is necessary. The *absence* of satisfaction with the way

---

26　This is in contrast to the usual discussion of OLS regressions, where either values or performance indicators are deemed more important.

27　"A case is uniquely covered if it holds a membership value higher than 0.5 in only one sufficient path" (Schneider and Wagemann 2012: 137).

government is handling unemployment (~SU) and the agreement with the statement that there is widespread corruption among those who govern (C) contradict our assumptions. Yet, as indicated by the coverage of necessity, the conditions SV, ~SU and C are trivial in most of the Central Asian countries. This means that the majority of respondents in our sample of the Asia Barometer Survey are satisfied with the right to vote in Kazakhstan, Kyrgyzstan and Uzbekistan, are dissatisfied with the way government is handling unemployment in Kyrgyzstan, Tajikistan and Uzbekistan and believe that there is high corruption among those who govern in all four countries. Therefore, unlike suggested by Fuchs' model, neither political nor socio-economic performance are *relevant* necessary conditions for high trust in national government (TG), highlighting the need to take into account the difference between necessary and sufficient conditions when studying the conditions of political trust.

With regard to the question of sufficient conditions, as outlined earlier, Fuchs' model suggested that there are exclusively performance-based trusters. As the unique coverage scores of the sufficient conjunctions of conditions show, there are indeed exclusively performance-based sufficient conjunctions of conditions: SI*SE*SL in Kazakhstan and SE*SI as well as SE*SH in Tajikistan. These uniquely cover the 'performance-driven trusters'. However, the unique coverage is very low, which shows that there are very few cases to which these conjunctions of conditions apply, i.e. they are theoretically interesting but empirically almost irrelevant. Furthermore, there are no 'value-driven trusters'. This means that there are no individuals who base their high trust in national government (TG) exclusively on intrinsic support of authoritarian values. Instead, authoritarian values always occur in conjunction with instrumental aspects as well as the other dimension of political support.

In line with our assumption, the results show that high trust in parliament (TP), support of strong leadership (L) and satisfaction with socio-economic and political performance interact. In Kyrgyzstan and Uzbekistan, the sufficient conjunctions of conditions that include all of these dimensions have high raw coverage (L*TP*SH*SV in Kyrgyzstan, SC*SH*SI*~L*TP and SI*SH*SU*~L*TP in Uzbekistan). In Kazakhstan and Tajikistan, the sufficient conjunctions of conditions that cover support of strong leadership (L) and satisfaction with socio-economic and political performance also have high raw coverage (L*SI*SL in Kazakhstan, L*SI* ~SH and ~L*SI*SH in Tajikistan). However, in Kazakhstan and Tajikistan, high trust in parliament (TP) has the greatest explanatory power by itself which does not corroborate our assumption regarding the profound interaction of the conditions.

In order to substantiate these results and ensure that these conjunctions of conditions are not also sufficient for the non-occurrence of the outcome, we also carried out analyses of sufficiency for no trust in national government (not shown here). In Tajikistan, Kyrgyzstan and Kazakhstan, none of the conjunctions of conditions passed the sufficiency threshold of 0.9 and the PRE threshold of .79, indicating that they are not sufficient for explaining no trust in national government. In Uzbekistan, the analysis of sufficiency showed that: ~TP*~SU*~ SH*~SC+~TP*~SI*~SU*~SH+~TP*~L*~SU*~SC are sufficient for no trust in national government. These results highlight that high trust in national government and no trust in national government are two qualitatively different states of mind that are not subject to the principle of symmetric causation. Furthermore, with the exception of Uzbekistan, no trust in national government appears to derive from factors other than those included in this analysis. This also underlines the need to account for asymmetric causation in future analyses of the causes of political trust (Schneider and Wagemann 2012, 81–83).

Implications

In our article, we set out to determine the conditions of high trust in national government in authoritarian regimes in Central Asia. In order to do so, we adapted Fuchs' model of political support, which applies to democracies, to authoritarian regimes. First, the results contribute theoretically to the model of political support as developed by Fuchs as they show the need to revise the model when it is applied to authoritarian regimes. Second, the study clearly reflects the methodological need to allow for equifinality by taking country-specific conditions into account and to distinguish between necessary and sufficient conditions. Third, the results of the analysis of necessity give important insights into the use of survey data in authoritarian regimes.

As justified theoretically, the first thing that should be taken into account when studying the conditions of political support in authoritarian regimes is that political trust in the political authorities is the essential dimension that should be studied due to its relevance for the persistence of the authoritarian regime in a given country: In authoritarian regimes the values as well as the institutions of the regime are associated with the political authorities.

In general, the chosen conditions explain high trust in national government well in Kazakhstan and Tajikistan. The degree to which political values, institutional trust, socio-economic and political performance explain high political trust in government is considerably lower in Kyrgyzstan and Uzbekistan. Methodologically, this finding highlights the need for a context-sensitive choice of conditions of high trust in national government. With regard to the model of political support in general, this leads us to conclude that there may be other conditions in Central Asian authoritarian regimes that explain high trust in national government to a greater extent beyond the conditions suggested by the theoretical model.

As for the assumptions regarding the manner in which political values, trust in institutions, socio-economic and political performance affect high trust in national government, the results of the analysis provide a mixed picture. Generally, they support our assumption that these conditions interact. This is particularly evident in Kyrgyzstan and Uzbekistan. In Kazakhstan and Tajikistan, political values and satisfaction with socio-economic and political performance are also important but comparatively less so than institutional trust.

Beyond these model-specific assumptions regarding the sufficient conditions, the fact that each country exhibits its own specific conjunctions of conditions underlines the usefulness of the application of the principle of equifinality. This takes into account both within- and between-country variations in the conditions of high trust in national government but allows for a test of a general theoretical model all the same.

The analysis of the necessary conditions yielded findings that are pertinent both from a substantial and a methodological perspective. High satisfaction with the current scope of the right to vote, the *absence* of the conviction that the government is dealing well with unemployment and the belief that there is widespread corruption among those who govern is common among the respondents in the Central Asian countries. All four countries exhibit high rates of corruption, which the public clearly perceives and judges negatively. Even though all four countries have similar unemployment rates, Kazakhstan is the wealthiest in resources among the four, which may account for the fact that dissatisfaction with unemployment is not as omnipresent in Kazakhstan as in the other three countries which are comparatively poorer. As for satisfaction with the scope of the right to vote, Kazakhstan and Kyrgyzstan provide these rights to the greatest extent compared to Uzbekistan and Tajikistan which is again reflected in the survey responses. Methodologically, it is important to note that the survey respondents stated their opinion regarding the socio-economic and political performance of their regimes very openly. This is indicated by the overall negative assessment of the treatment of corruption and unemployment. This provides greater confidence in the survey responses in these authoritarian regimes.

As for the generalizability of the results, it is possible to "formulate propositions that we can then apply, with appropriate caution, to other similar cases – that is, cases that share a reasonable number of characteristics with those that were the subject of the QCA" (Berg-Schlosser et al. 2009, 12). Since socio-economic and political performance, authoritarian values and trust in parliament are included in the conjunctions of conditions in all countries, our assumption that the people do not discern clearly between national government and parliament as well as political values is generally sustained. Therefore, the results suggest that our model outlines the conditions whose interactions should be taken into account when performing analyses of high political trust in multiparty authoritarian regimes in future research.

Appendix A: Conditions and Calibration Rules

Concept	Quest.	Set	Abbr.	Resp. Cat.	Fuzzy set M.ship score	Linguistic qualifiers
Outcome						
	Q27a	High political trust in central government.	TG	1	1	Trust a lot
				2	0.66	Trust to a degree
				3	0.33	Don't really trust
				4	0	Don't trust at all
Conditions						
Political support						
	Q27f	High political trust in parliament.	TP	1	1	Trust a lot
				2	0.66	Trust to a degree
				3	0.33	Don't really trust
				4	0	Don't trust at all
	Q34a	Having a government by a powerful leader without the restriction of parliament or elections is good.	L	1	1	Very good
				2	0.55	Fairly good
				3	0	Bad
Political performance						
	Q31b	There is widespread corruption among those who govern the country.	C	1	1	Strongly agree
				2	0.75	Agree
				3	0.55	Neither agree nor disagree
				4	0.25	Disagree
				5	0	Strongly disagree

Appendix A (cont.)

Concept	Quest.	Set	Abbr.	Resp. Cat.	Fuzzy set M.ship score	Linguistic qualifiers
	Q31g	Government officials pay little attention to what citizens like me think.	A	1	1	Strongly agree
				2	0.75	Agree
				3	0.55	Neither agree nor disagree
				4	0.25	Disagree
				5	0	Strongly disagree
	Q35a	Very satisfied with the current scope of the right to vote.	SV	1	1	Very satisfied
				2	0.66	Somewhat satisfied
				3	0.33	Somewhat dissatisfied
				4	0	Very dissatisfied
	Q35d	Very satisfied with current scope of the right to be informed about the work and functions of government.	SI	1	1	Very satisfied
				2	0.66	Somewhat satisfied
				3	0.33	Somewhat dissatisfied
				4	0	Very dissatisfied
	Q28c	The government is dealing well with human rights.	SR	1	1	Very well
				2	0.66	Fairly well
				3	0.33	Not so well
				4	0	Not well at all
Socio-economic performance						
	Q6d	Very satisfied with the standard of living.	SL	1	1	Very satisfied
				2	0.75	Somewhat satisfied
				3	0.55	Neither satisfied nor dissatisfied
				4	0.25	Somewhat dissatisfied
				5	0	Very dissatisfied

Appendix A (cont.)

Concept	Quest.	Set	Abbr.	Resp. Cat.	Fuzzy set M.ship score	Linguistic qualifiers
	Q6e	Very satisfied with household income.	SH	1	1	Very satisfied
				2	0.75	Somewhat satisfied
				3	0.55	Neither satisfied nor dissatisfied
				4	0.25	Somewhat dissatisfied
				5	0	Very dissatisfied
	Q28e	The government is dealing with crime very well.	SC	1	1	Very well
				2	0.66	Fairly well
				3	0.33	Not so well
				4	0	Not well at all
	Q28a	The government is dealing with the economy very well.	SE	1	1	Very well
				2	0.66	Fairly well
				3	0.33	Not so well
				4	0	Not well at all
	Q28d	The government is dealing with unemployment very well.	SU	1	1	Very well
				2	0.66	Fairly well
				3	0.33	Not so well
				4	0	Not well at all

SOURCE: OWN CALIBRATION BASED ON ASIA BAROMETER 2005

Appendix B: Analysis of Necessity

B.1: Kazakhstan

Condition	Consistency	Coverage
TP	0.813079	0.922853
~TP	0.578464	0.751763
L	0.479302	0.763759
~L	0.657449	0.642687
SV	0.916302	0.765672

Appendix B (cont.)

Condition	Consistency	Coverage
~SV	0.391285	0.862247
SI	0.749072	0.835296
~SI	0.589673	0.782318
C	**0.908082**	**0.691978**
~C	0.322112	0.952354
A	0.880400	0.700996
~A	0.362336	0.918238
SR	0.635063	0.928860
~SR	0.706250	0.730484
SE	0.825458	0.885257
~SE	0.563031	0.784082
SU	0.496522	0.916572
~SU	0.812462	0.732734
SC	0.440671	0.966990
~SC	0.857916	0.718035
SL	0.802714	0.790592
~SL	0.475176	0.748082
SH	0.757130	0.804523
~SH	0.534796	0.753836

B.2: Kyrgyzstan

Condition	Consistency	Coverage
TP	0.772623	0.842796
~TP	0.621846	0.586843
L	0.597387	0.642617
~L	0.608431	0.581247
SV	**0.907304**	**0.640317**
~SV	0.357627	0.639277
SI	0.762160	0.697565
~SI	0.579412	0.655603
C	**0.899836**	**0.564884**
~C	0.317205	0.827289
A	0.879402	0.564657
~A	0.357895	0.854216

Appendix B (cont.)

Condition	Consistency	Coverage
SR	0.617240	0.881313
~SR	0.738372	0.578652
SE	0.563940	0.907012
~SE	0.781030	0.576564
SU	0.267214	0.895683
~SU	**0.917901**	**0.547005**
SC	0.357180	0.872815
~SC	0.852439	0.543940
SL	0.799005	0.656466
~SL	0.490295	0.645760
SH	0.742307	0.693877
~SH	0.556071	0.613366

B.3: Tajikistan

Condition	Consistency	Coverage
TP	0.768202	0.867634
~TP	0.541993	0.752059
L	0.538036	0.749271
~L	0.622801	0.701354
SV	0.807733	0.812273
~SV	0.501880	0.820511
C	0.882257	0.696539
~C	0.306823	0.903886
A	0.851182	0.716441
~A	0.380144	0.909420
SR	0.627767	0.891914
~SR	0.710942	0.787978
SE	0.590331	0.942346
~SE	0.751093	0.766712
SC	0.571089	0.913440
~SC	0.761180	0.776024
SL	0.766495	0.787015
~SL	0.499901	0.790795

Appendix B (cont.)

Condition	Consistency	Coverage
S I	0.602085	0.890930
~S I	0.722541	0.776689
S U	0.290607	0.933923
~S U	**0.920197**	**0.710627**
S H	0.690225	0.825615
~S H	0.604258	0.784685

B.4: Uzbekistan

Condition	Consistency	Coverage
T P	0.796990	0.857247
~T P	0.661999	0.535053
L	0.312031	0.608743
~L	0.848739	0.513024
S V	**0.898278**	**0.662456**
~S V	0.520502	0.641814
S I	0.603866	0.781210
~S I	0.804417	0.577065
C	**0.894165**	**0.549660**
~C	0.468323	0.866932
A	0.860034	0.533613
~A	0.473909	0.853510
S R	0.581705	0.893962
~S R	0.838180	0.552794
S E	0.640330	0.879956
~S E	0.828358	0.575535
S U	0.340330	0.922923
~S U	**0.939653**	**0.522548**
S C	0.656720	0.771138
~S C	0.794411	0.603958
S L	0.842109	0.683848
~S L	0.580538	0.620538
S H	0.747757	0.681074
~S H	0.662736	0.619925

Appendix C: Truth Tables[28]

C.1: Kazakhstan

Row	Conditions					Outcome	Number of individuals	Consistency	PRE
	TP	L	SI	SE	SL	TG			
1	1	1	1	1	1	1	78	0.979464	0.952760
2	1	0	1	1	1	1	50	0.985451	0.954857
3	1	1	0	1	1	1	42	0.967684	0.905339
4	0	0	1	1	1	1	28	0.969413	0.853813
5	0	1	0	1	1	1	24	0.955220	0.796246
6	0	0	0	0	0	0	22	0.850061	0.258314
7	0	0	0	0	1	0	22	0.890967	0.404693
8	1	0	0	1	1	1	19	0.976856	0.903121
9	0	1	1	1	1	1	18	0.965579	0.845638
10	0	0	1	0	1	0	15	0.945466	0.664123
11	1	1	1	0	1	1	15	0.968583	0.886741
12	0	0	1	0	0	0	14	0.910163	0.504420
13	1	0	0	0	1	1	14	0.987413	0.928260
14	1	1	0	0	1	1	14	0.984750	0.933523
15	1	1	1	1	0	1	13	0.976318	0.917289
16	1	0	1	0	1	1	11	0.985928	0.925027
17	0	1	0	0	1	0	10	0.942332	0.602441
18	1	0	1	0	0	1	10	0.975050	0.851182
19	0	1	0	0	0	0	9	0.897946	0.342447
20	1	1	0	1	0	1	9	0.977087	0.891510
21	0	0	0	1	1	0	8	0.954100	0.719709
22	0	1	1	0	1	1	8	0.971858	0.828359

---

28   The following truth tables might give the impression that we used csQCA since the conditions are only represented in terms of '0' (not present) and '1' (present). However, this is not the case. Each individual has partial membership in all rows but is assigned to a single truth table row where he has a set membership of > 0.5, as reflected by the column 'number of individuals'. The set membership score in the conjunctions of conditions is derived from the individuals' fuzzy set membership in the sets described by the individual conditions. The consistency and coverage values of the conjunctions of conditions are also based on fuzzy set membership scores. For a detailed outline of the procedure, see Ragin (2008, Chapter 7) and Schneider and Wagemann (2012, Chapters 4 and 5).

Appendix C (cont.)

Row	Conditions					Outcome	Number of individuals	Consistency	PRE
	TP	L	SI	SE	SL	TG			
23	0	1	1	1	0	0	8	0.951613	0.722749
24	1	0	1	1	0	1	8	0.978420	0.900000
25	0	1	1	0	0	0	7	0.948125	0.676018
26	0	0	0	1	0	0	6	0.937869	0.604576
27	0	1	0	1	0	0	6	0.947718	0.660168
28	1	0	0	1	0	1	6	0.985255	0.915645
29	1	1	1	0	0	1	6	0.978015	0.897716
30	1	1	0	0	0	1	4	0.970714	0.820195
31	0	0	1	1	0	0	2	0.952006	0.695524
32	1	0	0	0	0	1	2	0.980801	0.852731

C.2: Kyrgyzstan

Row	Conditions					Outcome	Number of individuals	Consistency	PRE
	L	SH	TP	SI	SV	TG			
1	1	1	1	0	1	1	39	0.942996	0.808241
2	1	1	1	1	1	1	67	0.939141	0.839896
3	0	1	1	0	0	0	3	0.935093	0.601828
4	0	1	1	1	1	1	31	0.931888	0.804707
5	0	1	1	0	1	0	12	0.9263	0.6917
6	1	0	1	1	1	0	21	0.918549	0.726751
7	1	1	1	1	0	0	2	0.914573	0.610374
8	1	0	1	0	1	0	16	0.913406	0.64154
9	1	0	1	0	0	0	2	0.91219	0.530928
10	1	1	1	0	0	0	5	0.907526	0.57647
11	0	0	1	1	1	0	8	0.906578	0.652897
12	0	0	1	0	1	0	6	0.902893	0.561498
13	0	0	1	0	0	0	3	0.895954	0.460674
14	1	1	0	0	1	0	17	0.855836	0.46746
15	0	1	0	0	1	0	10	0.854481	0.390068
16	1	1	0	1	1	0	52	0.849473	0.55946
17	0	1	0	1	0	0	2	0.836132	0.384802

Appendix C (cont.)

Row	Conditions					Outcome	Number of individuals	Consistency	PRE
	L	SH	TP	SI	SV	TG			
18	0	1	0	1	1	0	24	0.835867	0.467185
19	1	0	0	0	1	0	10	0.83193	0.372409
20	1	1	0	1	0	0	9	0.818954	0.371527
21	1	0	0	1	1	0	25	0.814674	0.416548
22	0	1	0	0	0	0	8	0.807599	0.285122
23	1	1	0	0	0	0	10	0.800098	0.308475
24	0	0	0	1	1	0	16	0.794332	0.352107
25	0	0	0	0	1	0	12	0.792533	0.272588
26	0	0	0	1	0	0	3	0.749033	0.22921
27	1	0	0	1	0	0	7	0.747564	0.22012
28	1	0	0	0	0	0	6	0.746256	0.198214
29	0	0	0	0	0	0	16	0.710994	0.208956
30-32	Logical remainders					0			

C.3: Tajikistan

Row	Conditions					Outcome	Number of individuals	Consistency	PRE
	TP	L	SI	SE	SH	TG			
1	1	0	1	1	1	1	12	0.998074	0.991859
2	1	0	0	1	1	1	14	0.992681	0.971584
3	0	1	0	1	1	1	8	0.993590	0.944840
4	1	1	1	1	1	1	35	0.983393	0.943864
5	1	0	1	1	0	1	5	0.987769	0.939560
6	0	0	1	1	1	1	1	0.993200	0.936210
7	1	0	0	1	0	1	9	0.982085	0.931226
8	0	1	1	1	1	1	10	0.989816	0.929205
9	1	1	1	1	0	1	5	0.983010	0.915310
10	1	0	0	0	1	1	12	0.978785	0.909540
11	1	1	0	0	1	1	36	0.977347	0.904403
12	1	0	1	0	1	1	10	0.977355	0.902203
13	0	1	1	1	0	1	3	0.985647	0.900685

Appendix C (cont.)

Row	Conditions					Outcome	Number of individuals	Consistency	PRE
	TP	L	SI	SE	SH	TG			
14	1	0	1	0	0	1	4	0.979411	0.896552
15	0	0	1	1	0	1	1	0.985655	0.891981
16	1	1	0	1	1	1	17	0.976993	0.882517
17	1	1	1	0	1	1	30	0.970885	0.879631
18	1	1	0	1	0	1	7	0.976618	0.874158
19	0	0	0	1	1	1	6	0.976475	0.841270
20	0	0	1	0	1	1	10	0.975244	0.841010
21	1	1	1	0	0	1	6	0.968831	0.836799
22	1	1	0	0	0	1	17	0.963590	0.835901
23	0	1	0	1	0	1	4	0.976855	0.833606
24	1	0	0	0	0	1	21	0.950293	0.831792
25	0	1	1	0	0	1	12	0.970699	0.827161
26	0	0	0	1	0	0	2	0.958021	0.755459
27	0	0	1	0	0	0	3	0.954361	0.728796
28	0	0	0	0	1	0	18	0.934140	0.702415
29	0	1	1	0	1	0	20	0.949027	0.702382
30	0	1	0	0	1	0	27	0.939960	0.658122
31	0	1	0	0	0	0	12	0.932408	0.612567
32	0	0	0	0	0	0	37	0.837200	0.480155

C.4: Uzbekistan

Row	Conditions						Outcome	Number of individuals	Consistency	PRE
	TP	L	SI	SU	SC	SH	TG			
1	1	1	1	1	1	0	1	1	1.000.000	1.000.000
2	1	1	0	1	1	1	1	1	1.000.000	1.000.000
3	1	1	1	1	1	1	1	5	1.000.000	1.000.000
4	1	0	1	1	1	0	1	1	0.982312	0.853535
5	1	0	1	1	1	1	1	3	0.974595	0.840909
6	1	0	1	0	1	1	1	13	0.965793	0.811089
7	1	0	1	1	0	1	1	1	0.981706	0.800677
8	1	1	0	1	1	0	1	2	0.974419	0.797546

Appendix C (cont.)

Row	Conditions						Outcome	Number of individuals	Consistency	PRE
	TP	L	SI	SU	SC	SH	TG			
9	1	1	0	0	1	1	0	7	0.955674	0.760766
10	1	1	1	0	1	0	0	2	0.969438	0.750000
11	1	0	0	0	1	1	0	19	0.948702	0.737342
12	1	1	1	0	0	1	0	6	0.953074	0.721448
13	1	0	1	0	1	0	0	3	0.962904	0.711628
14	0	1	0	1	1	1	0	1	0.950783	0.690141
15	1	0	1	0	0	1	0	10	0.950923	0.675339
16	1	1	1	0	1	1	0	2	0.950254	0.671642
17	1	0	1	0	0	0	0	6	0.953084	0.664179
18	1	1	0	0	1	0	0	1	0.958457	0.644068
19	1	1	0	0	0	1	0	13	0.923765	0.612022
20	0	1	0	1	0	1	0	1	0.946860	0.571429
21	1	0	0	0	1	0	0	4	0.942738	0.570895
22	1	1	0	0	0	0	0	4	0.934035	0.567639
23	1	0	0	0	0	0	0	13	0.924259	0.562945
24	1	0	0	0	0	1	0	23	0.906971	0.560945
25	1	1	1	0	0	0	0	7	0.916667	0.497076
26	0	1	1	0	1	1	0	2	0.913649	0.421642
27	0	0	0	1	1	1	0	3	0.942074	0.418182
28	0	0	1	0	1	1	0	7	0.922006	0.348609
29	0	1	1	0	1	0	0	2	0.903280	0.340909
30	0	0	1	0	1	0	0	2	0.913471	0.276316
31	0	1	0	0	1	1	0	15	0.801932	0.272852
32	0	1	0	0	0	1	0	18	0.817402	0.255930
33	0	0	0	0	1	1	0	20	0.845005	0.247713
34	0	1	1	0	0	1	0	9	0.848420	0.212861
35	0	0	0	0	1	0	0	10	0.837791	0.193966
36	0	0	1	0	0	0	0	8	0.871275	0.185557
37	0	1	0	0	1	0	0	6	0.827545	0.180266
38	0	0	0	0	0	1	0	34	0.784494	0.162551
39	0	0	0	0	0	0	0	36	0.732458	0.162433
40	0	0	1	0	0	1	0	13	0.875122	0.157550
41	0	1	0	0	0	0	0	16	0.741506	0.142723
42	0	1	1	0	0	0	0	3	0.844573	0.030641
43–64	Logical remainders							0		

References

Almond, Gabriel A. 1980. "The Intellectual History of the Civic Culture Concept." In *The Civic Culture Revisited*, edited by Gabriel A. Almond and Sidney Verba, 1–36. Boston: Little, Brown and Company.

Almond, Gabriel A., and Sidney Verba. 1963. *The Civic Culture: Political Attitudes and Democracy in Five Nations*. Princeton: Princeton University Press.

Anderson, Christopher J., André Blais, Shaun Bowler, Todd Donovan, and Olaf Listhaug. 2005. *Losers' Consent: Elections and Democratic Legitimacy*. Oxford: Oxford University Press.

Berg-Schlosser, Dirk and Gisèle de Meur. 2009. "Comparative Research Design. Case and Variable Selection." In *Configurational Comparative Methods: Qualitative Comparative Analysis (QCA) and Related Techniques*, edited by Benoît Rihoux and Charles C. Ragin, 19–32. London: Sage Publications.

Berg-Schlosser, Dirk, Gisèle de Meur, Benoît Rihoux, and Charles C. Ragin. 2009. "Qualitative Comparative Analysis (QCA) as an Approach." In *Configurational Comparative Methods: Qualitative Comparative Analysis (QCA) and Related Techniques*, edited by Benoît Rihoux and Charles C. Ragin, 1–18. London: Sage Publications.

Catterberg, Gabriela, and Alejandro Moreno. 2005. "The Individual Bases of Political Trust: Trends in New and Established Democracies." *International Journal of Public Opinion Research* 18(1):31–48. doi: 10.1093/ijpor/edh081.

Chu, Yun-Han, and Min-Hua Huang. 2007. "A Synthetic Analysis of Sources of Democratic Legitimacy." *Asian Barometer Working Paper Series* 41. Accessed March 31, 2011. http://www.asianbarometer.org/newenglish/publications/workingpapers/no.41.pdf.

Citrin, Jack. 1974. "Comment: The Political Relevance of Trust in Government." *The American Political Science Review* 68(3):973–88.

Citrin, Jack, and Samantha Luks. 2001. "Political Trust Revisited: Déjà Vu All Over Again?" In *What is it About Government that Americans Dislike?*, edited by John R. Hibbing and Elizabeth Theiss-Morse, 9–27. Cambridge: Cambridge University Press.

Coppedge, Michael, John Gerring, David Altman, Michael Bernhard, Steven Fish, Allen Hicken, Matthew Kroenig *et al.* 2011. "Conceptualizing and Measuring Democracy: A New Approach." *Perspectives on Politics* 9(2):247–67. doi: 10.1017/S1537592711000880.

Dadabaev, Timur. 2005. "Central Asia Reconsidered: Old Problems, New Paradigms." *Annals of the Japan Association for Middle Eastern Studies* 20(2):375–85.

Dahl, Robert A. 1971. *Polyarchy: Participation and Opposition*. New Haven: Yale University Press.

Dalton, Russell J. 2004. *Democratic Challenges, Democratic Choices: The Erosion of Political Support in Advanced Industrial Democracies.* Oxford: Oxford University Press.

Dalton, Russell J. and Doh Chull Shin. 2003. "Democratic Aspirations and Democratic Ideals: Citizen Orientations toward Democracy in East Asia." Accessed March 31, 2011. http://www.worldvaluessurvey.org/wvs/articles/folder_published/publication_500.

Diamond, Larry. 1993. *Political Culture and Democracy in Developing Countries: Textbook Edition.* Boulder, CO: Lynne Rienner Publishers.

Dononbaev, Alim, and Asel Naskeeva. 2004. "Political Culture and Modernization in the Central Asian States." Accessed March 31, 2011. http://www.ca-c.org/journal/2004-01-eng/01.donprimen.shtml.

Easton, David. 1965. *A Systems Analysis of Political Life.* New York: John Wiley & Sons Inc.

———. 1975. "A Re-Assessment of the Concept of Political Support." *British Journal of Political Science* 5(4):435–57.

Freedom House. 2012. "Country Ratings and Status." Last modified 2012. http://www.freedomhouse.org/sites/default/files/FIW%20All%20Scores%2C%20Countries%2C%201973-2012%20%28FINAL%29.xls.

Fuchs, Dieter. 1989. *Die Unterstützung des politischen Systems der Bundesrepublik Deutschland.* Opladen: Westdeutscher Verlag.

———. 1999. "The Democratic Culture of Unified Germany." In *Critical Citizens: Global Support for Democratic Government,* edited by Pippa Norris, 123–45. Oxford: Oxford University Press.

———. 2002. "Das Konzept der politischen Kultur: Die Fortsetzung einer Kontroverse in konstruktiver Absicht." In *Bürger und Demokratie in Ost und West: Studien zur politischen Kultur und zum politischen Prozess,* edited by Dieter Fuchs, Edeltraud Roller, and Bernhard Wessels, 27–49. Wiesbaden: Westdeutscher Verlag.

———. 2007. "The Political Culture Paradigm." In *The Oxford Handbook of Political Behavior,* edited by Russell J. Dalton and Hans-Dieter Klingemann, 161–84. New York: Oxford University Press.

Geddes, Barbara. 1999. "What Do We Know About Democratization After Twenty Years." *Annual Review of Political Science* 2:115–44.

Grotz, Florian, and Ferdinand Müller-Rommel. 2011. "Die Regierungssysteme der mittel- und osteuropäischen EU-Staaten als Gegenstand der Vergleichenden Demokratieforschung." In *Regierungssysteme in Mittel- und Osteuropa: Die neuen EU-Staaten im Vergleich,* edited by Florian Grotz and Ferdinand Müller-Rommel, 11–24. Wiesbaden: Verlag für Sozialwissenschaften.

Hadenius, Axel, and Jan Teorell. 2006. "Authoritarian Regimes: Stability, Change, and Pathways to Democracy, 1972–2003." *Kellogg Institute Working Paper Series* 331.

Accessed March 31, 2011. http://kellogg.nd.edu/publications/workingpapers/WPS/331
.pdf.

Haerpfer, Christian W. 2008. "Support for Democracy and Autocracy in Russia and the
Commonwealth of Independent States, 1992–2002." *International Political Science
Review* 29(4):411–31. doi: 10.1177/0192512108095721.

Inglehart, Ronald F., and Christian Welzel. 2005. *Modernization, Cultural Change and
Democracy: The Human Development Sequence.* Cambridge, UK; New York:
Cambridge University Press.

Inoguchi, Takashi, ed. 2008. *Human Beliefs and Values in Incredible Asia: South and
Central Asia in Focus: Country Profiles and Thematic Analyses Based on the
AsiaBarometer Survey of 2005.* Shohan. Tokyo: Akashi Shoten.

Inoguchi, Takashi, et al. 2005. "AsiaBarometer Survey Data 2005. AsiaBarometer
Project." Accessed March 21, 2009. https://www.asiabarometer.org/data/abdl.php.

Inoguchi, Takashi, and Jean Blondel. 2008. *Citizens and the State: Attitudes in Western
Europe and East and Southeast Asia.* London: Routledge.

Inoguchi, Takashi, and Seiji Fujii. 2008. "The AsiaBarometer. Its Aim, Its Scope and Its
Development." In *Barometers of Quality of Life Around the Globe: How are We Doing?*,
edited by Valerie Møller, Denis Huschka, and Alex C. Michalos, 187–232. Heidelberg:
Springer.

Kaase, Max, and Kenneth Newton. 1995. *Beliefs in Government.* Oxford: Oxford
University Press.

Klingemann, Hans-Dieter, and Dieter Fuchs. 1995. *Citizens and the State.* Oxford:
Oxford University Press.

Kotzian, Peter. 2011. "Conditional Trust: The Role of Individual and System-Level
Features for Trust and Confidence in Institutions." *Zeitschrift für Vergleichende
Politikwissenschaft* 5(1):25–49. doi: 10.1007/s12286-011-0094-1.

Linz, Juan J. 2000. *Totalitarian and Authoritarian Regimes.* Boulder, CO: Lynne Rienner
Publishers.

Lipset, Seymour M. 1959. "Some Social Requisites of Democracy: Economic
Development and Political Legitimacy." *The American Political Science Review*
53(1):69–105.

Luhmann, Niklas. 1970. *Soziologie als Theorie sozialer Systeme. Soziologische Aufklärung.
Aufsätze zur Theorie sozialer Systeme. Band 1.* Opladen: Westdeutscher Verlag.

———. 1984. *Soziale Systeme. Grundriß einer allgemeinen Theorie.* Frankfurt a.M.:
Suhrkamp.

Mackie, John L. 1965. "Causes and Conditions." *American Philosophical Quarterly*
2(4):245–64.

Marshall, Monty G., Keith Jaggers, and Robert T. Gurr. "The Polity IV Project: Political
Regime Characteristics and Transitions, 1800–2010." Accessed March 31, 2011. http://
www.systemicpeace.org/polity/polity4.htm.

Mazaheri, Mehrdad, and Peter Theuns. 2009. "Effects of Varying Response Formats on Self-ratings of Life-Satisfaction." *Social Indicators Research* 90(3):381–95. doi: 10.1007/ s11205-008-9263-2.

Miller, Arthur H. 1974a. "Political Issues and Trust in Government: 1964–1970." *The American Political Science Review* 68(3):951–72.

——. 1974b. "Rejoinder to "Comment" by Jack Citrin: Political Discontent or Ritualism." *The American Political Science Review* 68(3):989–1001.

Mishler, William, and Richard Rose. 2001. "What Are the Origins of Political Trust? Testing Institutional and Cultural Theories in Post-Communist Societies." *Comparative Political Studies* 34(1):30–62. doi: 10.1177/0010414001034001002.

Norris, Pippa. 1999. "Introduction: The Growth of Critical Citizens?" In *Critical Citizens: Global Support for Democratic Government*, edited by Pippa Norris, 1–27. Oxford: Oxford University Press.

Norris, Pippa. 2011. *Democratic Deficit. Critical Citizens Revisited.* New York: Cambridge University Press.

Nye, Joseph S., Philip D. Zelikow, and David C. King. 1997. *Why People Don't Trust Government.* Cambridge, MA: Harvard University Press.

Pappi, Franz U. 1986. "Politische Kultur. Forschungsparadigma, Fragestellungen, Untersuchungsmöglichkeiten." In *Politische Wissenschaft und politische Ordnung. Analysen zu Theorie und Empirie demokratischer Regierungsweise*, edited by Max Kaase, 279–91. Wiesbaden: Westdeutscher Verlag.

Parsons, Talcott. 1971. *The System of Modern Societies.* Englewood Cliffs, NJ: Prentice-Hall.

Pharr, Susan J., and Robert D. Putnam. 2000. *Disaffected Democracies: What's Troubling the Trilateral Countries?* Princeton, NJ: Princeton University Press.

Pickel, Susanne, and Gert Pickel. 2006. *Politische Kultur- und Demokratieforschung. Grundbegriffe, Theorien, Methoden: Eine Einführung.* Wiesbaden: Verlag für Sozialwissenschaften.

Polity IV. 2011. "Polity IV. Annual Time Series 1800–2011." Accessed December 20, 2012. http://www.systemicpeace.org/inscr/p4v2011.sav.

Ragin, Charles C. 1987. *The Comparative Method: Moving Beyond Qualitative and Quantitative Strategies.* Berkeley: University of California Press.

——. 2008. *Redesigning Social Inquiry: Fuzzy Sets and Beyond.* Chicago: University of Chicago Press.

——. 2009. "Qualitative Comparative Analysis Using Fuzzy Sets (fsQCA)." In *Configurational Comparative Methods: Qualitative Comparative Analysis (QCA) and Related Techniques*, edited by Benoît Rihoux and Charles C. Ragin, 87–121. London: Sage Publications.

Rihoux, Benoît, Charles C. Ragin, Sakura Yamasaki, and Damien Bol. 2009. "Conclusions – The Way(s) Ahead." In *Configurational Comparative Methods: Qualitative Comparative Analysis (QCA) and Related Techniques*, edited by Benoît Rihoux and Charles C. Ragin, 167–77. London: Sage Publications.

Rose, Richard, William Mishler, and Christian W. Haerpfer. 1998. *Democracy and its Alternatives. Understanding Post-Communist Societies.* Cambridge: Polity Press.

Sartori, Giovanni. 1997. *Demokratietheorie.* Darmstadt: Wissenschaftliche Buchgesellschaft.

Schneider, Carsten Q., and Claudius Wagemann. 2007. *Qualitative Comparative Analysis (QCA) und Fuzzy Sets. Ein Lehrbuch für Anwender und alle, die es werden wollen.* Opladen: Verlag Barbara Budrich.

———. 2010. "Standards of Good Practice in Qualitative Comparative Analysis (QCA) and Fuzzy-Sets." Comparative Sociology 9(3):397–418. doi: 10.1163/156913210X124935387 29793.

———. 2012. *Set-Theoretic Methods for the Social Sciences. A Guide to Qualitative Comparative Analysis.* Cambridge: Cambridge University Press.

Verba, Sidney. 1965. "Conclusion. Comparative Political Culture." In *Political Culture and Political Development,* edited by Lucian W. Pye and Sidney Verba, 512–60. Princeton, NJ: Princeton University Press.

Wagemann, Claudius, and Carsten Q. Schneider. 2010. "Qualitative Comparative Analysis (QCA) and Fuzzy-Sets. Agenda for a Research Approach and a Data Analysis Technique." *Comparative Sociology* 9(3):376–96. doi: 10.1163/156913210X124 93538729838.

Welzel, Christian, and Ronald F. Inglehart. 1999. "Analyzing Democratic Change and Stability: A Human Development Theory of Democracy." Discussion Paper FS III 99–202. Wissenschaftszentrum Berlin für Sozialforschung (WZB). Accessed March 31, 2011. http://edoc.vifapol.de/opus/volltexte/2009/1972/pdf/iii99_202.pdf.

———. 2009. "Political Culture, Mass Beliefs, and Value Change." In *Democratization,* edited by Christian W. Haerpfer, Patrick Bernhagen, Ronald F. Inglehart, and Christian Welzel, 126–144. Oxford: Oxford University Press.

Westle, Bettina. 1989. *Politische Legitimität – Theorien, Konzepte, empirische Befunde.* Baden-Baden: Nomos.

Wong, Timothy Ka-ying, Po-san Wan, and Hsin-Huang Michael Hsiao. 2011. "The Bases of Political Trust in Six Asian Societies: Institutional and Cultural Explanations Compared." *International Political Science Review* 32(3):263–81. doi: 10.1177/0192512110378657.

Index

Alienation 101, 121, 131

American National Election Study (ANES) 59, 59n2, 60, 61, 63–65, 164–171, 171n12, 174, 176, 178, 179, 179n16

Asia Barometer 15, 186, 194, 195, 195n18, 195n19, 196, 197, 201, 204

Authoritarian regimes 83, 184–217

Boycotting 11, 34, 38–40, 42–44, 47, 85, 85n4, 93

Central Asia 10, 15, 184–187, 191–194, 197–206

CPS. *See* Current Population Study (CPS)

Crisis of democracy 21

Culture, political 184, 184n1, 185

Current Population Study (CPS) 164–167, 178, 179

De-commodification 130–153

Democratic satisfaction 20

Demonstrating 1, 11, 32–35, 38, 42–45, 55

Direct democracy 90, 96, 98–101, 104

Disenchantment 1–26, 31n1, 32, 42n2, 54, 59n1, 63n4, 75n11, 83, 88, 101, 109, 112, 125, 131–133, 135, 143, 147, 153

Disproportionality 113n2, 122

District magnitude 114, 116, 116n6, 123, 126

Efficacy 4, 5, 17, 112, 113, 124, 125

Efficacy, political 16, 89, 111–113, 112n1, 124, 125

Electoral system 10, 13, 17, 89, 90, 96–101, 104, 109–126

Electoral threshold 114, 116

Emerging 34, 159, 176

Equifinality 187, 199, 205, 206

Equivalence 33, 35–36, 40–46, 53, 55

European Social Survey (ESS) 10, 11n4, 13, 33, 36–40, 42, 43, 46–49, 51, 52, 114, 115, 135, 136n1, 136n2, 137, 142, 148, 150

Evaluations of president 62, 65, 66, 75

Exit 4–9, 12, 13, 17, 133

Factor analysis 64, 66, 66n7

Federalism 89, 96–99, 101, 104

Fremskrittspartiet (Norway) 111

Fuzzy Set 15, 186, 194–197, 200, 207–209, 213

Gini Index 165, 168, 175

Governance 1

Guttman scaling 40

Hirschman, Albert O. 4–8, 10, 12, 13, 16, 18

Income inequality 10, 146–148, 151, 156–180

Interest, political 96–100, 103, 115, 119, 120, 130–133, 136–138, 141, 152, 169, 174

Internet 39, 55

Item difficulty 43

Item response theory 41

Kazakhstan 15, 191, 192, 194n17, 198–206, 209, 213

Kyrgyzstan 15, 191, 191n12, 194n17, 198–206, 200n25, 201–206, 210, 214

Loevinger's Hi 41, 42

Longitudinal equivalence 41, 53

Loyalty 4–8, 8n2, 16–18

Majoritarian electoral system (FPTP) 97

Marginalization 114, 121, 130–134, 141, 152, 153

Mobilization 157, 159, 160, 164, 167–177

Mokken scale analysis 40, 53

Multilevel modelling 84, 86, 92, 95, 95n15, 102, 115

Necessity 194, 197–198, 203–205, 209

Participation

conventional 5, 5n1, 7, 8, 10–12, 35, 36, 38, 39, 46, 47

electoral 10, 12, 14, 89n7, 109–126

institutionalized 33, 34, 84–86, 88, 90, 91, 101, 102

non-institutionalized 84, 86, 90, 94

unconventional 5, 5n1, 7, 8, 10–12, 31–80

Party membership 32, 34, 35, 85, 93

Petition(s)   5, 33–35, 38, 42, 47, 85n4, 88, 90, 93, 96, 98, 100, 101, 103, 156

Petitioning   11, 12, 33, 34, 42, 43, 45, 55, 86, 93, 97, 99, 101

Policy conflict   157, 159, 169, 170, 172–174, 176, 177

Political attitudes   8, 17, 19, 20, 59, 62, 109, 112n1, 194

Political behaviour   6, 8, 110, 115, 156–180

Political detachment   14, 130–153

Political interest   96–100, 103, 115, 119, 120, 130–133, 136–138, 141, 152, 169, 174

Political system   2, 5–7, 11, 14, 31, 32, 34, 60, 61, 64–68, 72, 75n10, 87, 88, 101, 109, 111, 124, 125, 130, 132, 137, 153, 156, 185–189, 194, 198

Political trust   1–24, 31, 31n1, 32, 42n2, 59–79, 83–104, 109–126, 130, 131, 136–138, 141–143, 152, 185–187, 187n5, 189, 190, 193–195, 197–205, 207

Populist parties   114

Predictors for trust   23

Presidential evaluations   60–62, 74, 79

Presidential performance   15n7, 60, 62, 65–66, 72, 75, 78

Proportionality   112, 151n61

Proportional representation (PR)   13, 89, 112–114, 116–126, 116n6

Protest   7, 12, 23, 32, 87, 88, 90, 90n9, 96–101, 103, 109–111, 113, 114, 123–125

Public deficit   91, 96–100, 104

Qualitative Comparative Analysis (QCA)   15, 186, 187, 186n6, 194, 199, 207

Reduction of poverty   140, 141, 144, 145, 148, 149, 151

Rosenberg scale   20, 25

Scale H   41–45

Social capital research   20

Social expenditure   140, 144, 145, 147–149, 151

Social risk   130–153

Social services   23

Sufficiency   194, 198–205

Support
diffuse   60, 61
political   1, 5, 132, 184–217
specific   11, 60, 61

Tajikistan   15, 191, 194n17, 198, 198n23, 199, 201–206, 211, 215

Trust
dimensions   62, 72, 78, 131, 136
general   19, 25, 26, 64, 65, 67, 75, 86, 109, 130, 132, 190, 205
leaders   63, 65, 66, 68–70, 72, 74, 75, 106–108
measurements   7, 9, 59–114
national government   62, 65, 67, 68, 74, 75, 185–187, 189–195, 197–206
political   1–24, 31, 31n1, 32, 42n2, 59–79, 83–104, 109–126, 130, 131, 136–138, 141–143, 152, 185–187, 187n5, 189, 190, 193–195, 197–205, 207
social   9, 14n6, 20, 22, 24, 86
state government   62, 64, 67, 68, 72, 107

Turnout   32, 35, 54, 85, 90, 109, 110, 112–115, 117–125, 156–160, 164–167, 169, 174–177, 179n15

Turnout
electoral   110–114
participation   110–115, 117–125

Unemployment   16, 23, 91, 96–101, 104, 133, 134, 139, 140, 164, 198, 203, 204, 206, 209

United States   32, 34–36, 53, 54, 134, 156, 159, 161–164

Uzbekistan   15, 191, 194n17, 198–206, 212, 216

Values, political   8, 184–217, 184n1

Voice   1, 4–8, 12, 13, 17, 90, 111, 125, 133

Volunteering   19, 33

Voting   7, 11–14, 17, 32–36, 38, 40, 41, 44, 45, 50, 52, 54, 60, 78, 84, 85n2, 86–88, 93–103, 111, 115, 116, 118–121, 124–126, 156, 157, 159, 160, 164–167, 172–177

Welfare state   23, 130–153

Printed in the United States
By Bookmasters